Robert R. Carkhuff
William A. Anthony

94012

the skills of
helping

22 Amherst Rd.
Amherst, Massachusetts 01002 413-253-3488
Copyright © 1979 by
Human Resource Development Press, Inc.

First Edition, First printing February 1979

First Edition, Second printing August 1979

First Edition, Third printing July 1981

First Edition, Fourth printing October 1983

First Edition, Fifth printing May 1984

First Edition, Sixth printing October 1984

First Edition, Seventh printing October 1985

Library of Congress Catalog Card No. 78-73987

International Standard Book Number 0-914234-08-0 *paper*

the skills of helping

CONTENTS

About the Authors

Robert R. Carkhuff, Ph.D. is an internationally known authority on human resources development. The most-cited author in counseling psychology in the last decade, he is the author of more than three dozen books, including *Beyond Counseling and Therapy, Helping and Human Relations, The Development of Human Resources, The Art of Helping III,* and *The Skills of Teaching Series.*

William A. Anthony, Ph.D. is Associate Professor and Director of Rehabilitation Counseling at Boston University. He is also currently project director of a three year NIMH grant to develop the specific skills involved in psychiatric rehabilitation and to train practitioners in these skills. He has published over three dozen articles in professional journals and is the author of *The Art of Health Care* and *The Principles of Psychiatric Rehabilitation.*

John R. Cannon, Ph.D. is Director of Management Systems, Carkhuff Institute of Human Technology (CIHT). A specialist in counseling and mental health, Dr. Cannon is the author of *The Kiddie Kurriculum for Keeping Kids Out of Trouble* and co-author of *The Art of Helping III.*

Richard M. Pierce, Ph.D. is Director of Human Technology, CIHT. A lifelong counselor and counselor educator, he is the author of *Helping Begins at Home* and *Teacher as Person.*

F. Jack Zigon, M.A. is Research Associate, CIHT, and Consulting Graduate Professor, Human Relations and Community Affairs Department, American International College. Mr. Zigon is co-author of *The Art of Helping III Trainer's Guide.*

TO THE READER

The aim of this text is to enable every helper to develop that repertoire of concrete and functional skills needed to make a difference — for the better rather than the worse — in the lives of individual helpees. The term "helper" here is not a reference to credentialed professionals alone. Trained therapist or "hotline" worker, guidance or vocational counselor, rehabilitation practitioner or even teacher: All are united as helpers in a mutual commitment to achieving positive, meaningful, and measurable outcomes on the part of their respective helpees. If you see yourself in any of these groups, either now or in the future, this book is for you. If you are simply an individual who wishes to acquire the skills needed to help others in any situation where such help might be needed, this book is also for you.

As a brief survey of the table of contents will reveal, the text is organized into eight chapters. The first chapter presents a basic model outlining the major phases or stages of helpee activity — from initial involvement in the helping process through constructive action to reach a goal. Chapters two through seven focus on the specific substages of this helpee activity as well as on the specific skills that the helper should use to promote each activity. Chapter eight reviews the entire helping model; presenting each of the phases of helpee activity and growth in conjunction with the sequence of helper skills that facilitate the helpee's growth.

Individual chapters are developed in parallel fashion. Each begins with an "Overview," which outlines the major substantive elements within that chapter. Following this, a brief narrative presents some of the specific weaknesses in the relatively unskilled "common sense" approach to helping. Next come the substantive elements of the chapter, presented in terms of particular helpee goals and the helper skills required to facilitate achievement of these goals. "Bette and Jimmy" provides a continuing illustration of the ways in which each set of helper skills can be used in real-life situations. Following this narrative section is a section devoted to "The Research Background," which links particular helpee outcomes and helper skills to the appropriate empirical evidence. Readers interested in a first-hand examination of some of the relevant research should read the references. Finally, each chapter ends with a "Summary," which outlines the major points covered in the chapter and suggests ways of practicing the skills.

The best approach to take to the materials in this text involves using the "SQ3R" method. Begin by *surveying* the "Overview," "Summary," and section headings and sub-headings in each chapter. Develop a brief list of specific *questions* suggested by your survey. Then *read* the chapter with a sharp eye for the answers to your questions, *recite* to yourself the answers to your questions and any other statements of particular importance, and *review* your questions and answers and the chapter itself to ensure that your understanding is complete.

The real test of your mastery of **The Skills Of Helping,** of course, lies in your ability to put these skills to practical use. In the end, the degree to which you have understood these materials can only be measured in terms of the positive difference you make in the lives of others. For that is what helping is all about.

RRC
WAA
JRC
RMP
JZ

Amherst, Mass
January 1979

helping begins with learning: THE MODEL

Overview

1. *All helping is for better or worse* — there is no middle ground.

2. The immediate aim of all effective helping is to promote measurable and constructive *changes in helpee behavior.*

3. The four phases of helpee activity during the prehelping and helping processes are *involvement, exploration, understanding,* and *action.*

4. *Involvement* is the essential prehelping of helpee activity, without which no progress or change is possible.

5. The initial phase of the helping process itself requires the helpees to *explore* their immediate situations.

6. The second phase of the helping process entails the helpees achieving an *understanding* of their problems in relation to their desired goals.

7. The final phase of the helping process is characterized by *action* designed to enable the helpees to reach their goals.

8. The key ingredient in promoting helpee involvement, exploration, understanding, and action is the helper's repertoire of concrete and functional *skills.*

Introduction

Only in this century have people and institutions begun to recognize *helping* as a professional (and therefore accountable) activity involving the use of specific and functional (and therefore teachable) skills. The definition of helping that is gaining wider recognition and acceptance all the time is as simple in form as it is profound in its implications.

Helping: The act of promoting constructive behavioral changes in an individual, which enhance the affective dimension of the individual's life and permit a greater degree of personal control over subsequent activities.

More constructive patterns of behavior; enhancement of emotional sensitivity; greater control of one's life: These are the primary and secondary outcomes of all effective helping, regardless of whether the helper is a teacher or a parent, a counselor or a credentialed therapist. And, far from being vague or elusive, these outcomes have been shown by the overwhelming weight of empirical evidence to be as objectively verifiable as they are personally meaningful. The helpee's development of new and more constructive patterns of behavior is reflected in his or her ability to reach previously unattainable goals. The enhancement of the helpee's emotional life is shown through his or her improved energy level and self-expressed feelings. The development of personal control is exhibited in the helpee's ability to recycle newly acquired skills for use in areas beyond those that were the focus of the original helping session.

Effective helping, then, results in meaningful and measurable outcomes. Yet we must also recognize that poor or ineffective helping results in negative outcomes that are equally meaningful, equally measurable. *One of the most documented principles of helping is that all helping is for better or worse.* No helpee is left unchanged by any helping interaction. The helpee has either developed new skills and behaviors — or has been confirmed in the belief that such development is impossible. The helpee either experiences more positive feelings about her or his situation and capability — or stoops even lower under the burden of increased negativity. The helpee either acquires a greater degree of self-control and self-guidance — or is rendered more impotent and ineffectual than ever.

All helping is for better or worse. And the critical ingredient — the factor that most determines whether helpee outcome will be positive or negative — is the helper's repertoire of *skills*. Neither degrees nor years of experience nor any other element even begins to approach the determinative role of helper skills.

As we shall see, helping entails a developmental process that takes helpees through four major phases. Helpees begin by becoming *involved* in the helping experience. Once full involvement is achieved, the helpees *explore* where they are in terms of the immediate situation and the various factors affecting it. Next, the helpees learn to *understand* the personal deficit or deficits that stand between them and the desired goal. Finally, the helpees learn how to outline and implement a course of *action* designed to take them to the goal. Involvement. Exploration. Understanding. Action. These are the phases of helping through which helpees progress. At each point in this progression the helper must be able to employ certain specific skills in order to promote the necessary activity on the part of the helpees. The aim of this text is to outline each of these skills in some detail for the present or prospective helper.

There are, of course, those people who still cleave to the old "common sense" approach to helping. To such people, talk of helper skills and helpee phases of activity may seem formal, artificial, even unnecessary. We may be in a better position to appreciate the critical issues facing today's helper or counselor — and the crucial need for helper skills — if we begin by examining a familiar type of "common sense" helping situation.

Helping
as
Common Sense

Harry is a young man in his senior year in college. Home for spring vacation, he only has a couple of months to go before completing work for his B.A. degree in sociology. It has been a long four years for Harry, but right now he's feeling pretty good about everything. Even the job market, marked by expressions of gloom and doom in past months, is looking up. Just this morning Harry had an excellent interview at Horizon House, a storefront drop-in center for local youth. Although most of Harry's work as an under-graduate has involved academic research and intellectual analysis, he feels sure he could handle the freewheeling counseling that the position with Horizon House would involve.

Four-thirty on a warm April afternoon. Heading back to his parents' house, Harry checked the gas gauge and hung a quick left into Bessom's Shell station. Damn! The old man couldn't be getting more than 10 or 12 miles to the gallon with this gas guzzler! Oh well, couldn't very well bring it back to him empty.

"Hey, Harry! How's the boy?" Frank Bessom, recognizing Harry as he got out of the car, came over to give the young man a handshake and a big grin. "Long time no see. You home on vacation or something?"

"Hi, Mr. Bessom. Yep, got ten days before I go back." Force of habit made Harry slip the gas hose off the tank and flip the register back to zero. All of Frank Bessom's "regulars" pumped their own gas.

"How much longer you got to go, Harry?" Frank asked.

"Oh, just a few more weeks, really. Be all finished up by the first of June!"

"Graduated and all?" Frank shook his head wonderingly. "Damn — it doesn't hardly seem possible. That's great, boy, just great! Your folks must be plenty proud." Then he shook his head again, this time reflecting frustration rather than wonder. "I wish my Jimmy had your sense, I gotta say that."

Jimmy Bessom. Harry's memory dredged up an image of a skinny kid in jeans and scruffy T-shirt riding his bicycle in great looping figure-eights around the concrete-and-gas-pump islands in front of Bessom's. "Jimmy? Why, what's wrong with him?"

"Ah, you know how these kids are today!" Frank Bessom's shrug bestowed an instant and equal maturity upon Harry. "You try to set 'em straight but they never listen. In the end, all you can do is hope they'll get some smarts before it's too late."

"What's Jimmy been up to, Mr. Bessom?"

The older man shrugged again, the picture of bewildered concern. "Well, we talked him into going to the Community College — the new one out on Tyler? So he went there for a year — or almost a year. Did real fine, too. Only now he says he may drop out and take a job driving a truck for Morris!" This last comment was bitter, contemptuous. "Hell, he could do like you and end up with a degree from a good school. But no, he'd rather drive a truck and hang around with the rest of those bums who work for Morris!"

"Gee, it's a shame for him to drop out if he was doing well," Harry said. And then, without thinking, "I don't know, maybe I could talk to him or something . . ."

The reaction was instantaneous. "Yeah?" Frank Bessom's voice was anxious. "Would you do that? Hey, great! Listen, he's just inside waiting for me to drive him downtown. Maybe you could give him a lift and talk to him at the same time, huh?" And before Harry could think twice, Frank Bessom had wheeled away and was moving toward the office calling, "Jimmy! c'mere a minute!"

And so it was that Harry found himself headed back downtown with Jimmy Bessom, still wearing scruffy jeans and T-shirt, sitting silently next to him. Nineteen now, Jimmy still looked as though he belonged on a bicycle rather than in a car.

"Where do you want to go?" Harry asked, uncomfortable with his passenger's continued silence.

"Oh, anywhere near the middle of town. I gotta wait for some friends." Jimmy's tone was neither friendly nor unfriendly, just guardedly neutral.

"If you're supposed to meet them at one particular place, I can drop you off right there," Harry told the younger boy. He snuck a sidelong glance but Jimmy showed no sign of answering. Then Harry had an inspiration. "I bet you're supposed to meet them at Delaney's Grill, aren't you?"

This got an immediate reaction. "How'd you know that?" Jimmy asked, his tone suspicious. "My old man talk to you about Delaney's?"

Harry shook his head. "Uh uh. I just remembered how much time I used to spend in Delaney's. In fact, there's lots of times when I was away I actually missed that old dump!" He snuck another glance at Jimmy. "I wouldn't mind stopping in for a beer — that is, if you don't mind."

Jimmy looked at him hard, then looked away. "Suit yourself," he said, back in neutral again. "It's a free country — or at least that's what people say."

Now settled on a destination, Harry postponed any talk with Jimmy about the latter's plans. Reaching the center of town, he swung right onto Federal and began looking for a parking spot. He was in luck as someone pulled a Ford van out of a spot directly in front of Delaney's.

"Well, here we are!" he said, trying to sound cheerful. "It's like coming home all over again . . ."

Once through Delaney's heavy doors, the light of April died and a wave of familiar smells assaulted Harry's nose: stale smoke, spilled beer, cheap liquor; the dehumanized fragrance of pitted chrome, old wood and dry, cracked plastic; the all-too-human fragrance of men who seemed to come alive only in the subterranean glow of jukebox neon and low-wattage bar lights.

"Good old Delaney's," Harry murmured. "It sure doesn't change much." Then, spotting a couple of aging regulars at the far end of the bar, their expressions flat, pale, and vacant like those of dynamited fish, "The customers don't change much either, I guess."

"No?" The note of suspicion was back in Jimmy's voice. He turned away and headed for the bar.

"Hey, how about grabbing a table?" Harry suggested.

"I'd rather sit at the bar."

"Oh." Harry shrugged. "Sure, why not?" He followed Jimmy to the bar and perched beside him on a wobbly stool that seemed about to cave in after years of uncomplaining service. They ordered beers. When Harry's arrived, he took a long gulp, unsure of how to begin with Jimmy now that they were here together. But Jimmy saved him the trouble.

"I guess my old man put you up to giving me a ride so's you could lay some rap on me about school, huh?" The younger boy's eyes were bright with resentment.

"Huh?" Confused, Harry took another swallow of beer. "Well, yeah, he did say something about your wanting to quit school and go to work . ."

"And you think I'm dumb to do that?"

"Of course not! Why should I think you're dumb?"

Jimmy looked away. "That's what my old man thinks. He told me so flat out the first time I even talked about maybe quitting school to go to work for Morris."

"How come you want to go to work instead of finishing school?" Harry asked. "Is it the money?"

"Huh!" Jimmy snorted contemptuously. He pulled a pack of cigarettes from his T-shirt pocket, took one out, and lit it. "No one who works for Morris makes good money. It's just a job, that's all."

"So how come you want it, then?"

Jimmy blew smoke, then looked over at Harry for a moment before turning away again. "That's where my friends are at," he said. "They're not into school. They're into working. And so am I!"

"I see . . ." But Harry didn't. As far as he could tell, Jimmy was making a foolish decision for equally foolish reasons. "If you stay in school," he said at last, "you're bound to make new friends, aren't you? I mean, you can make friends anywhere."

"Huh!" Jimmy snorted again, this time in contempt. "Maybe you college guys change your friends the way you change your clothes, but not me!"

By now Harry was getting restless. He was also finding the smoky barroom atmosphere oppressive. "Well listen, Jimmy," he said. "Will you do one thing at least? Will you really think things over carefully before you make any final decision? For your father's sake? And for your own, too. It could be your whole life you're messing with!"

"Sure, sure," Jimmy responded. "I'll think about it!" And before Harry could say anything else, the younger boy had spun on his stool and was greeting a group of his friends who chose that minute to make their noisy entrance.

"Oh well," Harry said to himself, once more driving toward his parents' house. "At least I tried. And who knows? Maybe it'll do some good . . ."

Here we have what might be termed the "common sense" approach to helping: a few beers, a little conversation, an indication by one person that he's ready and willing to help another. This sort of approach is probably familiar to all of us. Equally familiar is Harry's epilogue: "I did my best . . . Who knows? Maybe it'll do some good."

Unfortunately for Harry — and even more unfortunately for young Jimmy — the informal helping session related above probably did far more harm than good. Given the "Principle of Inevitable Effect," that which does not help must hurt! Jimmy was clearly at odds with his father already concerning his tentative plan to drop out of school. Now, confronted by Harry as the personification of academic success, Jimmy will almost certainly resent his father even more for wishing this do-gooder upon him. Far from thinking about his decision more carefully, Jimmy may well move toward a more hasty and irrational decision as the result of Harry's "help."

The lesson for us here is as clear as it is crucial: Real helping or counseling requires more, far more, than common sense and a willingness to try. Real helping makes it possible for clients or helpees to *resolve their problems*. The resolution of a problem is the only meaningful *outcome* of counseling. The interaction of helper and helpee and their cumulative movement toward such a resolution is the *process* of counseling. By taking a closer look at Harry's session with Jimmy, we can better understand how process and outcome are inextricably linked.

A Closer Look

To begin with, we can use a simple five-point scale to rate the level of any helper's interaction with the helpee or client.

Level 1: There is no evidence of any helper effort to attend to the helpee's needs.

Level 2: There is evidence of the helper's effort to *involve* the helpee in the helping process.

Level 3: There is evidence of the helper's effort to facilitate the helpee's *exploration* of her or his experiences.

Level 4: There is evidence of the helper's effort to facilitate the helpee's *understanding* of previously explored material.

Level 5: There is evidence of the helper's effort to facilitate the helpee's *action* based on her or his understanding.

Given this scale, we can see at once that Harry was functioning somewhere below Level 3. Far from facilitating Jimmy's understanding or action, Harry did not even help Jimmy to explore where he really was in terms of his school situation, his family, his friends. For exploration means uncovering new material, new ideas or insights. And all Harry elicited from Jimmy was a pat, clearly defensive response concerning his present position: "Maybe you college guys change your friends the way you change your clothes, but not me!"

What about Level 2, then? Did Harry manage to get Jimmy involved in the helping process? If involvement meant nothing more than sitting together and exchanging a few comments, we might be able to say yes. But real helpee involvement means far more than this. It means that the helper or counselor, by communicating genuine interest and concern to the helpee, gets that helpee to suspend for a moment the stock defenses and postures and consider the possibility of help with an open mind. Harry failed to do this. Such involvement, as we shall see, requires the helper to identify and enter the helpee's own private frame of reference, his or her particular way of viewing and responding to experiences. More than this, helpee involvement can occur only when the helper is fully attentive to the helpee in ways that are both physical and psychological. By communicating a "hovering attentiveness" that is receptive rather than judgmental, interested rather than insistent, the helper can draw the helpee into the counseling process and move him or her toward the beginning stages of exploration.

Harry did none of this. He did not think to arrange to talk with Jimmy in a quiet, comfortable setting free from ordinary distractions. Instead, he let Jimmy draw him into an exceedingly distracting setting, the barroom at Delaney's, where any conversation would inevitably be interrupted. He did not make any effort to come to terms with Jimmy's own frame of reference. Instead, he took a "common sense" approach to helping and wound up functioning at Level 1 — which is, alas, the level at which far too many people function. Like Harry, such people mistake amiability for attentiveness. And again like Harry, they leave their clients or helpees with little more than vague concepts and well-meant advice — "Think about your decision carefully" — which at best sounds pointless and at worst condescending.

Yes, Harry showed that he was a nice guy by giving Jimmy a chance to talk out his problems. But a helper has to be more than just another "nice" person. And a helpee must have more than a "chance" to work out a problem. For a "chance" is just that — a random opportunity that may result in growth but may equally well result in irreparable harm and helpee deterioration.

Helping cannot afford to be a lottery operating according to the fickle rules of chance. Yet the bulk of research evidence indicates that this is precisely how most counseling sessions do operate. They provide helpees or clients with a chance — no more, no less. And in statistical terms, these chances seem to pay off in no more than one or two cases out of ten. As if this were not bad enough, the evidence also shows that in those cases where clients do make substantial gains, the positive effects are more often the result of what the clients themselves brought to the sessions than the result of any specific behaviors of the counselors.

Yet the picture is not entirely gloomy. On the contrary, there is ample evidence to show that those few helpers who have developed specific and functional skills are able to promote helpee or client gains *consistently*. Such helpers or counselors do more than provide a chance. And their clients receive more than random benefits. By putting to use the skills that they have acquired, these helpers are able to help their helpees to get *involved* in the helping process itself, to *explore* where they really are in terms of their own world, to *understand* where they are in relation to where they want to be and, finally, to *act* in a systematic fashion to reach the goals that they have set for themselves.

The Phases of
Helping: A MODEL

Helpee involvement — helpee exploration — helpee understanding — helpee action: These four related phases provide us with the beginnings of a skeletal framework through which to view the entire prehelping and helping process.

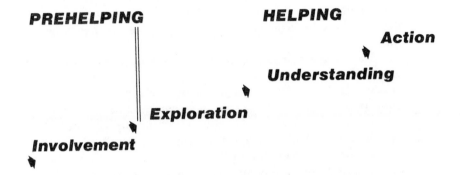

Figure 1-1: Four main phases of helpee activity.

As this figure indicates, helping is a developmental process. Initial client or helpee involvement paves the way for a period of exploration during which the helpee recognizes and expresses a wealth of personal feelings, reasons for feelings, and related circumstances; this is essentially an expansive phase as more and more material is presented by the helpee. Eventually, exploration gives way to understanding as the counselor helps the client to recognize how one or more specific behavioral deficits are contributing to those negative feelings or problems that are the focus of the counseling session; here the thrust is one of narrowing rather than expanding possibilities as the helpee learns to identify his or her personal responsibilities in the situation in order to assume control over it. Finally, understanding yields to action as the counselor helps the client to develop a step-by-step program of activity designed to move the client toward the client's unique goals.

This is all well and good. Yet helpee involvement, exploration, understanding, and action clearly do not occur spontaneously. Rather, the helpee's movement through these four main phases of activity can be seen as a carefully designed sequence of developmental steps orchestrated by the skills of the helper. To understand these steps and thereby flesh out our skeletal model of the helping process, let us consider a hypothetical counseling situation.

The Helping Process from the Helpee's Perspective

A helper — a woman, let us say — is working with a man who has a problem with alcohol. He has failed to control his drinking in the past and will do so in the future unless he learns a different way to cope with his problems. He realizes that his first step must be to get *involved* with someone who can help him.

By involvement we mean the client must *appear* for counseling rather than find some excuse for avoiding the session. He must relax enough to *express himself nonverbally* in terms of specific visual cues communicated by his appearance and behavior. He must *express himself verbally* by voluntarily talking about anything. And eventually, becoming fully involved, he must begin to *express personally relevant material* and begin using words like "me," "my," and "I." These are the four steps of involvement that characterize helpee movement through the prehelping process.

Phases of Helpee Activity

PREHELPING ǁ **HELPING**

Action
Understanding
Exploration

INVOLVEMENT
Expresses personally relevant material
Expresses self verbally
Expresses self nonverbally
Appears

Figure 1-2: The steps of helpee involvement.

Once the client or helpee has become involved, he must move into the next phase of the helping process. Here the aim is the exploration of where he really is in terms of his unique feelings, his problems, his overall experience of the world. He must begin by discussing his *immediate situation* — the facts that cause him to want to drink, that reflect how he tends to deal with problems, that show how he gets along with people. Having described the present situation fully, the helpee must move on to consider the *immediate meaning* that this situation has for him. Perhaps he recently lost a job because of his drinking problem. Does he tend to view this loss as a financial threat? As a sign of the hostility that others have shown him? He must answer the question: "What does this situation or fact really mean to me?" The helpee must begin next to organize his experience by labeling the *immediate feelings* that he has concerning the situation. Finally, the client must identify the *immediate reasons* that seem to explain why he feels the way he does and tie a reason to each feeling.

To develop our hypothetical case a bit more fully, the helpee exploring his drinking problem might begin by describing a situation involving the loss of a job, bills mounting, his kids getting sick, and the resulting financial pressures. He might go on to comment on the way in which this has affected his family and how his wife treats him. From the client's point of view, the immediate meaning of this set of circumstances might be, "My life is really out of my control." The immediate feelings flowing from this experiential meaning could well include anger, helplessness, even depression. And the immediate reasons for these feelings might be expressed in terms of "the way my wife hassles me about money" and "the way employers treat me, like I was worthless." Ultimately, the helpee must tie the feelings and the

Phases of Helpee Activity

PREHELPING

HELPING

Action

UNDERSTANDING

EXPLORATION

Explores immediate reasons for feelings
Explores immediate feelings
Explores immediate meaning
Explores immediate situation

INVOLVEMENT

Expresses personally relevant material
Expresses self verbally
Expresses self nonverbally
Appears

Figure 1-3: The steps of helpee involvement and **exploration**.

reasons together: "I'm angry because of the way my wife hassles me about money and I'm depressed with the way my boss treats me, like I was worthless."

Here, then, we have an outline of the developmental stages through which the helpee must pass during the process of exploration. We can add these to our model.

The earlier discussion of personally relevant material signaled the client's full involvement and led directly to his presentation of situationally specific material — the first phase of exploration. Now the final phase of exploration, the client's consideration of his immediate feelings and their reasons, leads in a similar fashion to the beginnings of a more personalized understanding. Whereas initially the client finds a host of external causes for his situation — the world is against him, his family puts pressure on him — he must now begin to recognize the ways in which *he* himself is responsible for his situation and therefore has the opportunity to change it for the better.

During the first phase of understanding, the man must translate his awareness of his immediate feelings and their reasons into more *personalized meanings*. He must begin to answer the question: "How am I at fault here?" The resulting shift is from a statement like "My wife hassles me about how little money we have" to "I only bring in half of what I used to each week." Thus, personalizing meaning expresses the meaning that a situation has for the helpee in terms that omit external agents; the helpee forgets about blaming

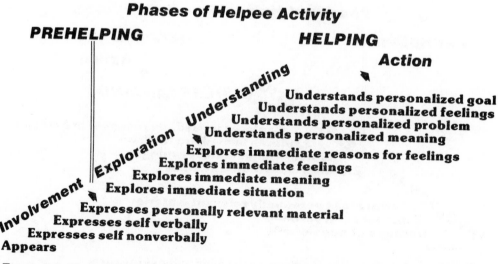

Phases of Helpee Activity

PREHELPING　　　　　　　　　　　**HELPING**

Action

Understands personalized goal
Understands personalized feelings
Understands personalized problem
Understands personalized meaning
Explores immediate reasons for feelings
Explores immediate feelings
Explores immediate meaning
Explores immediate situation
Expresses personally relevant material
Expresses self verbally
Expresses self nonverbally
Appears

Understanding
Exploration
Involvement

Figure 1-4: *The steps of helpee involvement, exploration and* **understanding.**

others and focuses on the situation in terms of how he is responsible. Next the helpee must begin to formulate his *personalized problem* in terms of a specific behavioral deficit: "I can't hold a job and make enough money to suport my family." A recognition of the real problem prompts the client to express more *personalized feelings.* Instead of railing against the external forces that prompted his original anger, the man might now say, "I really feel incompetent because I can't hold a job and make enough money to support my family." Having come to this point, the client must now flip over his personalized feelings, meaning, and problem in order to focus on a *personalized goal:* "I really feel incompetent because I can't hold a job and I want to be able to make enough money to support my family."

Now we can flesh out the "understanding" column in our skeletal model of the helping process.

The helpee has a goal. More than this, he has arrived at a personalized understanding of his situation that recognizes the way in which a specific behavioral deficit has held him back. To reach his goal, the man must address this deficit directly. This can be accomplished by further defining the personalized but still vague goal in terms that are concrete, measurable, and meaningful. This is the first of four action phases that will culminate in the helpee's achievement of the goal itself. Here the helpee translates his general goal — to be able to support his family — into concrete and specific terms along the lines of, "I want to be able to acquire a job that pays at least two hundred fifty dollars a week after taxes." Only by having a measurable goal will the man be able to recognize when he has achieved the goal. In the absence of some fairly strict parameters, the helpee may struggle to improve himself yet end up asking, "Have I really gotten anywhere?"

Once the goal has been defined, the helpee must consider the many ways in which this goal might be approached. There are many ways of reaching almost every goal. The helpee's aim here is to *choose a course of action* that will lead directly to the goal while enhancing (or at least not conflicting with) personal values. Thus the helpee must expand his awareness of both alternatives and personal values and then take a systematic approach to selecting that course of action that best suits his unique situation and purpose.

Having defined an appropriate goal and chosen an op-

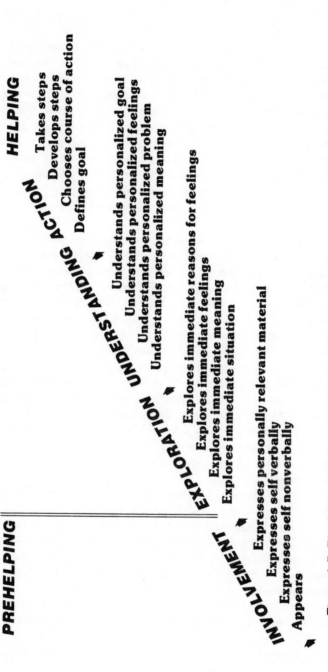

Phases of Helpee Activity

PREHELPING

INVOLVEMENT
Appears
Expresses self nonverbally
Expresses self verbally
Expresses personally relevant material

EXPLORATION
Explores immediate situation
Explores immediate meaning
Explores immediate feelings
Explores immediate reasons for feelings

UNDERSTANDING
Understands personalized meaning
Understands personalized problem
Understands personalized feelings
Understands personalized goal

ACTION
Defines goal
Chooses course of action
Develops steps
Takes steps

HELPING

Figure 1-5: The full model showing all steps of helpee involvement, exploration, understanding, and action.

timum course of action, the helpee must *plan a sequence of primary and secondary action- or "do-steps"* that will lead him directly toward his goal. For our sample helpee, this may involve mapping a systematic campaign whereby he expands a list of potential employers, writes his résumé, and acquires interviewing skills. Once these do-steps have been outlined, the client must chart an accompanying series of systematic *check- or "think-steps"* that will serve to tell him whether he is, at any given point, really on track and moving toward his goal. Thus, if any early do-step involved creating a list of 100 potential employers, the accompanying think-step might involve asking himself some questions: "Where do I want to work? What kinds of employers usually hire people with my skills? What specific employers of these types are in my chosen geographical area?"

Finally, of course, the helpee must begin to *take the steps* he has charted; for no program is any better than the helpee's ability to put it into action. Knowing this, the helpee should make sure that his program of action contains sufficient steps, each of which is relatively easy for him to take.

We can now complete our initial version of the basic helping model by adding the phases of helpee or client action.

The result of any truly effective helping session is a positive and measurable change in helpee behavior. In terms of our hypothetical situation, the helpee's attainment of his goal would reflect his acquisition and use of specific skills. His behavior would be different — that is, he would be able to acquire a job that would allow him to support his family because he learned to act differently. No longer the misunderstood, maligned victim who has a problem, he would be a man who had at least begun to come to terms with the ways in which his own actions affect his own life.

Needless to say, our helper in this situation would almost certainly have to work with her helpee for a number of sessions. Although effective help can be given in some situations during a three-minute exchange, the type of help required by a man like our sample client cannot be doled out in this way. Nor should any single helping session, whether it lasts three minutes or is stretched over three months, be viewed by any counselor as an end in itself. For one of the key features of the model we have examined is the way in which the three major phases of the actual helping process can be *recycled.* New behaviors inevitably produce new feelings and situations. And these in turn provide a new focal point for further exploration, understanding, and action. Thus, what may at first seem a linear process—

INVOLVEMENT EXPLORATION UNDERSTANDING ACTION
(I) ▶ **(E)** ▶ **(U)** ▶ **(A)**

— must in the end be viewed as a continuous spiral of helpee activity and growth:

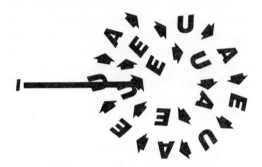

This completes our discussion of what steps a helpee must complete in order to resolve a problem: getting involved; exploring; understanding; acting. Most helpees are helpless precisely because they cannot complete one or all of these four activities. The effective helper knows this and uses specific skills designed to promote helpee success in each area.

We have seen something of the results of a "common sense" approach to helping. Now let us take a brief preliminary look at a helping session involving a skilled helper. We should find quite a difference, even in its initial stages.

Helping
as a Set of
Skills: Bette and Jimmy

Harry wasn't the only person to learn of Jimmy Bessom's plan to drop out of college. Bette Simmons, the young career counselor at the Community College, had also learned of this plan. And because she had ample opportunity to observe Jimmy while he was at school, she suspected that his feelings fell far short of the clear-cut "I know what I want and I'm going to get it" variety.

Bette did some checking before deciding to approach Jimmy openly.

She knew that she had to find out as much as possible about the way *he* felt before going any further. A couple of Jimmy's teachers commented that the quality of his work had fallen off in recent weeks and that Jimmy frequently cut or was late to classes. Remembering some of Jimmy's friends from the previous semester, Bette checked and found out that several of them had dropped out after Christmas to go to work. The final link was provided by Jimmy's father, Frank Bessom, who called Bette one afternoon and related the same story that he had given to Harry.

Although Bette understood Frank Bessom's concern for his son, she was by no means ready to make the sort of snap judgment that the older man wanted. After all, some people set goals for themselves that have nothing whatsoever to do with school. Yet if Jimmy himself was so determined to drop out, Bette reasoned, he would probably have done so at the same time as his friends. The records showed, however, that Jimmy had done quite well in many of the same courses that his friends had flunked. There was, she decided, a very good chance that Jimmy did not know *what* he wanted to do. And this was an area in which she felt she could provide help.

Having made up her mind, Bette approached Jimmy one day as he sat out on the lawn eating lunch.

"Hi, Jimmy. How's it going?"

"Oh — hi, Ms. Simmons. OK, I guess." But the hesitancy of Jimmy's answering smile told her that things could be better.

"There's a rumor going 'round that you're planning to drop out," Bette said. "If that's true, I thought maybe we could talk about it. After all, I'm supposed to be some kind of career counselor around here."

Jimmy's expression turned sour. "You want to talk me out of it!"

Bette shook her head. "You're angry because you think your father sicced me on you," she responded. "But he didn't. Oh, sure, he called me. And I told him I'd talk with you. But I also told him that dropping out might be the best thing for you."

"Yeah?" Jimmy looked incredulous but relieved.

Bette nodded. "Uh huh. Of course, staying in might also be the best thing. But it seems to me like that sort of a decision could be a real hassle. And I thought I could help you make it the best way possible. How about it? You feel like getting together?"

Jimmy looked around uncertainly. "You mean — now?"

Bette shook her head. "Uh uh. Why don't you come see me — oh — tomorrow afternoon at three, after class. That way we wouldn't have to cut things short." That way, too, they wouldn't have to cope with the distractions of the lawn at lunchtime.

"At three?" Jimmy considered. "Sure, that'd be all right." He looked at Bette. "You're sure you're not just trying to snow me, Ms. Simmons?"

Again Bette shook her head. "I know you're under a lot of pressure, Jimmy," she said, her eyes finding his. "And I know you want to make the

19

right decision for yourself. All I want to do is help you make that choice — and then help you get where you want to go."

Jimmy returned her gaze for a long moment. "OK then, I'll be there," he said at last.

"You know how to find my office OK?"

"Sure — main building, third floor, last office on the right. Right?"

Bette grinned. "I guess you know your way around," she said, getting up and brushing vagrant blades of grass off her slacks. "Then I'll see you at three tomorrow."

Bette did see Jimmy at 3:00. He arrived looking apprehensive and hopeful at the same time. They had a good session — one in which Bette put to good use the specific helping skills that she had developed. And when Jimmy left at a little after 4:30, it was with a totally new expression on his face. An expression of confidence and new-found pleasure.

The Helping Process from the Helper's Perspective

With Bette's help, Jimmy had made his choice. He now knew where he wanted to go and how to get there. But how had all this taken place? What went on in Bette's office between 3:00 and 4:30? And what were the specific skills that she was able to use in Jimmy's behalf? The answers to these questions foj. the substance of this book. In each succeeding chapter, we will address ourselves to one particular set of skills. And at the end of each chapter, we will return to the session between Bette Simmons and Jimmy Bessom. Thus our consideration of specific skills will be echoed in a brief consideration of the ways in which Bette used these same skills. Yes, we will learn the precise outcome of Bette's work with Jimmy. But not until the end of the book — not until, that is, we can see this *outcome* in terms of the fundamental *process* of helping. For the separation of process and outcome is finally as futile, as impossible, as the separation of the dancer and the dance. The growth that our helpees or clients achieve, as we shall see, is inextricably bound up in the ways that we, as helpers or counselors, help them to go.

Process and outcome — and the concrete skills that, by creating the former, make it possible for us to achieve the latter — are what this text is all about. For in the end, neither common sense nor good intentions are enough! If we are to make a lasting and constructive difference in the lives of our helpees, it will only be because we have mastered *The Skills of Helping* and are able to put them to practical use.

The Research Background

The research that will be most helpful to counselors or helpers will be that which deals with the outcomes and processes of helping. Simply stated, we have found it most effective to look at *helping outcomes* and trace back through their recorded *helping processes* to find the effective ingredients.

Helping Outcomes

Historically, Eysenck (1960) and others (Levitt, 1963; Lewis, 1965) confronted the helping professions with the challenge that *counseling and psychotherapy really did not make a difference.* About two-thirds of the patients remained out of the hospital a year after treatment, *whether or not they were seen by professional psychotherapists.* These effects held for adult and child treatment.

One answer to this challenge was the finding that the variability or range of effects of the professionally treated groups on a variety of psychological indices was significantly greater than the variability of the "untreated" groups (Rogers, Gendlen, Kiesler, & Truax, 1967; Truax & Carkhuff, 1967). This meant that professional practitioners tended to spread the effects on the patients. This suggested one very consoling conclusion: *Counseling and psychotherapy really did make a difference.* It also suggested one very distressing conclusion: *Counseling and psychotherapy have a two-edged effect — they may be helpful or harmful* (Bergin, 1971).

Follow-up research by Anthony and his associates (Anthony, Buell, Sharratt, & Althoff, 1972; Anthony, Cohen, & Vitalo, 1978) has shed some light on the lasting effects of counseling, rehabilitation, and psychotherapeutic techniques. This research was based upon data indicating that within three to five years of treatment *65 percent to 75 percent of the ex-patients will once again be patients.* Also, regardless of the follow-up period, *the gainful employment of ex-patients will be below 25 percent.*

The major conclusion that might be drawn from these data on outcome is that *counseling and psychotherapy — as traditionally practical — are effective in about 20 percent of the cases.* Of the two-thirds of the clients and patients who initially get better, only one-third to one-quarter stay better.

Multiplied out, this means that psychotherapy has lasting positive effects in between 17 percent and 22 percent of the cases. Counseling and psychotherapy may indeed be "for better or for worse." In most instances, the lasting effects are not facilitative.

In order to understand the reasons for these outcomes, we examined the process of counseling and psychotherapy. When we looked at effective helping processes from the perspective of the helpee, we found that helping is simply a *learning* or *relearning process* leading to change or gain in the behavior of the helpee (Bergin, 1971; Carkhuff, 1969).

Learning Processes

The phases of effective counseling and psychotherapy are really the phases of effective learning (Carkhuff, 1969, 1971; Carkhuff & Berenson, 1967, 1977). The helping processes by which helpees are facilitated or retarded in their development involve their *exploring where they are* in their worlds; *understanding* and specifying *where they want to be;* and developing and implementing step-by-step *action programs to get there.*

Exploring is perhaps the most significant activity of the helpee in helping (Carkhuff & Berenson, 1976). It is a precondition of understanding, giving both helper and helpee an opportunity to get to know the helpee's experience of where he or she is in the world. In this respect, exploration is a self-diagnostic process for the helpee. Exploration is in part under the control of the helper and in part under the control of the helpee. High-level functioning helpees explore themselves independent of the level of interpersonal skills offered by the helpers while moderate to low-level functioning helpees are dependent upon the helper's skills for their level of exploration.

Understanding is the necessary mediational process between exploring and acting (Carkhuff & Berenson, 1976). It serves to help the client focus upon personalized goals from among the many alternatives made available through exploration. The basic foundation for understanding rests with insights as discriminative stimuli — insights revealing the helpee's own deficits and role in the situation — which increase the probability that related behaviors will occur. Unfortunately, action does not always follow insight. For one thing, insights promoted by "common sense" techniques are usually not developed systematically in such a way that each piece of explored material is used as a base for the next level of understanding. Therefore the individual helpee, aided only by change and common sense, does not "own" the insights and cannot act upon them.

Acting is the necessary culminating process of helping (Carkhuff & Berenson, 1976). The helpees must act upon their newly personalized understanding in order to demonstrate a change or gain in their behavior. In doing so, they are provided with the opportunity to acquire new experience and thus stimulate more extensive exploration, more accurate understanding, and more effective action. Any discrepancy between understanding and acting is, in part, a function of the lack of systematically developed action programs that flow from systematically developed insights.

In conclusion, both helpers and helping programs are effective in facilitating the helping process to the degree that they incorporate and emphasize the phases of learning: involving the helpees in exploring where they are in their worlds; understanding and specifying goals for where they want or need to be; and developing and implementing step-by-step action programs to achieve their goals. The helpers who have the helping skills and the skills to develop helping programs are, for the most part, those individuals who have learned them in systematic help in skills-training programs, whether professional or paraprofessional (Anthony & Carkhuff, 1978; Carkhuff, 1968).

The number of models of helping based upon this simple paradigm of helping as learning have proliferated the literature of counseling and psychotherapy (Anthony, 1979; Brammer, 1973; Combs, Avila, & Purkey, 1978; Danish & Hauer, 1973; Egan, 1975; Gazda, 1973; Goodman, 1972; Guerney, 1977; Ivey & Authier, 1978; Kagan, 1975; Patterson, 1973; Schulman, 1974). Though varying their terminology, most attribute the effectiveness of counseling and psychotherapy to those helper skills that facilitate the helpee's self-exploration. Very few of these helping approaches have identified and operationalized the helper dimensions of personalizing and programming that culminate in helpee behavior change or action. Indeed, most major therapeutic orientations, we will find, tend to emphasize exclusively one phase of helping or the other.

And what about the "common sense" approach to helping that is employed by the well-intentioned helper? Perhaps the best illustration of the potential dangers and harm of the "common sense" approach are several research studies that

23

investigated the helping skills of hot-line volunteers (Carothers & Inslee, 1974; Augelli, Handis, Brumbaugh, Illig, Shearer, Turner, & Frankel, 1978; Genther, 1974; Rosenbaum & Calhoun, 1977; Schultz, 1975). Volunteers such as these would certainly seem to be concerned and well-intentioned. Yet despite such assumptions, the research suggests that untrained volunteers do not normally possess a high level of helping skills to combine with their good intentions. In order to be effective, helpers must combine their good intentions with helping skills; for it is the helper's skills that make the difference. Concern is clearly not enough.

None of this is intended to imply that volunteers or other types of uncredentialed helpers cannot be expert in the skills of helping. As a matter of fact, uncredentialed helpers who have buttressed their good intentions with a training program in the skills of helping can be as helpful or more helpful than the typical credentialed professional (Anthony & Carkhuff, 1978; Carkhuff, 1968).

References

Anthony, W.A. *The principles of psychiatric rehabilitation.* Amherst, Mass.: Human Resource Development Press, 1979.

Anthony, W.A., Buell, G.J., Sharratt, S., & Althoff, M.E. Efficacy of psychiatric rehabilitation. *Psychological Bulletin,* 1972, *78,* 447-456.

Anthony, W.A., & Carkhuff, R.R. The functional professional therapeutic agent. In Gurman and Razin (Eds.), *Effective psychotherapy: A handbook of research.* Oxford, England: Pergamon Press, 1978, pp. 103-119.

Anthony, W.A., Cohen, M.R., & Vitalo, R. The measurement of rehabilitation outcome. *Schizophrenia Bulletin,* 1978, *4,* 365-383.

Augelli, A., Handis, M., Brumbaugh, L., Illig, V., Shearer, R., Turner, D., & Frankel, J. Verbal helping behavior of experienced and novice telephone counselors. *Journal of Community Psychology,* 1978, *6,* 222-228.

Bergin, A.E. The evaluation of therapeutic outcomes. In A.E. Bergin & S.L. Garfield (Eds.), *Handbook of psychotherapy and behavior change.* New York: Wiley & Sons, 1971, pp. 217-270.

Brammer, L. *The helping relationship.* Englewood Cliffs, N.J.: Prentice-Hall, 1973.

Carkhuff, R.R. The differential functioning of lay and professional helpers. *Journal of Counseling Psychology*, 1968, *15*, 117-126.

Carkhuff, R.R. *Helping and human relations*. New York: Holt, Rinehart & Winston, 1969.

Carkhuff, R.R. *The development of human resources*. New York: Holt, Rinehart & Winston, 1971.

Carkhuff, R.R., & Berenson, B.G. *Beyond counseling and psychotherapy*. New York: Holt, Rinehart & Winston, 1967, 1977.

Carkhuff, R.R., & Berenson, B.G. *Teaching as treatment*. Amherst, Mass.: Human Resource Development Press, 1976.

Carothers, J.E., & Inslee, L.J. Level of empathic understanding offered by volunteer telephone services. *Journal of Counseling Psychology*, 1974, *21*, 274-276.

Combs, A.W., Avila, D.L., & Purkey, W.W. *Helping relationships*. Boston: Allyn & Bacon, 1978.

Danish, S., & Hauer, A. *Helping skills: A basic training program*. New York: Behavioral Publications, 1973.

Egan, *The skilled helper*. Belmont: Brooks-Cole, 1975.

Eysenck, H.J. The effects of psychotherapy. In J.J. Eysenck (Ed.), *The handbook of abnormal psychology*. New York: Basic Books, 1960.

Gazda, G. *Human relations development: A manual for educators*. Boston: Allyn & Bacon, 1973.

Genther, R. Evaluating the functioning of community hot lines. *Professional psychology*, 1974, *5* (4), 409-414.

Goodman, G. *Companionship therapy*. San Francisco: Jossey-Bass, 1972.

Guerney, B. *Relationship enhancement*, San Francisco: Jossey-Bass, 1977.

Ivey, A., & Authier, J. *Microcounseling*. Springfield, Ill.: Thomas, 1978.

Kagan, N. *Influencing human interaction*. Washington, D.C.: APGA, 1975.

Levitt, E.E. Psychotherapy with children: A further evaluation. *Behavior Research and Therapy*, 1963, *1*, 45-51.

Lewis, W.W. Continuity and intervention in emotional disturbance: A review. *Exceptional children*, 1965, *31*, 465-475.

Patterson, C.H. *Theories of counseling and psychotherapy*. New York: Harper & Row, 1973.

Rogers, C.R., Gendlen, E.T., Kiesler, D., & Truax, C.B. *The therapeutic relationship and its impact*. Madison, Wisc.: University of Wisconsin Press, 1967.

Rosenbaum, A., & Calhoun, J. The use of the telephone hotline in crisis intervention: A review. *Journal of Community Psychology*, 1977, *5*, 325-339.

Schulman, E. *Intervention in human services.* St. Louis: Mosby, 1974.

Schultz, J.L. Hotlines: Is concern enough? *The vocational guidance quarterly,* 1975, *23* (4), 367-368.

Truax, C.B., & Carkhuff, R.R. *Toward effective counseling and psychotherapy.* Chicago: Aldine, 1967.

What is this chapter all about?

This first chapter equates helping with learning in that the individual who has truly been helped has learned to function more effectively. Thus the four phases of the pre-helping and helping processes are identical to the phases of individual activity reflected in all learning processes: involvement in the process, exploration of the situation, reaching an understanding of personal deficits and responsibilities, and taking action to reach new goals.

Where does the overall helping model come in?

The model outlined in this chapter is a developmental one showing the four phases of helpee activity — involvement, exploration, understanding, and action — and the specific subprocesses that each of these major phases entails. Such a model is not presented as an arbitrary and restrictive structure but, rather, as an accurate reflection of the stages of activity that any individual will complete as he or she learns to function more effectively.

INVOLVEMENT EXPLORATION UNDERSTANDING ACTION
(I) ➧ **(E)** ➧ **(U)** ➧ **(A)**

Why is the helping model important?

As is indicated in this chapter, many credentialed and uncredentialed helpers alike fall victim to two erroneous beliefs: that efforts that do not help will at least not hurt; and that good intentions and common sense are all the helper really needs. In fact, there is ample evidence to show that counseling sessions that do not help must always hurt — and that helper skills rather than good intentions or common sense are the critical ingredients in helping. The model presented in this chapter is crucially important in that it shows how and when the focus of helpee activity must shift if helpees are to learn how to function effectively — that is, if they are to be helped rather than hurt. The model also shows the particular phases of helpee activity that the helper must promote through the use of those skills that are the substantive concern of this text.

Who must do what in terms of the model?

As indicated, the basic I-E-U-A model shown here reflects the four primary phases of helpee activity. The skills that the helper must employ are treated individually in each of the following chapters. Helpees vary according to the phases of the helping model in which they need the most help. Not all helpees require that the helper use all the various helping skills in any one helping situation. However, because helpees vary so tremendously in terms of their own unique needs, a helper must be proficient in all the skills related to the helping model. In this way the helper can call on those particular helping skills that are appropriate to the specific needs of each individual client.

Also, though the actual helper skills are learned in discrete stages, this does not imply that the actual implementation of these skills in the helping process is perfectly sequential. However, what the helping model does is to keep the helper on track. It provides helpers with a guide as to what skills they should be using as well as the activities in which helpees should be engaged.

When should a helper use the model?

Whenever the helper is involved with an individual or a group that needs help! The model is sequential and thus reminds the effective helper of precisely what outcome to promote at any given stage. Helpees cannot act until they understand the personalized situation. Helpees cannot achieve such understanding until they have explored the immediate situation. And helpees cannot undertake any real process of exploration until they have become involved in the helping process itself.

What can you do to gain insight into the basic helping process?

As indicated, helping begins with learning. The pattern of helpee movement through the phases of helping is precisely the same as the pattern of individual growth and learning. Thus you may be able to gain insight into the model by observing and/or reflecting upon any learning process.

For example, you might think about how you have gone about mastering any body of new material in school. Chances are you began by getting involved. After all, you could not master the materials unless you had enrolled in the course and attended some classes. Once you were involved, you probably spent some time exploring the more external aspects of the course: names, dates, facts, important concepts, and so forth. This exploration paved the way for a greater and more personalized understanding of what the materials were all about; at this level you probably stopped thinking of all the material as abstract and external to your own situation and started thinking instead of how the material related to you as a unique individual. Finally, your real mastery of the material was reflected in the action you took based upon your new level of understanding. Like all of us, you learned more than theories or concepts or principles or facts — you learned to *do* something!

Look for the basic I-E-U-A pattern in your own learning activities. Look for it as well in the learning activities of other people with whom you are familiar. You will find that, far from being arbitrary or abstract, the basic model reflects what is really going on when any individual grows and learns — and especially when that individual is receiving the help truly needed!

helping people get involved: ATTENDING SKILLS 2

Overview

1. Full helpee *involvement* is the essential aim of prehelping activity.

2. The helper can promote full helpee involvement by employing basic *attending* skills.

3. The first phase of helpee involvement requires that each helpee make and sustain an *appearance*.

4. To promote helpee appearance, the helper uses those attending skills involved in *preparing* for the helpee by informing him or her of the availability of help, encouraging the helpee's appearance, and arranging the helping setting in the most effective manner.

5. The second phase of helpee involvement focuses on the helpee's *nonverbal expressions*.

6. The helper promotes and learns from these nonverbal expressions by using those attending skills involved in *positioning*, i.e., posturing oneself at the appropriate angle, level, inclination, and maintaining eye contact.

7. The third phase of helpee involvement is signaled by the helpee's presentation of *verbal expressions*.

8. The helper promotes the helpee's verbal expressions by using those attending skills involved in *observing* the helpee and thus communicating interest and concern.

9. The fourth and final level of helpee involvement is reflected in the helpee's *expression of personally relevant material*.

10. The helper promotes the helpee's expression of such material by continuing to position and observe while actively *listening* to both the tone and content of helpee statements.

11. The attending skills of positioning, observing, and listening allow the helper to accomplish a dual aim: *to promote greater helpee involvement and to gather important information about the helpee.*

Helping is a process of learning: learning to *explore,* to *understand,* and to *act.* Before clients or helpees can begin this process of learning, however, they must become *involved.* They must be drawn into an initial helping session and made to see that the aid a counselor or helper is offering can and will make a real and tangible difference in their lives. Contrary to what may be popularly believed, a majority of helpees either never appear for helping or quit the helping process prematurely. They either never become involved or do not stay involved. Thus, the first skills the helper/counselor needs to develop are the prehelping skills required to involve clients in the learning process. These are the skills on which we will focus our attention in this chapter.

Here as elsewhere, of course, many counselors feel that all they need to do is adopt a "common sense" approach. Such a feeling is clearly reflected in the approach taken by Linda Goodman in the following account. Check to see how effective her common sense is in getting her helpees involved.

Linda is a second-year history teacher at Mathias High School. Having largely overcome the nervousness that characterized her first year at Mathias, she has recently begun to gain considerable self-confidence. Like many teachers, Linda came to realize that not all meaningful work with students is confined to the academic classroom. In terms of her own history classes, her students' verbal and mechanical skills are profoundly influenced by such "external" factors as TV and outside reading. Then, too, Linda discovered that even her slowest students were capable of good work if they were sufficiently motivated. And their varying degrees of motivation, it turned out, were directly linked to their plans for the future.

In recent weeks, Mathias High had been without a placement counselor. Seeing this as a golden opportunity to motivate some of her lagging seniors, Linda decided to act as unofficial counselor and help these students concretize their plans for the future. If she can help them see the difference that academic work can make to their educational or career goals, Linda reasoned, she can improve the quality of their work in her class. This is all quite commendable.

Linda's first move in this motivational campaign was to choose six students whose past efforts had been less than inspiring. Rather than risk a fuss in class by issuing a verbal invitation ("Hey, Ms. Goodman, how come you wanta see him?" "Hey, what's going on, anyway?"), she posted an announcement on the central bulletin board asking the six — Harry Daniels, Jim Cruikshank, Debby LePetre, Shari Bullit, Mark Tessa, and Lou Johnson — to meet with her at 2:30 that afternoon in her classroom. Her next move was to bring in a collection of brochures and pamphlets she had gathered that dealt with a variety of colleges and career possibilities.

Feeling quite pleased with herself — after all, this definitely *was* above and beyond the call of contractual duty — Linda returned to her classroom at 2:30 to wait for her six helpees. One — Harry — was already there.

"Hey, Ms. Goodman, how come you want to see me and the other kids?"

"Well, Harry — you're Harry, right?" (Linda still had some trouble with names; after all, she saw some 150 students each day.) "Yes. Well, I thought I might help you out by going over some of your plans for next year. Now that Mr. Spezik isn't here, you really don't have anyone to work with you on placement things. So I thought I could fill in, that's all."

"You mean find out about colleges and jobs and stuff? Hey, that's good! We really need someone like that!" Harry plunked himself down in the center seat in the front row and waited to be instructed.

"I wasn't sure what the best time would be to meet," Linda said, sneaking a look over her shoulder at the clock high over the chalkboard. "I hope that this is a convenient time for you and the others . . ."

"Oh, yeah, it's cool," Harry hastened to assure her. "If I wasn't here, I'd just have to be down at my old man's store working for him. I'm always glad to stick around after school!"

"I see . . ." Linda wasn't quite sure how to respond to this. Fortunately, Jim, Debby, and Lou chose this moment to appear.

"Hi, Ms. Goodman. What'd you wanta see us about?" Debby asked. Linda repeated the explanation she had given Harry. Debby and Lou shrugged and took seats, apparently willing to stick around and see what developed. But Jim was considerably less enthusiastic.

"Aw, Ms. Goodman, I don't have time for that stuff. I gotta work all day and night too if I'm gonna get my English paper done. Besides, I *know* what I'm gonna do after graduation. I'm gonna go work for my uncle in Hastings, servicing oil burners! I don't need none of this placement stuff."

Jim left, shaking his head and muttering to himself about how "everyone wants to to do somethin' different!" Linda snuck another look at the clock: 2:45. "Has anyone seen Shari Bullit or Mark Tessa?"

"Who?" Debby asked.

"I don't know about Shari what's-her-name," Harry volunteered. "But Mark Tessa's on the track team and they've got a meet today."

"Oh . . ." Linda hesitated, then came to a quick decision. "Well, let's begin and maybe Shari'll show up. Harry, why don't you start by telling us a little bit about your plans for next year. Do you have any idea what you want to be doing?"

33

As it developed, Harry did. In fact, he had quite a few ideas. For the next 10 minutes he held the floor, outlining the program of studies he planned to take at the State University — courses designed to qualify him for a career in business.

"Have you thought at all about applying to other colleges that might have a better business curriculum?" Linda asked at one point. But Harry shook his head vehemently.

"Uh uh. State's the only place I can afford to go. Besides, that's where my brother Mike went, and he's earning twenty thou' a year with the degree he got! That sounds all right to me!" And Harry proceeded to explain to one and all just how his brother Mike went about earning his "twenty thou'."

Finally, with Harry starting to run down, Linda decided to reassert her control over the group. "What about you, Debby? What are your plans?" As it turned out, however, Debby's plans for the immediate future centered around her ride home.

"I'm sorry, Ms. Goodman, but I really gotta go! My ride won't wait for me!"

Having said his piece, Harry apparently felt it was time for him to leave as well. Lou Johnson was the only student left. Linda considered getting Lou to talk about his plans but decided that there wasn't much point in the absence of what she thought of as essential "peer support."

"I'm sorry, Lou," she said. "Listen, I'll arrange another session for — oh, say next Tuesday. And you can go first, OK?"

Lou shrugged and got up. "Yeah, I guess so." He looked around the room uncertainly. "If I can make it. I'll have to see how — how my school work and stuff is going, huh? I'll let you know. . . ."

Linda watched Lou's figure retreating down the hall. "Oh, well," she murmured. "Not a great start, maybe — but not a bad one. At least they found out they can come to me for help . . ."

Not a bad start? Perhaps the saddest thing about situations like this is that the "helper" often feels that he or she has accomplished something positive when actually the effects on helpees are quite the reverse. The Harrys leave convinced that "placement counseling" is just another chance to brag or blow off steam. The Debbys and Lous leave convinced that the "counselor" could not care less about them. The Jims do not bother to stick around, feeling that anyone who really wanted to help would not schedule such a session at such an inconvenient time. And the Sharis and Marks, having cut one session, decide that there would be even less point in attending a second.

Linda was unable to help any of the six students with whom she met. How could she help when — with the possible exception of Harry — she didn't even succeed in getting them involved?

Remember the way in which we outlined the helpee's movement through the prehelping phase? In reviewing this outline, we would have to conclude that Linda failed to promote or sustain the appearance of three helpees, failed to promote the verbal expression of two helpees, and failed to move even the one helpee who did express himself into the area of personally relevant discussion.

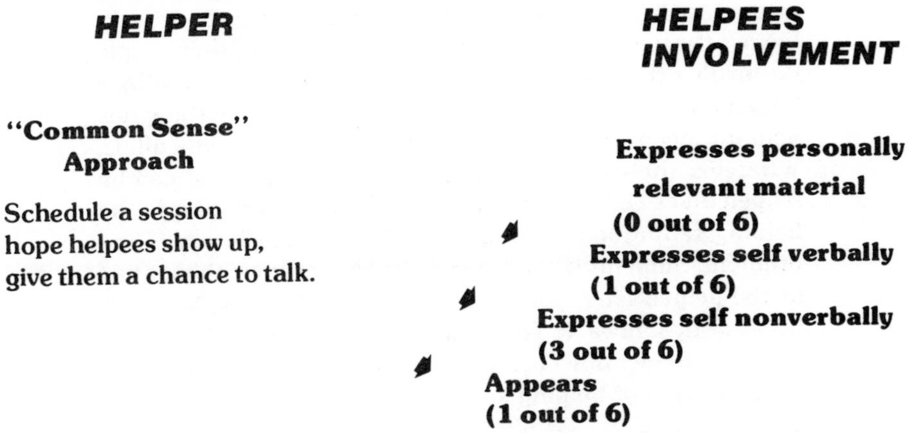

HELPER

"Common Sense" Approach

Schedule a session hope helpees show up, give them a chance to talk.

HELPEES INVOLVEMENT

Expresses personally relevant material (0 out of 6)

Expresses self verbally (1 out of 6)

Expresses self nonverbally (3 out of 6)

Appears (1 out of 6)

Figure 2-1: Impact of Linda's "Common Sense" approach on helpee involvement.

We cannot criticize Linda's intentions. She *wanted* to help her students. In the end, however, she was unable to do so because she did not have the professional skills needed to involve her people in the helping process. It is to these specific skills, then, that we must now turn our attention. In dealing with these skills, the counselor's aim should be to learn what he or she needs to know and do to *get people involved!*

Involving helpees or clients in the helping process entails two separate functions. On the one hand, the helper must communicate real interest and concern in order to get helpees to relax and "open up." On the other hand, the helper must function in such a way as to develop her or his own understanding of where these particular helpees are in terms of their own problems and unique frames of reference. Stated somewhat differently, the helper must give assurance and take in information. To accomplish these dual purposes, the helper can and should make use of basic *attending skills.* Such skills involve four main areas of activity: *preparing, positioning, observing,* and *listening.* We will consider these four areas in turn.

Preparing

Helpee Goal:

To appear for help and remain in the helping setting.

There are many, many individuals who experience severe difficulties of one sort or another yet never come to a counselor or helper for the assistance they need. In some cases they may simply be unaware of the availability of such help. In other cases they may be vaguely or even acutely aware that help is available but be apprehensive about seeking out the people who are there to help them. Other people do involve themselves in an initial meeting or two with a helper but then "drop out" or fade away before anything has actually been done to resolve their individual difficulties. Whatever the case, one fact is clear: No individual can be helped unless he or she appears for help and remains in the helping setting long enough to achieve a resolution of the problem. Such initial and sustained appearance, then, must be the helpee's first goal — albeit one of which the helpee is necessarily unaware. To promote and sustain such appearance, the helper must use specific attending skills to *prepare* for a delivery of helping services.

Helper Skills:

Informing, encouraging, and arranging the setting.

The first thing any helper must do to promote helpee involvement is *inform* each helpee of the helper's availability, either on a continuing basis or in relation to a specific situation or set of problems. Linda chose to inform her students about the meeting by posting a notice on the bulletin board at her school. Such an approach is usually as ineffective as it is familiar. We have all seen this sort of bland, depersonalized notice. And we have all experienced at either first or second hand the sort of "Ah, why bother?" reaction that such notices prompt.

Some clients or helpees, of course, are anxious to receive help and only need to be informed about the availability of such help. Other helpees, however, may not even suspect that a real or potential source of help for their unique area of concern exists. These people will invariably react in a far more positive fashion to a *personal invitation* than to an impersonal notice of some kind. A personal invitation — delivered either verbally or in writing — tells each person that the helper is aware of him or her as an individual. This initial contact is critically important in creating an atmosphere of true concern and interest.

Linda could have taken steps to issue a personal invitation to each of the six students if she had bothered to check the records available in the school office. Such a check would have let her know where each of the six could be reached during the school day — assuming, that is, that Linda could not have simply spoken to each of the six before or after her class. This check would also have revealed any potential scheduling conflicts — as with Mark's track team involvement, for example. Armed with the necessary information, Linda could then have issued a personal invitation to each of the six several days before the meeting date in order to give them plenty of "lead time" — again, a way to say, "I'm dealing with this with *your* convenience in mind!" Had she done this, Linda might have had six people in attendance rather than the four who actually showed up.

The content of an invitation is no less important than the personal manner in which it is delivered. Such an invitation can *encourage* the physical appearance of helpees if it stresses the specific benefits that appearance may bring. In other words, the emphasis should be on one or another version of the familiar "If you contact me, you will learn something to your advantage" approach.

Since two of Linda's six prospective helpees never put in an appearance, her possible success rate once the meeting started was never greater than 66 percent. Had she issued a personal invitation to each of the six that stressed what was in the meeting for them, she could have done a great deal to improve these odds. Again, some preliminary checking might have helped her learn about individual student's interests and concerns. She might have learned, for example, that Debby was in a college preparatory program and hoped to be a teacher while Lou was in a vocational program that emphasized various metalwork courses. Linda could then have personalized the six invitations in order to stress the individual benefits for each student: "As you probably know, Debby, the teaching market is not very good these days. However, I have a few ideas that might help you get out in front of the competition."

Once a helpee or a group of helpees has put in an initial appearance, the helper must ensure that such appearance is sustained. One key way in which the helper can prepare for this is by *arranging the helping setting.*

The best setting for any counseling interaction is one in which each person can see and hear each other person equally well. In a one-to-one helping situation, then, the optimal setting will require two comfortable seats — preferably separate chairs placed three to four feet apart rather than a couch, since counselor and client can face one another this way without needing to turn their bodies in toward one another in what might become an awkward position. In working with a group of helpees — and all of our own extensive work has shown that any helping that can be done individually can be done more effectively in a group context — the helper should avoid the one-row-behind-another arrangement found in classrooms and use instead a seating arrangement where chairs are placed in an open arc (for helpees) facing the helper's own seat or in an oval where the helper can sit at one end. Arrangements of this sort make it possible to attend to each helpee in turn while ensuring that no other helpee will feel left out or ignored.

In general, a helper should use the arc arrangement of helpee seats when all helpees can fit within a 90-degree angle of her or his own seat. This is the maximum angle allowing the counselor to turn easily from one person to another without placing her or his shoulder or back to someone at the opposite end of the arc. Whether employing the arc or oval, the helper can check the effectiveness of the seating arrangement by asking two questions: "Can each person see and hear me and each other?" and "Can I see and hear each person equally well?" If the answer is yes in each case, the seating arrangement is probably quite effective.

In addition to the seating arrangement, the helper must control and focus what might be termed the "decorative" aspects of the helping setting. To begin with, each helpee should be able to look around the room and find evidence of the helper's commitment to the helpee's own area of concern. An individual seeking vocational counseling should find specific career-oriented materials. A couple visiting a marriage counselor should find materials related to interpersonal skills, family problem-solving, and the like. An outpatient with a drinking problem who visits a clinic should find materials concerned with approaches to that problem. In most cases a helper can anticipate the general types of helpees with whom she or he will be working. All supportive materials (pamphlets, wall posters, and the like) should reflect the helper's commitment to dealing with problems that fall within the typical helpee's area of concern.

It is equally important for the helper to make sure that the setting does not contain any distractions or irrelevant materials. The helper's office is not a private sanctuary into which he or she can retreat; it is the place where the helper carries out the greater part of his or her work. Thus, everything about this setting should reflect the helper's awareness of helpees' probable frames of reference rather than simply reflecting the helper's own personality or private concerns. This means no provocative political posters, no distracting wall clocks — and no signs of counselor confusion like overflowing wastebaskets or heaps of paperwork.

If the helper prepares effectively for the helpee, the helpee will probably appear initially and continue to appear. But this is only the first step in helpee involvement. The helper can and should promote greater involvement by using those attending skills that involve *positioning*.

Positioning

Helpee Goal:

To express himself or herself nonverbally.

It has been argued that no individual can avoid a certain amount of nonverbal communication. There is certainly some truth in such an argument. Even the helpee who sits slumped in a chair without moving throughout an hour-long session is expressing something about his or her experience of the world. Nevertheless, there are degrees of nonverbal expression, just as there are degrees of fluency and articulation, fullness and accuracy, in the area of verbal expressions. The more relaxed a helpee is — and the more he or she recognizes the genuineness of the helper's concern — the more the helpee will express nonverbally. Such nonverbal expression represents the helpee's goal at this second level of involvement — albeit a goal of which the helpee is once again unaware. The helper can promote (and subsequently learn from) such nonverbal expressions by employing those attending skills that involve physical *positioning*.

Helper Skills:

Positioning with respect to level, angle, inclination, and eye contact.

All of the positioning skills the helper uses assume an optimum distance between the helper and helpee or helpees. In general, the best distance is three to four feet in a one-to-one situation. The helper may have to increase this distance to avoid crowding when working with several helpees at once. When responding to any individual helpee within such a group, however, the helper should try to narrow the gap somewhat to achieve this optimum distance. Staying three to four feet from a helpee allows the helper to see and hear all visual and verbal cues without infringing on the helpee's "private space." With this requirement as to distance in mind, let us look at the specific positioning skills involving level, angle, inclination, and eye contact.

When Linda spoke to her helpees, she took a position half-sitting, half-leaning on the corner of her desk. We might call this familiar position the "professional perch." Such a position may seem helpful when helpees are seated in rows. Given an effective seating arrangement, however, the position is often unnecessary and even counterproductive. Instead, the helper should try whenever possible to take a position that puts him or her on the same *level* with the helpees. For one thing, the helper can see helpees' faces better this way. For another, he or she can communicate a "helpful equality," which is quite different from the "remote superiority" of a higher position. When using the chalkboard or making some type of group presentation, of course, the helper will want to assume a standing position even if the helpees are seated. When the presentation is over, however, the helper should go back to the helpees' level again to remind them in physical terms of his or her accessibility and interest.

Next there is the matter of helper positioning in terms of *angle*. We have all run into the supposed helper — teacher, parent, counselor, or just a friend — whose favorite "attentive" position is one in which he or she leans back or turns away. Many people defend such a position: "I'm just relaxed, that's all — I can really hear better this way!" In practice, however, it seems that such turning away often succeeds in "turning off" individual helpees or clients. This should not surprise us. After all, who seems more interested in the closing moments of an exciting movie — the guy who is looking the other way or the guy leaning forward and facing the screen directly?

The best angle the counselor or helper can take with a helpee is one that has her fully squared with that helpee: her right shoulder directly across from his left and vice-versa. When working with a group of helpees, the helper should take and hold this position with each helpee in turn, demonstrating quite graphically that she is really paying attention, that she is really focusing her concern.

Inclination, like angle, says a good deal about the quality of our attending. When we lean back, we put ourselves "out of reach" in visual terms. Our posture says, "I'm willing to stick around, but I'm not really going to get involved." At the same time, we are less able to see the helpees and take note of important visual cues.

Rather than leaning back or even sitting totally erect, the helper should incline his upper body toward each helpee to whom he is attending. When seated, he should lean forward about 30 degrees until he can comfortably rest his forearms on his thighs. When standing, he should incline his upper body about 10 degrees forward — not enough to appear uncomfortable but enough to say, in effect, "I am inclined to help you." Again, such a posture is natural for anyone genuinely involved in what is going on. The forward inclination of the body signals a helper's real interest, just as it signals the interest of the genuine movie fan. And at the same time, it allows the helper to take in maximum information about each helpee.

The counselor should attend to each helpee by putting herself at the same level, by adopting a squared-off angle, by inclining her body forward — and by making frequent *eye contact.* Such contact is perhaps the single most effective way of saying, "I'm really here with you, I'm really involved, I really care."

We are all familiar with the practiced gazes that seem to take us in while actually focusing just over our shoulder or just to one side or another of our eyes. What a difference when we actually make eye contact! It is as if a tiny electrical spark leaped between us and the other person. The helper or counselor should make frequent eye contact with each helpee for periods of at least 20 seconds. Doing so will communicate real concern — and at the same time, allow the helper to learn something about the helpee by seeing whether he or she meets or avoids this contact.

At this point let us briefly review. The first attending skills the effective helper needs to develop are those bound up in the acts of *preparing* and *positioning.* Activities such as informing, encouraging, and arranging the setting should be specifically designed to get clients or helpees involved in the overall process of helping. The other attending behaviors or skills — those concerned with positioning through level, angle, inclination, and eye contact — provide a continuing basis for subsequent helping. In developing such skills, the helper is systematizing the several ways in which he can promote greater helpee involvement by communicating interest while gathering information for his own consideration. But just how can this process of information gathering be accomplished? To answer this, we must move on to a third major area of concern: *observing*.

Observing

Most of us — especially if we lean toward the "common sense" approach to helping — tend to think of observation as a natural and automatic capability. In actual practice, however, we are often far less observant than we think. We meet someone and later can recall only the most obvious features: sex, general size, approximate age, and so on. Or we meet the same person and immediately leap to some sweeping conclusion concerning her or his character — "What a grouchy guy!" — on the basis of only the most limited sort of observational data.

"Ah," we may be tempted to say. "Sure, some people aren't very observant. But it's an easy skill to acquire. Look at all the professionals who have to be observant as part of their job!"

If we find that our thoughts run in this direction, we might want to consider an actual situation that occurred during an in-service training program for experienced police officers. During one class period, a senior police administrator lectured to the assembled officers on the importance of visual observation. By previous arrangement, a young man slipped quietly into the room in the middle of the lecture. This man had a mustache, wore his long hair in a ponytail, was slender and about six feet tall, and wore blue coveralls with the legend "ACE WINDOW SERVICE" on the back. Without interrupting the lecture, he crossed behind the speaker and proceeded to wash the large window. Having performed this task, he left as quietly as he had come.

At this point the speaker abruptly halted his lecture and asked each of his "students" to write out a brief description of the person who had just spent five minutes in full view of the class. Of the 16 police officers in the class, 8 identified the visitor as a woman, 3 others omitted any reference to his large droopy mustache, and only 1 recalled the legend on the back of his coveralls. As if this were not bad enough, 7

42

officers were unable to specify any task he had performed while most of the others indicated he had done things like "empty wastebaskets" and "move chairs around." In the end, not 1 of the 16 experienced police officers was able to give anything approaching an accurate description of the visitor and his actions while in the room!

So much for the observational skills of many professionals. Such a deficiency is bad enough when it occurs among trained police personnel. But it is even more disastrous and intolerable when it exists among the ranks of professional counselors or helpers. After all, can any of us reasonably expect to help someone if we are not even able to *see* that person fully and accurately? Of course not! The plain truth is that we cannot begin to help people until we have developed the functional skills needed to observe that person. As helpers, we accomplish two things by using observing skills. We promote our helpees' verbal expressions by signaling our attentiveness and concern; and we learn a good deal about the helpees by taking in visual information.

Helpee Goal:
To express her/himself verbally as well as nonverbally.

A helpee's initial appearance and nonverbal expressions signal at least tentative involvement in the helping process. Yet no helpee can gain much simply by putting in an appearance and expressing through nonverbal behavior his or her experience of the world. It is obviously important for the helpee to go beyond these initial stages of involvement and begin to "open up" verbally as well as nonverbally. At first the helpee's conversation may be superficial and largely irrelevant in terms of her or his problem. Such conversation — about the weather, about the counseling setting, about a host of topics — represents a natural transition for the helpee from simple appearance and nonverbal expression to the eventual discussion of personally relevant material. Such conversation represents as well the helpee's goal at the third level of involvement. The helper can promote the helpee's achievement of this verbal goal through his or her own nonverbal *observing,* which continues to express the helpers attentiveness and genuine concern.

Helper Skills:
Observing to draw inferences concerning helpee energy level, feelings, and relationship with helper.

The skilled helper knows that the simple act of attentive *observing* will promote her verbal expression. But the helper also knows that she must identify and ultimately enter each helpee's unique frame of reference — the particular way in which that helpee views and responds to the world. In order to accomplish this, the counselor must first observe specific aspects of the helpee's appearance and behavior and then, having amassed as much observational data as possible, use this data to draw some careful inferences concerning the helpee's frame of reference.

Again, many of us find it easy to draw inferences — but not so easy when these inferences are required to have a firm observational basis. For this reason, the helper should limit his initial observations to concrete and tangible aspects of helpee appearance and behavior: not "he looks happy," but "he is smiling;" not "she must be worried," but "she continuously clenches and unclenches her hands." The first statement in each pair represents a fairly typical — and often grossly inaccurate — assumption. A smile is neither a necessary nor sufficient proof of happiness. Only observations focusing on verifiable data are helpful at this point. If a helper is not sure of the validity of an observation, he should ask, "Would anyone else who was here agree with exactly what I see?" Only when the helper has gathered as much data as possible should he attempt to draw any inferences — and even then, these should be considered highly tentative, subject to later support or contradiction.

Although any number of different kinds of inferences can be drawn, we will limit ourselves to three areas: *energy level, helper-helpee relationship,* and general "feeling" state. We observe for energy level because this is the best indicator of the helpee's potential for new and more constructive action. We observe for cues concerning the helper-helpee relationship because this is our source for understanding how the helpee experiences both us and the world. Finally, we observe for cues that will allow us to respond later to the ever-changing "feeling" states that the helpee is experiencing.

In making observations, the counselor or helper must ask and answer the following question: "Does this feature of the helpee's behavior or appearance tell me about his level of energy, his relationship to me, or his general feeling?" Five specific areas on which to concentrate are *body build, posture, grooming, focus* (where the helpee's attention is directed), and continued *nonverbal expression.* Again, observations in each of these five areas should be tied to specific and objectively verifiable visual cues.

In terms of *body build*, the helper can begin by answering the question: "Clothes and grooming aside, how can I describe this individual's physical appearance?" One person, for example, might be described as "about 5'6" and approximately 190 pounds." Note that the helper would not use a term like "overweight" here — at this point, any such term would still be far too subjective, a value judgment rather than an observational fact. Another person might be "about 6' and 150 pounds." Again, the counselor would use objective terms like these as opposed to subjective terms like "slender" or "skinny" to avoid making too hasty a value judgment.

Posture, of course, means the way in which the helpee holds his or her body. Here the helper can ask and answer the question, "What is the shape of this person's body while sitting or standing?" By dealing with the shape of the body, the helper is again able to avoid hasty and subjective discriminations. Thus she or he can answer, "He sits low in his seat with his spine curved forward and his shoulders drooping," or "She stands erect with one shoulder pushed slightly forward." As with body build, posture can reveal a good deal about a helpee. In particular, it is eventually possible to draw inferences on the basis of posture related to the helpee's energy level, feelings, and even his or her relationship with the counselor.

Grooming here may be taken to involve both mode of dress and level of personal hygiene. Since we are all tempted quite often to make value judgments based on a person's style of dress and degree of cleanliness, the helper must be particularly careful in gathering observational data related to grooming. She might try categorizing observations by asking, "Is this person clean?" and "Is this person neatly dressed and groomed?" and settling for two simple yes/no answers. Thus a person who appeared in a sharp suit, hair combed, looking as if he just took a shower, would get a yes on cleanliness and another yes on neatness. And a person who looked scrubbed yet appeared in grubby jeans and a sweatshirt would get a yes (cleanliness) and a no (neatness) in that order.

The direction of a helpee's *focus* can obviously reveal a lot about her potential relationship with the helper as well as a good deal about her own feelings. The question to ask and answer here is a simple one: "Where is she looking most of the time?" Thus one helpee may sit slumped in a chair with his eyes on his shoes while another may sit back and keep looking from the helper to a clock that is visible to her. (Needless to say, the helper's own eventual aim is to get the helpee to be able to focus on him even as the helper is using his attending and observing skills, focusing on the helpee.)

Finally, there is the area of continued *nonverbal expressions*. There is ample evidence showing that the various ways in which we move our bodies and our faces reflect a good deal about what we are feeling and thinking. But we cannot assume that any complete and standardized "vocabulary" of nonverbal expressions exists. Different people express themselves in different ways. For example, most Westerners indicate agreement by nodding the head up and down. But many people in Asian societies indicate just the opposite, complete disagreement, by using the same head motion. By the same token, there is the story about the New York City high school principal who, having accused a young Puerto Rican girl of a particular action, was convinced of her guilt because she refused to meet his gaze and looked down at the floor instead. He failed to understand that this girl's cultural background included a strong injunction against looking an adult in the eyes — something no "good" Puerto Rican girl would do!

In identifying nonverbal expressions, then, the counselor must again limit herself to strict observational data. The question to ask here is, "What is this person doing that might be seen as an instance of nonverbal expression?" Is she looking at the ceiling? Is he covering most of his mouth by leaning on his hand whenever he speaks? Is she clutching her books against her chest all through the counselor's initial talk? The helper should not, at this point, attempt to draw any inferences or interpretation from the nonverbal signals perceived. Instead, she should wait until all the evidence is in and then try to determine the direction in which this evidence collectively points.

Once the helper has gathered as much observational data as possible concerning a helpee's behavior and appearance — data reflecting the three categories of energy, relationship, and feeling — he can work to draw one or two careful inferences by asking: *"How energetic would I feel if I looked like or did this?"; "How would I feel about my helper if I looked like or did this?"*; and *"What feeling would I feel if I looked like or did this?"* The answers to such questions make it far easier for the helper to enter the helpee's own frame of reference.

The helper attending activities of *preparing* and *positioning* draw the helpee into initial involvement in the helping session. Helper *observing* promotes the helpee's transition from nonverbal to verbal expression while allowing the helper to amass visual data from which tentative inferences can be drawn. But the helpee at this point is still not fully involved. Such full involvement requires that the helpee begin to express personally relevant material. The helper can promote the helpee's attainment of this final level of involvement by continuing to observe the helpee and, at the same time, demonstrating her ability to *listen* to the helpee. By actively listening to what the helpee is saying, the helper communicates continued attentiveness and concern while at the same time gathering additional valuable information concerning the helpee and his situation.

Listening

Like observing, listening often seems to be a simple, automatic matter: "Sure, I'm listening!" In a helping situation, however, it is critically important that the counselor or helper recognize the way in which auditory as well as visual cues reveal each helpee's actual condition. How people look and what they do are inextricably linked to how and what they feel; in the same way, *what* helpees say and *how* they say it tells us a lot about how they perceive the world around them. The helper must also recognize the way in which his active listening can promote the helpee's expression of personally relevant material.

Helpee Goal:
To begin talking about things that really matter to him or her.

Few helpees will begin a helping session by launching immediately into a discussion of those things that are troubling them. In general, there would seem to be an inverse relationship between the seriousness of a given helpee's problem and the willingness of that helpee to initiate discussion of the problem. Simply stated, helpees with minor difficulties may be far readier to express themselves on these topics than helpees with severe problems — although there are, needless to say, many exceptions to this generalization.

Up to now the helpee has appeared, expressed herself nonverbally, and begun to talk. Expressions concerning personally relevant or meaningful material represent the help-ee's transition from what may have been only idle chatter to an initial exploration of the helpee's specific situation. Thus such personally relevant expressions represent the helpee's goal at the highest level of involvement. By actively listening to the helpee while continuing to use basic positioning and observing skills, the helper can promote the helpee's shift to this new level of involvement — and can, moreover, gain additional insight into the helpee's unique situation and experience.

Helper Skills:

Listening to draw inferences based on the content and tone of personally relevant helpee expressions.

As with observing, the counselor should not attempt to draw any inferences until he has taken in as much tangible data as possible concerning what a helpee has said (the *content* of expression) and how the helpee has spoken (the voice *tone* of expression).

Concerning content, the helper should practice listen-ing until she is able to repeat short helpee expressions word-for-word — not approximately but exactly! In the case of longer expressions, the helper should be able to summarize all the important elements of each statement, especially any words expressing feeling. A helpee may say, "Gee, my older brother's such a pain! He really makes me mad. He's always telling me I should be doing stuff the way he did it. He never lets me do it my own way!" The counselor should then be able to summarize the expression as follows: "He says he gets mad with his brother because the brother won't let him do things his own way but instead tries to make him do everything his (the brother's) way." Leaving out the word "mad" or omitting the helpee's specific relationship with the other person distorts the data and can render any later inference invalid.

The keys to capturing the content of a helpee's state-ment, then, are *repetition* and *summary*. In particular, the counselor must be able to remember the precise words of expressed feeling employed by the helpee. "Confused" is not the same as "confusing." And "foolish" does not always mean the same as "dumb" or "stupid." By developing the ability to accurately repeat or summarize a helpee's expres-sion, a counselor will have gone a long way toward entering that helpee's frame of reference.

But listening requires more than attention to content. A

helper must also be able to recognize the *tone of voice* used in a helpee's expression.

The key things to listen for concerning tone are the *loudness* or *softness* of the helpee's voice, *rapidity of speech,* and any *changes* in these two indicators. The helper is trying to determine how much the helpee seems to be involved in what he or she is saying. We tend to show our changes in involvement by changing the loudness and rapidity of our tone of voice:

> Helpee: "Yeah, today went OK, I guess. (low, slow monotone) *But boy am I excited about what's happening tonight!!* (loud and fast)

As careful listeners, helpers will notice the fact that the helpee was initially uninvolved (as evidenced by the low, slow monotone) but changed radically to a fast, loud tone indicating a greater involvement in what was to occur tonight. Cues like these and any radical change in the way a helpee usually expresses himself or herself help the counselor focus attention on the most important parts of a helpee's expressions.

As with observation, the helper should wait until all possible data are in before attempting to draw any inferences. Nor should such inferences ignore the data already collected through observation. Identifying and entering a helpee's unique frame of reference is a cumulative rather than a disjointed process; the more a counselor sees and hears, the better equipped he or she will be to understand and relate to the ways in which each helpee experiences her or his life.

We have noted the dual purpose of most attending skills: to communicate concern while gathering information. Both observing and listening play this dual role. By observing and listening to a helpee closely, the helper not only takes in essential data but also shows the helpee in the clearest way possible that she or he is vitally interested in helping. The helper is fully present, fully awake and alert, fully concerned. And in response, the helpee gradually becomes fully involved. The helpee is able to move off dead center and begin to take an active role in the overall helping process.

Bette and Jimmy

Now, how did Bette Simmons go about getting Jimmy Bessom involved in the helping process? To begin with, she *informed* Jimmy of her availability as a helper by issuing a personal invitation. Remember how she met him outside at lunchtime? Bette wasn't about to put her trust in an impersonal notice of some kind! She also made sure that her invitation contained some *encouragement* for Jimmy: "I know you're under a lot of pressure. . . . All I want to do is help you make a good decision." Finally, Bette knew how to *sustain* Jimmy's physical presence once he appeared in her office. All of the visible materials, whether texts or decorative posters, were relevant to the type of situation in which Jimmy found himself. "HOW TO FIND *THE JOB* THAT'S RIGHT FOR YOU" and "EDUCATION = SKILLS = INCOME." The setting was comfortably nonacademic: no "teacher's" desk and "student's" seat but, instead, a pair of comfortable chairs facing each other with a table beside them on which rested several pamphlets related to career and educational programs.

Needless to say, Bette had the skills she needed to attend fully to Jimmy. Despite his initial nervousness and even a vague suspicion that this woman might try to "railroad" him into choosing one course of action over another, Jimmy soon relaxed and was able to express himself to Bette. The way she sat forward, intent upon his words, her eyes constantly finding his — all this seemed strange at first but gradually served to convince Jimmy that Bette was sincere in her interest and concern. For her own part, Bette saw the way Jimmy sat with his arms wrapped across his chest, saw the way he kept shaking his head, heard the way he kept repeating words like "hassled" and phrases like "what a drag." And she was gradually able to identify the specific ways in which Jimmy viewed the chaos and frustration of his private world of indecision. She did not push or try to rush things. Bette's initial goal was to get Jimmy to express personally relevant material about himself and his problem. Once he was able to do this, she felt sure she would be able to help.

Bette attended to Jimmy — before the session to promote his appearance and during the session to communicate her concern and to encourage his nonverbal expression of himself. She observed his appearance and behavior in order to understand how he was experiencing the more troublesome aspects of his own life and to encourage his verbal expressions. Finally, she listened carefully in order to gain additional insight into his feelings and the reasons for these feelings, thus helping him discuss personally relevant material. In short, Bette succeeded in getting her client fully involved. The next step was to get him to explore his own feelings and attitudes. We will see how she goes about this at the end of our next chapter.

As illustrated below, we can see that *preparing* leads to helpee appearance, thus giving the helper an opportunity to use those *positioning* skills that facilitate the helpee's non-verbal expressions. The helper's use of *observing* skills encourages the helpee's verbal self-expression. Finally, the helper's ability to *listen* carefully to what is expressed prompts the helpee to discuss personally relevant material, signaling a full level of helpee involvement.

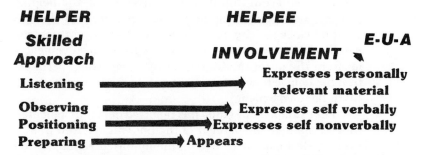

HELPER

**Skilled
Approach**

HELPEE

E-U-A

INVOLVEMENT

Listening ⟶ Expresses personally relevant material

Observing ⟶ Expresses self verbally

Positioning ⟶ Expresses self nonverbally

Preparing ⟶ Appears

Figure 2-2: A skilled helper like Bette uses attending skills to promote full helpee involvement.

The effective counselor must be familiar with all the simple yet essential attending skills needed to get any helpee involved in the helping process. The helper must spend time practicing these skills, all of which are outlined in this chapter: *preparing* by informing, encouraging, and arranging the setting; *positioning* through level, angle, inclination, and eye contact; *observing* cues related to helpee behavior and appearance; and *listening* to both the content and tone of helpee expressions. In time, the use of these skills become natural. The effective helper will be able to employ them to involve helpees and prepare them for the critical next step in the overall helping process: *exploration.*

The
Research
Background

At the prehelping or involvement stage of helping, the helping skills are essentially nonverbal. Except for the preliminary attending skills of informing and encouraging, these are all skills that the helper does "without opening his or her mouth." Perhaps because of the lack of verbal involvement, these attending skills are sometimes considered to be relatively simple and unimportant. Yet a number of research investigations suggest that these skills are more potent and more complex than is generally believed. (Barker, 1971; Birdwhistell, 1967; Carkhuff, 1969; Ekman, Friesen, & Ellsworth, 1972; Hall, 1959, 1976; Ivey & Authier, 1978; Mehrabian, 1972; Schefflen, 1969; Truax & Carkhuff, 1967.)

Getting and Keeping the Helpee Involved

It would seem that helpee involvement in the helping process should be a foregone conclusion. After all, helping is for the helpee — why not become involved? Unfortunately, significant data exist that indicate the helpee involvement is far from the norm (McClurek, 1978), suggesting, perhaps, that the helpee may not perceive helping as being totally for his or her own benefit.

For example, one study has reported data that indicated that as many as 66 percent of the patients referred from a psychiatric hospital to a community-based rehabilitation center chose not to attend the center (Wolkon, 1970). In addition, only half of those persons who began the program attended more than ten times. Other researchers have summarized data that indicated that a large number of clients prematurely drop out of counseling and psychotherapy of their own volition (Garfield, 1971). One such study found that of the 13,450 clients seen in 19 community mental health facilities, approximately 40 percent terminated treatment after only one session, and that the dropout rate for the nonwhite clients was significantly higher (Sue, McKinney, & Allen, 1976; Sue, McKinney, Allen, & Hall, 1974). Clearly, helpee involvement in the helping process cannot be taken for granted.

Positioning, Observing, and Listening

Some researchers (Genther & Moughan, 1977; Smith-Hanen, 1977) have investigated how different aspects of the helper's positioning skills affect how the helper is evaluated by the helpee. For example, Smith-Hanen (1977) found that certain leg and arm positions of the counselor do affect the helpee's judgment of counselor warmth and empathy. Genther and Moughan (1977) examined the effect of the counselor's forward leaning (incline) on the helpee's rating of attentiveness. In all instances the helper in the forward-leaning position was evaluated by the helpees as more attentive than the helper in an upright posture.

Additional research suggests that, besides attempting to get and keep the helpee involved, the positioning skills of the helper are also important because of their critical relationship to observing skills (Carkhuff, 1969). This relationship between helper positioning and observing skills is apparent in several key ways. First, an attentive posture and an appropriate environment facilitate observing, primarily by reducing the observer's possible distractions. Second, by making observations of a *helpee's attending position*, a helper can draw possible inferences about the helpee's feeling state and energy level. Third, positioning oneself so that you can pay attention to people can make people more nonverbally expressive, eliciting more nonverbal material to observe and verbal material to which to listen and from which to make inferences.

Obviously, attending by high-level functioning counselors produces different results from attending by low-level functioning counselors. In one project, the researchers (Genther & Saccuzzo, 1977) found that high-functioning counselors were significantly more accurate in their perceptions of the feelings and meaning of the client expressions than were low-functioning counselors. The clear implication of these results is that counselors must acquire attending skills in order to utilize effectively their observing skills.

Research findings in the area of verbal and nonverbal communication also support the contention that there is a relationship between positioning, observing, and listening skills (Barker, 1971; Mehrabian, 1972). Just as the helper's observing skills are in part a function of her or his positioning skills, a helper's listening skills are related to the skillfulness with which he or she positions oneself and observes. As a matter of fact, observing can be conceived of as a type of nonverbal listening. Interestingly, a person who indicates that she or he is listening nonverbally (observing) will increase the *verbal* output of the speaker. Additional research findings suggest that it is the listener's combined use of both observing and listening skills that allows the listener to identify discrepancies and incongruities between the speaker's verbal and nonverbal behaviors. The discovery of discrepancies of this type in the helpee's experience is an issue with which the helper and helpee will ultimately have to deal in the later phases of counseling.

In terms of listening skills, common sense would tell us that, because we have spent so much of our time in listening situations, we should be very good at it. (Approximately 40 percent of a person's daily verbal interaction is spent in listening.) Unfortunately, communication research suggests that immediately after listening to a short talk, a person remembers only one-half of what he or she has heard. This is not because the listener has not had time to listen. Most people are capable of comprehending speech at a rate three to four times faster than normal conversation. Thus the listener has plenty of time to think. The key to effective listening appears to be how the listener uses her or his extra "thinking time" (Carkhuff, 1972, 1977).

Attending behavior is an important core of behavior in a variety of counseling and therapeutic approaches. Some specific orientations such as Ivey and Authier's *Microcounseling* (1971, 1978) emphasize attending as the core of their counseling approach. In that approach the emphasis is on the counselor responding to the counselee's expression without stressing any of the more-advanced helping skills.

In summary, the research evidence suggests that the prehelping skills of positioning, observing, and listening appear to be both cumulative and causative skills. First of all, these prehelping skills are cumulative in that the helper can improve his or her observing skills through careful positioning; similarly, a helper can improve her or his listening skills by observing and positioning well. Second, these prehelping skills are causative in terms of their effect on the helpee. The successive implementation of each of these prehelping skills helps to bring about the desired developmental behavior in the helpee, which in turn allows for the more successful use of the helper's other helping skills. Preparing increases the chances of the helpee appearing for help. The helpee who appears for help becomes the subject of the helper's constant positioning skills, which in turn facilitate the helpee's expression of nonverbal behavior. The helpee, as he expresses himself nonverbally, becomes the subject of the helper's observing skills, which in turn facilitate the helpee's verbal expressions. The verbal expressions of the helpee become the target of the helper's listening skills. Finally, it is this combination of the helper's preparing, positioning, observing, and listening skills that facilitates the helpee's expression of personally relevant material to which the helper must skillfully *respond* — a skill that is the subject of the next chapter.

References

Barker, L.L. *Listening behavior.* Englewood Cliffs, N.J.: Prentice-Hall, 1971.

Birdwhistell, R. Some body motion elements accompanying spoken American English. In L. Thayer (Ed.), *Communication: Concepts and perspectives.* Washington, D.C.: Spartan, 1967.

Carkhuff, R.R. *Helping and human relations.* New York: Holt, Rinehart & Winston, 1969.

Carkhuff, R.R. *The art of helping III.* Amherst, Mass.: Human Resource Development Press, 1972, 1977.

Ekman, P., Friesen, W., & Ellsworth, P. *Emotion in the human face.* New York: Pergamon, 1972.

Garfield, S.L. Research on client variables in psychotherapy. In A.E. Bergin and S.L. Garfield (Eds.), *Handbook of psychotherapy and behavior change.* New York: Wiley & Sons, 1971.

Genther, R.W., & Moughan, J. Introverts' and extraverts' responses to non-verbal attending behavior. *Journal of Counseling Psychology,* 1977, *24,* 144-146.

Genther, R.W., & Saccuzzo, D.P. Accuracy of perceptions of psychotherapeutic content as a function of observers' level of facilitation. *Journal of Clinical Psychology,* 1977, *33,* 517-519.

Hall, E. *The silent language.* New York: Doubleday, 1959.

Hall, E. *Beyond culture.* Garden City, N.Y.: Doubleday, 1976.

Ivey, A., & Authier, J. *Microcounseling.* Springfield, Ill.: Thomas, 1971, 1978.

McClurek, R. Admitting personal problems and outcomes in hospitalized psychiatric patients. *Journal of Clinical Psychology,* 1978, *34,* 44-51.

Mehrabian, A. *Nonverbal communication.* New York: Aldine-Atherton, 1972.

Schefflen, A. *Stream and structure of communicational behavior.* Bloomington, Ind.: Purdue University Press, 1969.

Smith-Hanen, S. Nonverbal behavior and counselor warmth and empathy. *Journal of Counseling Psychology,* 1977, *24,* 87-91.

Sue, S., McKinney, H., & Allen, D.B. Predictors of the duration of therapy for clients in the community mental health center system. *Community Mental Health Journal,* 1976, *12,* 374-376.

Sue, S., McKinney, H., Allen, D.B., & Hall, I. Delivery of community mental health services to black and white clients. *Journal of Consulting and Clinical Psychology,* 1974, *43,* 794-801.

Truax, C.B., & Carkhuff, R.R. *Toward effective counseling and psychotherapy.* Chicago: Aldine, 1967.

Wolkon, G.W. Characteristics of clients and continuity of care into the community. *Community Mental Health Journal,* 1970, *6,* 215-221.

What is this chapter all about?

This chapter focuses on the basic attending skills — preparing, positioning, observing, and listening — which the helper must use to promote full helpee involvement on the one hand and to gather essential information about the helpee on the other.

Where does this fit in the overall helping model?

Helpee *involvement* represents the first of four major phases of helpee activity in the overall helping process. Such involvement is actually a prehelping phase that paves the way for subsequent helpee *exploration, understanding,* and *action.*

PREHELPING   **HELPING**

ACTION

UNDERSTANDING

EXPLORATION

INVOLVEMENT
Expresses personally relevant material
Expresses self verbally
Expresses self nonverbally
Appears

Figure 2-3: The steps of helpee **involvement.**

Why is helpee involvement important?

Obviously, of course, no individual can receive help until she or he has become involved in the helping process. Yet many of us tend to take helpee involvement for granted: "Anyone who needs help knows where to find me." Unfortunately, *the research evidence shows all too clearly that many individuals who need help never get involved with anyone who can give such help — and that many of those who appear for help drop out before they have become fully involved.* Thus it is essential that every helper acquire and be able to use the specific attending, observing, and listening skills that alone can assure full helpee involvement.

Who must do what to achieve full helpee involvement?

Involvement begins with the *appearance* of the helpee; the helper promotes and sustains such appearance by using those attending skills involved in *preparing* for the helpee — that is, informing him or her of the availability of help, encouraging the helpee to appear for help, and arranging the helping setting in the best possible way. Once the helpee appears, the helper promotes her or his *nonverbal expressions* by using the attending skills involved in *positioning* for optimum level, angle, inclination, and eye contact. At the third level of involvement, the helpee's *verbal expressions* are encouraged by the helper's use of those attending skills involved in *observing* the helpee; while communicating real attentiveness and concern, such observing skills allow the helper to focus on helpee body build, posture, grooming, focus, and nonverbal behavior and to draw tentative inferences concerning the helpee's energy level, feelings, and probable relationship with the helper. Finally, the helpee signals full involvement by beginning to *express personally relevant material*. The helper promotes such expression by continuing to position and observe while actively *listening* to both the content and tone of helpee statements; such listening also allows the helper to gather additional information about the helpee.

When should the helper take a skilled approach to helpee involvement?

Some helpees are already highly motivated to seek and obtain help. With such helpees, a helper can omit the preliminary attending activities designed to inform and encourage them — although the helper must, of course, make sure that each of these helpees knows precisely where to come for help. Once the helpees have appeared, the helper should use the basic positioning, observing, and listening skills. In the case of helpees who may not be motivated to seek help on their own, the helper should begin by using preparing skills to promote their appearance. It is important to note that *positioning, observing, and listening are fundamental skills that the helper continues to use throughout the entire helping session.*

How can you practice the skills of attending?

There is no need to set up elaborate and highly controlled lab sessions in order to practice these basic skills. Instead, you can put the skills to initial use in many of your daily interactions with other people.

Preparing.

Choose two or three people whom you see frequently yet know only slightly. Then select an area in which you feel you might help each of these people (e.g., an academic subject in which you are proficient). Then develop a personal invitation designed to *inform* the other person of your availability and to *encourage* him or her to contact you. Show each invitation to the person involved, explaining your own situation, and get positive or negative feedback. Finally, try arranging a room at home, work, or school in order to make it an effective counseling setting.

Positioning.

You can practice the skills of positioning during the course of an ordinary conversation with a friend or family member. First try a nonattending position — perhaps leaning back in your seat, looking away from the other person frequently, getting up and moving around, and so forth. Then shift to an attending position, taking care to maintain the proper level, angle, forward inclination, and amount of eye contact. Once the conversation is over, ask yourself, "When did the other person seem more open and communicative — more involved?" and "When was I able to learn the most about the other person?" The answers should certainly demonstrate the value of positioning skills — and the exercise should help you gain a good deal of valuable practice.

Observing.

Each day you have many interactions with many different people. Pick a day and engage in several interactions without making any particular effort to observe the other person. Then engage in other interactions while using all of your observing skills to focus on the other person's body build, posture, grooming, focus, and nonverbal expressions. At the end of the day, try to summon up a clear image of all the different people with whom you interacted. Which people appear to you as real individuals and which as vague (or hastily characterized) automatons?

Listening.

You can practice your listening skills by trying to repeat to yourself the exact substance of verbal expressions made to you in ordinary conversations and by trying to summarize the important elements of longer verbal expressions. After each such attempt, ask yourself if you have missed or left out anything of importance. It is critically important that your listening skills enable you to take in information that is both complete and accurate. And remember — you should be listening for the tone as well as the content of each verbal expression.

helping people explore where they are: RESPONDING SKILLS **3**

Overview

1. Full involvement paves the way for helpee *exploration* of the present situation — the first major phase of the actual helping process.

2. The helper promotes and directs helpee exploration by making use of specific *responding* skills.

3. The first stage of helpee exploration requires that the helpee discuss specifics related to her or his *immediate situation*.

4. Having encouraged helpee discussion of the immediate situation through continued use of attending, observing, and listening skills, the helper sustains such discussion by *responding to the content* of helpee expressions.

5. The second stage of helpee exploration involves the helpee's expression of the *immediate meaning* that the situation has for him or her.

6. Having promoted the helpee's presentation of meaning by responding to content, the helper now *responds to the meaning* that is inherent in the helpee's statements and nonverbal behaviors.

7. The third stage of helpee exploration involves the helpee's consideration and expression of those *immediate feelings* that each aspect of the situation arouses in him or her.

8. The helper promotes continued exploration of feelings on the helpee's part by *responding to these feelings*.

9. The fourth and final stage of helpee exploration is reflected in the helpee's discussion of the *immediate reasons* he or she finds for each feeling.

10. The helper encourages and sustains this final level of exploration by *responding to feelings and the reasons for these feelings* as expressed by the helpee.

11. Throughout this major phase of activity, the helpee's primary aim must be to expand her or his awareness of

the numerous ways in which her or his individual life is being affected by the outside world.

12. The helper's primary concern at this point must be to use responding skills that are not judgmental and threatening but that, rather reflect the helpee's own frame of reference or personal awareness in terms the helpee can immediately recognize and accept.

Up to this point we have focused our concern on the specific skills a helper or counselor can use to get his or her helpees *involved: preparing* for the helpee to promote helpee appearance; *positioning* oneself with the helpee to promote helpee nonverbal expression; *observing* to promote helpee verbal expression; and *listening* to promote helpee expression of personally relevant materials. All of these basic helper skills can be referred to collectively as *attending skills*.

As noted, full involvement is the essential prerequisite for any constructive helping. And — again as noted — the attending skills the helper develops in preparing, positioning, observing, and listening serve two related ends. They promote helpee involvement by convincing each individual that the helper is truly concerned and, more than this, that he is capable of approaching each helpee's situation on an individual basis. At the same time, the helper's use of the prehelping skills allows him to gain significant insight into each helpee's unique frame of reference — the particular way in which that person is experiencing the world at that time.

Although involvement is an essential step for helpees, it is far from sufficient in and of itself. Rather, involvement is the first in our series of four major steps leading from the helpee's original situation or problem to the development and implementation of a program of constructive action — the ultimate goal of all effective helping. Involvement is the first step. And full *exploration* is the second. In this chapter we will focus on the specific skills the helper needs to help clients explore where they are.

Before helpees can do anything about a problem or situation, they must explore where they are in terms of their own present feelings, ideas, and actions and the outside influences affecting them. There is a strong positive relationship between any helpee's depth of self-exploration and the subsequent helping outcome. The helper or counselor can promote such exploration by developiong and using the sequence of *responding skills* outlined in this chapter. These responding skills are designed to communicate to the helpee in a nonthreatening fashion the counselor's own understanding of where the helpee is at the moment. As a matter of fact, the relationship between helpee exploration and the helper's responding skills is so strong that a helper can easily and immediately change the helpee's level of exploration by subtly manipulating the level of responding skills — without the helpee even being aware of the helper's manipulation. Unfortunately, many aspiring counselors as well as any number of practicing counselors seem to feel that little more than common sense and good intentions are required in order to get a helpee to talk in depth about her personal life. We might take a moment here to consider a counseling session reflecting just such a belief on the counselor's part. In reading the following account, we should ask ourselves whether the counselor's responses are really helpful in promoting the helpees' exploration of their present situation.

Gil Thomas is not your run-of-the-mill college senior. To begin with, he is 25 — several years older than his typical senior class colleagues. Gil has had what an objective onlooker might call an "uneven" academic career. A bright, creative person, he quickly grew bored with the standardized "mush" that his high school teachers kept throwing at him and dropped out of school at 16. During the next few years his progress seemed a perfect reflection of the social unrest and vague, inarticulate longings of a whole generation of young Americans. Like many others, he took a flyer in the dope culture, pulling out only when a dose of horse tranquilizer, masquerading as a "fantastic trip," put him in cataleptic shock for eight hours one unforgettable winter night. Deciding that discretion was the better part of variety-for-its-own-sake, Gil went back to night school and, armed at last with a high school diploma, joined VISTA and spent two years in the Appalachians helping some local people to organize a crafts cooperative. During this period he met and was proselytized by advocates of every fringe and cult group on the scene: proponents of TM and EST; square-jawed Scientologists and passive outriders trying to resurrect the old Hog Farm Commune; Nader-Raider and Sierra Club types who sought to impose cosmic solutions on local problems; and even some hard-nosed representatives of the AFT, UMW, UFW, Teamsters. Gil saw them, he heard them, and in the end he rejected them all and determined to chart his own course. Which took him, eventually, back to his home state's university, an undergraduate degree program, and (starting in

63

his junior year) a paid position as resident advisor in a freshman dormitory.

Gil took his responsibilities as an RA seriously from the start. He was only too familiar with the sorts of pressure and general paranoia with which young people wre constantly bombarded. He also knew from bitter experience that most so-called adults had little real interest in dealing with the problems of these same young people. From the outset, Gil had resolved that he would be different. He was a good listener — again, something he had learned from long experience — and felt sure that this would help him make a real difference in the lives of the people he privately thought of as "his kids."

On the night in question, a mid-September evening during his final year, Gil had asked three of the new freshmen on his floor to stop in to see him: Fred Hayes, a shy, lanky kid with tousled hair the color of the corn in his native state; Roger Morris, a chunky black guy lured to State by the university's reputation in ethnomusicology; and Janet Sommes (yes, the dorm had gone coed), an outspoken girl from an urban center that she described as "Carcinoma City." At one point or another during the preceding few days, all three of these students had indicated varying degrees of dissatisfaction with their lives at the university — hence Gil's personal invitation.

Yes, Gill was sharp enough to know that you do not start to help people by pinning up depersonalized notices. He was also sharp enough to know that the setting for any helping session, however informal, had to be structured effectively. Although he had a room to himself as an RA, Gil had arranged two single beds on opposite sides of the small room. With people using these beds as sofas and with a couple of low desk chairs placed between the beds at the end away from the door, Gil was able to convert his room into a passable counseling setting. He also understood the ways in which room decorations could promote — or destroy — his own efforts to help students. As a result, he had avoided all the current crop of posters — W.C. Fields' mug shots, "SKI NEBRASKA," earnest politicians, and the perennial favorite, Salvador Dali's buring giraffes — in favor of two others, one over each bed. The first proclaimed the Newtonian approach to education: "You Get Back Just What You Put In." The second bore the message: "You're Going Where You Want To Go, Whether You Know It Or Not."

Now Janet and Roger sat on one bed, Fred on the other, While Gil sat facing them in one of the desk chairs. They had only arrived a few minutes ago, but they already seemed to be relaxing.

"God, the thing that gets me about this place is the way nobody in the administration ever *listens* to you!" Janet exclaimed.

"Yeah, that's a real bear, isn't it?" Gil responded. "I remember when I first came here, I thought they were all wearing ear plugs or something." Gil felt it was important to let the kids know he had been through similar experiences.

"That's funny," Roger said. "With me, it's just the opposite. Every time I go to talk to some teacher or administrator, I feel like they go 'Whup, here's a black kid! I better stay on my toes!' I mean, that's all they see is that I'm black. And you know, that's usually not what I want to get into with them. I mean, like yesterday I went up to this teacher I've got in English after class. The way he had given the assignment, it wasn't clear what we were supposed to do. But right away he comes on like 'OK, listen, why don't you just try *half* the reading assignment.' Like he saw that I was black and figured, 'Well, he's probably had a rotten education so far, I''ll just let him take it easy.' "

"Yeah," Gil agreed. "There's a lot of stereotyping going on still. And it doesn't make it any better when they're for you instead of against you."

"What's this 'ster- stereotyping' thing?" Fred asked, sounding confused.

"Oh, just like treating people in terms of their surface appearance," Gil explained. "You know, the old judging-a-book-by-its-cover thing."

Fred nodded. Now that the point was clear, he did not find it too interesting. "My problem doesn't have anything to do with listening or ster- stereotyping or like that. I'm just having a hard time all around. The work is real hard. And the people — I don't know, they just don't seem real friendly."

Gil nodded to indicate his understanding. Then he paused and looked around at the three faces confronting him. Time to lay it on them.

"It's tough getting started here," he began. "I know. Hell, I was older than any of you when I started as a freshman and it was still plenty tough. The thing of it is, though, you're here. That's the reality you've got to begin with. You're here. And it's up to you to make the best of it."

"How do we do that?" Janet wanted to know.

"By taking over from all the people who want to push you around. The people who want you to fit into the neat little boxes they've already built for you." Gil's voice got harder. "Listen, people, there's a million hucksters out there and they all want you to buy their product, join their group, ride their special train. The only way you can survive and grow is to stand up and say, 'Hold it! I'm an individual and I've got my own plans. Now either help me out or get out of my way!' "

"Yeah," Roger said, nodding his head slowly. "I guess I see what you mean. Janet and Fred looked somewhat skeptical. But when Gil looked at them directly, they both gave grudging nods of assent.

Their talk went on for another 10 or so minutes before winding down. Gil kept hitting at the same theme: take over, control your own life, don't let them get you down. By the time the three kids left, he was fairly sure he had helped to stiffen their spines. It was a tough world out there, Gil knew from experience. And he was convinced that only those people who could get tough in turn would survive for long. He had showed these three kids that he cared, that he had experienced many of the same things himself. And he had told them what they needed to do. That was, Gil felt, what being a resident advisor was all about.

All right. We have seen the way in which one highly motivated helper has taken a "common sense" approach to a counseling situation. The general question facing us, of course, is, "Did he help?" Alas, we must almost certainly answer this question with a loud no! For Gil did not provide his helpees with anything beyond some strong, conceptual advice. It does not matter whether we agree or disagree with Gil's cynical vision of the world. The thrust of his advice is, finally, irrelevant. What matters most is that *any advice, when divorced from a systematic program of action, is largely worthless.* All Gil really said to Fred, Janet, and Roger was "work harder, try harder, be yourself!" Marvelous. With advice like that, we would still need 25 cents to buy a cup of coffee!

The problem, of course, is that Gil never got his three helpees to the point where he and they could work together to develop a plan of action. They never reached the point where they really understood the personalized dimensions of their situations — the ways in which they themselves were responsible for their own feelings. They never even *explored* their situations fully! Instead, they made only the weakest of starts in this direction.

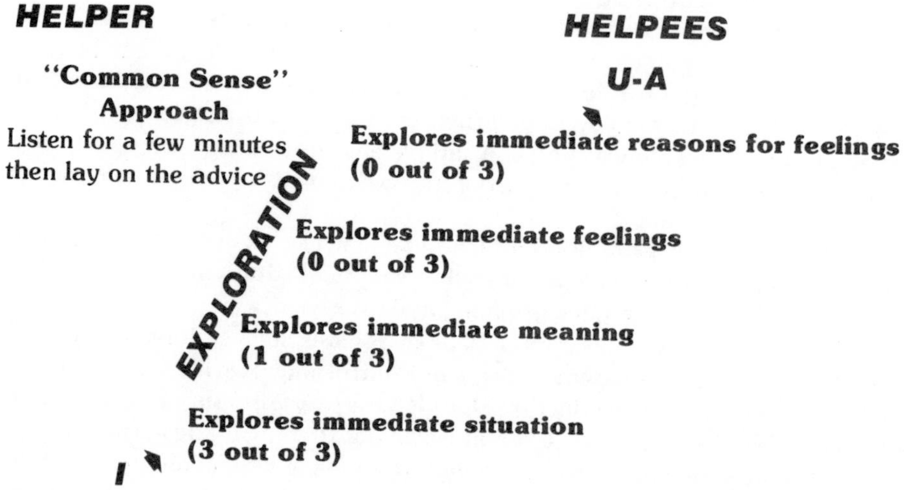

HELPER

"Common Sense" Approach

Listen for a few minutes then lay on the advice

EXPLORATION

HELPEES

U-A

Explores immediate reasons for feelings
(0 out of 3)

Explores immediate feelings
(0 out of 3)

Explores immediate meaning
(1 out of 3)

Explores immediate situation
(3 out of 3)

Figure 3-1: Impact of Gil's "common sense" approach on helpee exploration.

Using the session between Gil and the three freshmen as a starting point, let us take a look at some of the specific ways in which a counselor can respond to helpees in order to promote their full exploration. For if helpee exploration is the next essential step in the movement toward constructive action, *helper responsiveness is the key to this crucial step.*

Using What You've Learned

The helper uses his or her basic attending, observing, and listening skills in order to draw each helpee into full involvement in the counseling session and, at the same time, to gather necessary information about each helpee. This information, in combination with what he or she already knows, should enable the helper to recognize each helpee's initial *set*. This set may be summed up as the answer to the question, "Generally speaking, why is this person here?" At this point the helper does not have the depth of details that will eventually be needed. But the helper should have a good preliminary idea about why the helpee has presented himself or herself.

In many cases, of course, helpees may seek counseling or therapy because of specific problems they have recognized and with which they wish to come to terms: parents who are having trouble dealing with their children; children who are having equal problems with their parents; some difficulty with alcoholism or drug abuse, perhaps; or even a person with distinct suicidal tendencies. In other cases, real problems may exist that the helpees themselves have not yet recognized: a troublesome student who still says, "Leave me alone, I'm doing OK;" or a veteran, perhaps, whose reentry into civilian life is impeded by her or his refusal to recognize new priorities and situations. Finally, there are many helpees whom the helper meets who have only a vague sense of dissatisfaction, a premonition that unless "something is done" about their lives, things will just go gradually downhill.

It is critically important for the counselor to come to terms with each helpee's individual set. As we saw with Gil's three young students, each helpee will have a unique and personal reason for appearing. As indicated, the helper's initial attending, observing, and listening, together with any previous information that she or he has, should allow the helper to determine the general set of each helpee. The helper can also ask and answer some specific questions about each helpee. *"Is he here on his own?"* (He has probably recognized a specific area of difficulty.) *"Is she here because I invited her?"* (She may or may not have recognized any problem; and if the problem has been recognized, she may have been avoiding it.) *"Is he mentioning a particular set of circumstances again and again?"* (Chances are the problem is a concrete and immediate one.) *"Is she talking about a lot of things and feelings all at once?"* (It is likely that the problem is either broad based or particularly difficult for the helpee to identify.)

In general, of course, the basic set that all helpees or clients share is simply this: They have a situation that they have been unable to handle. By attending, observing, and listening to helpees during initial interactions, counselors can refine and individualize their understanding of each person's unique set. At the same time, helpers must keep clearly in mind the set that they need to have. *The helper's primary job at this point is to enter, understand, and respond to each helpee's set or frame of reference so that helpees can identify their feelings and the reasons for these feelings in relation to their problems.* Helpers should not, like Gil, concentrate on filtering helpees' experiences through their own to show them how much they have in common. Nor should helpers be judgmental in any way. Such approaches, though perhaps appropriate in another context, are not appropriate in a helping situation. The immediate goal is to help clients *explore.* At this point, helper agreement and disagreement are equally irrelevant. Responses should not be designed to talk helpees into or out of something but to promote their exploration. Counselors are not debaters — they are helpers!

In summary, then, a counselor should have a general idea of each helpee's initial set — why he or she is there — to serve as the basis for preliminary interaction. At the same time, the helper should remember that her or his own set must involve a suspension of personal judgment and a recognition of each helpee's frame of reference.

In the following sections we will consider both the several stages of helpee exploration and the several types of responsive skills that the effective helper must employ. Briefly stated, the helpee must explore his or her *immediate situation,* the *immediate meaning* this situation has, the *immediate feelings* prompted by this situation, and the *immediate reasons* for these feelings. The modifying term "immediate" here is designed to reflect a characteristic shared by almost all helpee exploration: the initial preoccupation with external or "immediate" factors. Most of us tend to view problems at first in "them against me" terms. Thus, in exploring a hypothetical situation, for example, we might begin by talking about how "they're always giving me a hard time." We might go on to convey the immediate meaning of this situation for us by saying "they're just not fair." We might then go on to present our immediate feelings as "anger" and "frustration" and cite specific actions by "them" as the immediate reasons for these feelings.

This initial concern with outside agencies or forces is quite natural. In exploring his or her immediate situation, its meaning, the feelings aroused by it, and the specific reasons for these feelings, the helpee is moving toward the point where he or she can attain a more *personalized* understanding — a "me against me" perspective, as it were — that will finally allow the helpee to take an active role in resolving the original problem. Thus the "personalized" dimension of helpee understanding — treated at length in chapter four — stands in direct contrast to the "immediate" nature of that helpee exploration treated here.

Responding to the Immediate Situation

Helpee Goal:

To express himself or herself concerning the immediate situation.

During the initial exploratory phase of any counseling session, the goal for the helpee should be *to discuss information related to specific situations*. Most clients are able to engage in this type of exploration fairly easily. After all, we all enjoy finding someone who seems genuinely interested in us and who, furthermore, seems capable of paying more than the superficial attention we so often get from others.

The most constructive helpee statements will be those that are in direct response to the basic interrogatives Who, What, Where, When, and How. Here the helpee articulates for the helper his or her awareness of the surrounding world — an essential complex of information for the counselor who is committed to entering and dealing with the client's own frame of reference. Without a clear understanding of the facts of the situation that brought the helpee for counseling in the first place, there will be little chance for understanding how the helpee feels about the situation.

Without actually intending it, Gil's meeting did result in some discussion of immediate situational specificity on the part of his helpees. Roger, for example, volunteered the following:

> . . . I went up to this teacher I've got in English after class. The way he had given the assignment, it wasn't clear what we were supposed to do. But right away he comes on like 'OK, listen, why don't you just try *half* the reading assignment.' Like he saw that I was black and figured 'Well, he's probably had a rotten education so far, I'll just let him take it easy.'

Gil's agreeable response, of course, is not really helpful in that it does not promote any further exploration on Roger's part: "Yeah, there's a lot of stereotyping going on" is a general comment rather than a response designed to reflect Gil's understanding of Roger's immediate situation. Below we look at how a skilled helper might have responded more effectively.

The presentation by a helpee of specific material related to the immediate situation serves two ends. It starts the helpee on a process of exploration that will eventually enable him to experience where he really is in terms of his own life and the surrounding world. And it gives the counselor new and valuable information concerning the helpee's situation.

Helper Skills:

Responding to the content of helpee expressions by using a format along the lines of, "So you're saying _____."

As indicated, the goal for the helpee at this stage is to explore specific material related to the immediate situation. The counselor or helper facilitates the attainment of this goal in several ways. To begin with, *he or she continues to position, observe, and listen.* The attitude of hovering attentiveness thus created enables the helpee to feel that he or she can express thoughts freely.

As the helpee expresses material that has clear situational specificity, the counselor should *respond to the content of these expressions.* Such a response may take one of two forms, both frequently beginning with the phrase, "You're saying that . . ." or "So you're saying . . ." For brief expressions, the helper can respond in terms of a repetition of the helpee's statement that involves only minor changes.

Helpee: "The other kids leave me all alone."

Helper: "You're saying that the other students leave you by yourself."

This type of response is clearly of limited value because of its repetitious quality. For variety — or when dealing with longer helpee expressions — the counselor or helper can respond by giving an accurate paraphrase or summary of the helpee's important points. The example below demonstrates a therapist at an outpatient clinic responding to the content of a client's statement.

> Helpee: "I've tried to deal with my kids. I told the oldest one, Barbara, I wanted her in no later than midnight on weekends, but it didn't seem to make any difference. She still stayed out till way after one A.M."

> Helper: "You're saying that you've really made an effort to tell your kids what you expect. But your oldest girl still stays out beyond your curfew."

In those instances where the helpee has difficulty volunteering the situationally specific details, the helper should consider utilizing a combination of questioning *and* responding to facilitate this phase of exploration. To encourage the maximum amount of discussion, the helper may use specific questions involving the basic interrogatives:

Who was involved?

What were they doing?

Where did this occur?

When did this happen?

Why did it seem to happen?

How did the whole thing end?

It must be emphasized that any such question must be followed up by at least a response to the content of the answer. The reason for this lies in an understanding of the helpee's experience. The helpee is already burdened with a situation he or she cannot handle and a series of cold, prying questions will only add to that burden. The helper will also find that responding to the content will enable him or her to clarify any points that are still unclear and encourage the helpee to continue to discuss the situation.

> Helpee: "I guess I'm stuck . . ."

> Helper: "What did you say when she did come home at one A.M.?"

> Helpee: "Well, I didn't say anything. I didn't know *what* to say. She doesn't listen to me!"

> Helper: "So you're saying that you couldn't think of anything that would get through to her."

Helpee: "Yeah. As hard as I try, Barbara just won't listen to me. Every time I try to sit down with her, she says she's too busy. It happened twice last week."

The effective counselor can let helpees know that he or she is really with them, really listening and attending, by responding to the content of their expressions. This will help them move beyond the stage of immediate situational specificity and begin to express something of the immediate meaning of the situations in which they find themselves.

Responding
to the Immediate
Meaning

Helpee Goal:

To explore the meaning of his or her immediate situation.

The helpee goal in exploring the immediate meaning is precisely that: *to find and express the immediate meaning that each particular experience has for him or her.* This meaning is what would be contained in a helpee's answer to the direct question, "What does this mean to you?" Going back to Roger in our brief sample session, for example, we might identify the immediate meaning in his statement in this way: "The teacher was treating me as a black instead of a person." In other works, the *meaning* Roger found in the situation was implicit in his original expression. Had Gil been able to respond effectively to Roger, the younger man would have been able to explore and develop this immediate meaning more fully.

It is important to recognize that meaning is not always the same as content: It is always implicit but not always explicit. In other words, meaning is reflected in the helpee's behavior and tone of expression as well as in the content of the expression. We can see this clearly by looking at the same expression spoken by three different people with different nonverbal behaviors accompanying their verbal presentations:

Helpee #1: (A girl worried about flunking an exam.) "I asked the teacher for extra help but he wouldn't help me."
(The implicit meaning is *"he wasn't fair."*)

72

Helpee #2: (A shy student with few friends.)
"I asked the teacher for extra help but he wouldn't help me."
(The implicit meaning is *"he doesn't like me."*)

Helpee #3: (A militant black student.)
"I asked the teacher for extra help but he wouldn't help me."
(The implicit meaning is *"he doesn't like blacks."*)

No counselor, of course, can pluck meaning out of thin air. The recognition of such meaning depends upon a cumulative recognition of every verbal and visual cue provided so far by the helpee. The first helpee above has already told her counselor about the exam and has been wringing her hands nervously; the second helpee has indicated his lack of friends and his belief that no one likes him; and the third helpee has already announced that a lot of the people she has met at school are prejudiced.

Helper Skills:

Responding to the helpee's meaning by using a format along the lines of, "You mean _____."

Although we may not realize it, we all respond to the meaning in other people's statements all the time. The unfortunate thing is that many of our familiar responses are as inaccurate as they are unhelpful.

Statement: "I can't stand any of the Democrats running for office!"

Response: "You mean you don't know about some of the really fine things they've done?"

That is, of course, not at all what the speaker means; the response, like so many that we hear, reveals far more about the *responder's* frame of reference than about the original speaker's. Indeed, the only good element in this sample response is the first two words. For the phrase "You mean —" is a perfectly valid way to begin a response to meaning.

In responding to a helpee's experiential meaning, the *helper must be able to communicate to that helpee the depth and accuracy of her or his own understanding.* The helper must say, in effect, "I not only hear what you're saying but what you mean as well." Such a response serves as further encouragement for the helpee in exploring the particular situation or problem at hand.

Again, one good way to begin a response to meaning is to employ the phrase "You mean —." When responding a number of times at this level — and he or she will want to do so whenever the helpee shows an interest in pursuing this phase of exploration — the helper can drop the "You mean —" and simply respond by giving what he or she perceives as the helpee's meaning. For example, a high school student exploring her parents' marriage:

Helpee: "Whenever they get mad at each other, they always end up yelling at me."

Helper: "You mean they take out their anger on you."

Such a response prompts further exploration and expression on the helpee's part:

Helpee: "Yeah — sometimes I wonder what they ever did to blow off steam before I came along."

Helper: "It seems like they need you — but only as a kind of verbal punching bag."

In practicing responding to meaning, the helper must rely heavily on her or his cumulative understanding of each helpee as well as her or his understanding of a specific statement. Only in this way will the helper's responses indicate to the helpee that she or he is an accurate as well as a willing listener. And only such an indication will prompt the helpee to move to the next level and begin to express her or his immediate feelings.

Responding to the Immediate Feelings

Helpee Goal:

To explore how he or she feels about the immediate situation.

At this level of exploration, the goal for helpees is to *express the immediate and specific feelings they have about their situations*. This is not always easy for helpees to do. After all, we have all been affected somewhat by the aura of "cool" detachment that has come into being in the last few decades. Many people think it a sign of weakness to let anyone outside of a small circle of friends see how they really feel.

"How do you feel about that?"

"All right, I guess."

Tossed off with customary nonchalance, such a statement does little to reflect a helpee's true feelings. Yet if the helpee has progressed developmentally from presenting personally meaningful material to discussing the immediate situation and the meaning that this situation has, then the helpee should be ready and relaxed enough to express his or her *feelings* openly. In addition, the helper should have been able to infer a good deal about the helpee's emotional state based on the data collected through observation and listening.

There are, of course, any number of specific words that a helpee may use to express various feelings. Some of the most common are terms like *happy, sad, angry, confused,* and *scared.* Yet terms like these are little more than the tip of some vast emotional iceberg in that, as general "feeling words," they do little to capture the unique nature and intensity of a helpee's feelings.

"I feel really good." Is the speaker's feeling related to a bright, sunny day — or does it reflect the far more profound and pervasive happiness of someone who, for example, is on the eve of a long-looked-forward-to wedding day?

"I don't feel so good." Is the speaker reacting to an exam he flunked — or to news of some personal tragedy with far-ranging implications?

When helpees express their feelings — through the way they move and handle their bodies, through the energy level in their voice, through their tone, and through the content of their statements — the helper must be able to recognize these feelings and respond to them. For *the helpee's immediate feelings are the heart of his or her experience of the world.* For better or worse, human feelings are perhaps the most fundamental characteristics of human experience. They are aroused by what we do and what is done to us; they are reflected in what we subsequently do and think; they condition how we act toward others and how we treat ourselves. And it is absolutely no good to tell someone not to have certain feelings.

"I get so damned mad at Jim sometimes!"

"Ah, you shouldn't feel like that. Jim means well!"

Our feelings and the feelings of our helpees are real — again, for better or worse. And it is with the reality of the helpees' feelings that the counselor must begin.

Helper Skills:

Responding to helpee feelings by using a format along the lines of, "You feel _____."

In responding to a helpee's feelings, the helper is *letting that person know that he is right there with the helpee, that he recognizes where s/he is, that he cares.* More important, the counselor is promoting the helpee's further exploration. For in many if not most cases, the initial feelings that a helpee has are changed and modified by the process of exploration itself. What starts out as "anger," for example, may well end up as "frustration" — quite a different feeling.

As indicated, there are many categories and levels of feelings. The following chart may serve to show something of the wide range of "feeling" words that a helper must be able to recognize and employ.

In order to recognize a helpee's emotional state, the helper should try to put himself in the client's place. In essense, the helper asks, "If I looked as the client looks, acted as he's acting, was in the situation he describes, and was saying what he's saying — how would I feel? When in doubt, counselors can use this short version: "If I looked as he looked, how would I feel?" This sort of empathic question is a helpful check even if the helpee has used one or more specific "feeling' words. Once the helper is fairly sure he understands the feeling, he can respond to the helpee.

The most direct way in which to introduce a response to feeling is to use the opening "You feel —," filling in the blank with what is the most accurate (i.e., most closely interchangeable) "feeling" word or phrase. For example, a recovering alcoholic has a helper who is responding to his feelings:

Helpee: "I just can't stand it when they treat me like that!"

Helper: "You feel furious."

Helpee: "Uh huh. And, like, it really mixes me up, because I want to tell them where to get off but I just can't seem to do it."

Helper: "You really feel conflicted."

Again, during a series of responses at this level, the helper may wish to vary the form they take.

Helpee: "Honestly, I work all these years to try to take care of them and now they act like they don't even went to be around me."

CATEGORIES OF FEELING

Levels of Intensity	Happy	Sad	Angry	Confused	Scared	Weak	Strong
STRONG	Excited Great Overjoyed	Hopeless Lost Crushed	Furious Disgusted Enraged	Numb Trapped Panicky	Terrified Afraid Fearful	Ashamed Vulnerable Exhausted	Powerful Potent Aggressive
MILD	Alive Proud Up	Lonely Hurt Upset	Frustrated Irritated Sore	Doubtful Mixed Up Uncomfortable	Shaky Worried Anxious	Embarrassed Helpless Powerless	Tough Confident Brave
WEAK	Calm Glad Pleased	Down Bad Dull	Annyoed Mad Uptight	Unsure Surprised Foggy	Nervous Shy Uneasy	Tired Shaky Worn Out	Healthy Firm Able

Helper: "That can really make you feel miserable."

The key element in any response to feeling is the inclusion of a specific *"feeling"* word or phrase that the helpee will recognize as being interchangeable with the feeling expressed in her or his own expression. Since there are, as we have noted, any number of different categories and varieties of feeling, the helper must work at expanding her or his effective vocabulary of *"feeling"* expressions. By using the skills of attending, observing, and listening — and by making a constant effort to see and understand the situation from the helpee's own frame of reference — the helper can learn to recognize specific feelings. By developing an effective "feeling" vocabulary and making it a part of his overall response repertoire, he can ensure his ability to respond to the real and immediate feelings of helpees. And by doing so, he can move helpees on to a consideration of the immediate experiential reason for their feelings.

Responding
to the Immediate Reasons
for Feelings

Helpee Goal:

To determine the immediate reasons for present feelings.

Here the helpee goal is *to explore the experiential reasons for his or her feelings.* Perhaps no other single construct is as fundamental to our understanding of daily life as the principle of cause and effect. Nothing occurs in a vacuum. There is a reason for every event that takes place. And a feeling, however elusive and insubstantial it may seem, is a real-life event. As such, it is prompted by some specific cause.

"I feel great" *because* my boss gave me a raise.

"I feel miserable" *because* my teacher just flunked me on a Biology exam.

"He's really angry" *because* one of his guest's dogs just threw up on the carpet.

"She feels rotten" *because* someone turned her in for cheating.

Many of our feelings are quite rational in the sense that most other people would feel the same way if the same things happened to them: "Who wouldn't feel frustrated, getting stuck for an hour in traffic like this with the temperature near ninety degress?" But we also have feelings that seem to make little or no sense. That is, whatever we see as the cause of our feeling does not really appear sufficient when viewed by other people: "How can you get so enraged just because he called you Miss instead of Ms.?" In still other cases, we cannot seem to find any tangible cause for our feelings at all: "I don't know why I'm so depressed. It's just that kind of a day, I guess."

The thing the helper must remember is this: *Regardless of the apparent nature of the cause of a particular helpee's feelings, each of those feelings will always turn out to have a sufficient and rational reason!* One of the most important goals of all helpee exploration is to identify — to the helper as well as to the helpee — the real reason for each of his or her real feelings.

The helpee's feelings and reasons for feelings are like separate hands on a clock. Neither stays firmly in place during the initial stages of the helping process. As one moves, the other moves as well. Thus the helpee's first attempts to come to terms with the reason for a feeling may eventually reveal a new level or type of feeling — which in turn may reveal a new reason. In the following example, a recently released prisoner expresses several levels of feeling and meaning:

Helpee: "I feel miserable because my boss fired me after three days on the job."

Helper: "It really depresses you because your employer didn't give you a chance."

Helpee: "Yeah. He acted like I was dumb or something for not knowing everything right off the bat."

Helper: "You feel pretty angry because he treated you unfairly."

The ultimate aim of all exploration is for the helpee to come to terms with his most fundamental feelings about each situation he explores — and with the real reasons for those feelings. For the helpee, the process is a bit like peeling one skin after another off a succession of onions: As the central core of each onion is approached, each skin is "tighter" in the same sense that each subsequent discovery by a helpee of a feeling and a reason for that feeling is a "tighter" approximation of reality. Throughout, the helpee expands and explores the whole range of situations related to his particular problem or area of concern; this exploration throws light into all the dark nooks and crannies of his complex existence.

Helper Skills:

Responding to helpee feelings and reasons by using a format along the lines of, "You feel ＿＿＿＿＿＿ because he/she/it/they ＿＿＿＿＿＿."

The helper must listen and respond to the helpee's expression of feelings while at the same time trying to pinpoint the underlying reason for each feeling. The helper knows that a reason or set of reasons exists — the feeling did not magically come into existence all by itself. She also knows that the first reason the helpee expresses may not be the most profound or basic reason. Thus she must continue to respond to feeling plus reason until both she and the helpee are sure that a "baseline" of some sort has been reached. The helper can invariably tell when such a line has been reached because the helpee's further exploration will be self-sustaining — he will just keep going on his own — and because the helpee's subsequent expressions will all be variations on a single theme. In terms of our earlier analogy, the hands on the clock will stop.

In responding to the helpee at this highest level of exploration, the helper can begin by using the simple format, "You feel *(feeling word or phrase)* because *he/she/it/they (reason for feeling.)*" The helper's job is not to supply a reason based on her own personal judgment; she is not, in other words, saying, "I *think* you feel ＿＿＿＿＿＿ because ＿＿＿＿＿＿." Rather, she is reflecting the helpee's own reason as seen from that helpee's own frame of reference; and she is doing so in a totally nonjudgmental, nonthreatening fashion. A newly admitted resident to a halfway house may have the following experience.

Helpee: "I just don't know what to do when they all look at me like that, just sitting around and waiting for me to say the right thing."

Helper: "You feel pressured because they're expecting something from you."

Responses to the reasons for helpee feeling, like responses to the feelings themselves, are only effective when the helpee perceives them as interchangeable with the reasons that he assigns to the feelings. Throughout this entire exploratory phase of helping, in other words, the effective helper is serving as a type of "mirror" for the helpee. The helper's reflection of what the helpee does, says, means, and feels is accurate to the point where the helpee can clearly recognize himself; at the same time, the helper's specific responses modify and help to clarify the helpee's own expressions, thus promoting continued exploration. Responding to feeling and content is different from any other type of response a helper can give. Such a response attempts to be based solely on what the helpee has expressed. Other types of responses often used to promote self-exploration in "common sense" helping interaction come in part from the helper's frame of reference. For example, a helper's question is based in part on what the helper thinks might be important; a helper's statement of advice is based in part on what the helper thinks should be done; a helper's attempt to reassure is based in part on what the helper thinks the helpee should be experiencing; a helper's sharing of information is based in part on what the helper thinks the helpee should know. In contrast to all these helper responses, a response to the helpee's feeling and content is based on the helpee's frame of reference. It accurately clarifies for the helpee what he or she has communicated and permits the helpee to continue in *whatever direction the helpee wants to go*. Most helpees have never had their self-exploration assisted in this manner. This freedom to talk about what they want to talk about, in a relationship with a helper who is assisting them by clarifying the essense of their remarks, leads many helpees toward a new and more personal level of self-exploration.

In terms of responding, there are several important qualifications. If the helper becomes confused at some point — unsure of why the helpee feels a certain way, perhaps — or maybe even unsure of how he or she is feeling, *the helper should drop back to a simpler level of response until she or he can once again respond effectively.* In the following example with a drug addict, the helper correctly retreats to a simpler level of responding.

Helper: "So you feel disappointed because your family and friends are always letting you down." (*A response to the helpee's previously expressed reasons for a particular feeling.*)

Helpee: "Yeah, I guess so. Maybe they're not really letting me down, though. Oh, I don't know — sometimes thinking about it gets me so messed up!" *(The helpee isn't sure about the real reasons for his feelings.)*

Helper: "You really feel pretty confused." *(The helper drops back and responds to the new feeling of confusion alone. He will continue to respond at this level until the helpee begins to express new reasons.)*

When the helper is feeling confused by the presentation of situationally specific data related to a helpee's highly technical job, for example, the best reaction involves dropping back to the level of simple observation. She can continue to observe the helpee until she is able to respond directly to his or her feelings concerning the material.

Thus, at the highest level of skills during the exploration stage the helper responds to feeling and the reasons for the feeling. However, when he is not able to formulate such a response, or when the helpee seems unable to use such a response, the helper can instead respond to only the feeling, the meaning, or the immediate situation.

Responding to the immediate situation in terms of content; responding to the meaning that a situation has for the helpee; responding to the feelings that the situation prompts in the helpee; responding to the reasons for these feelings — each of these activities builds upon the previous one. Thus the pattern of responding, like the overall pattern of the helping process itself, is developmental rather than discrete or isolated. The insight that both helper and helpee gain is cumulative; so, too, is the level of trust, of mutual respect, and awareness, which arises from their interaction. By the time the helpee has come to terms with her basic feelings and the reasons for those feelings, the helper has developed a clear and comprehensive understanding of the situation in which this helpee finds herself. Now the helper is ready to help the helpee understand this situation in terms that are both meaningful and personal. He is ready to move on to the next level of helping.

Bette and Jimmy

Bette had already gotten Jimmy Bessom involved in the helping process.

And by putting to use her own skills in attending, observing, and listening, she had learned a good deal about the young man who sat facing her in her office at the community college. The way he slumped in his seat with his arms folded across his chest told her something about the defensive wall he had built around himself. And the way he answered her initial questions with monosyllables and mumbled words told her that he was not going to trust her right off the bat. She would have to go slowly. And she did just that. Bette *attended*. She *observed*. She *listened*. Gradually, this strategy began to pay off as Jimmy reacted to her attentiveness by revealing more about his specific situation. Eventually he was able to produce a fairly clear capsule summary of his immediate situation.

"See, my old man has this bug about me going to college. I guess because he never had a chance to go, he really wants me to make it. And that wouldn't be so bad. I mean, I can get into going to school and all that. Some of the courses are pretty good — especially the math and engineering stuff. But all my friends quit to go to work. And I mean, these guys really are my friends. For the last couple of years we've done everything together. And in a lot of ways, I guess I'd just rather be with them than here in school."

Having made his statement, Jimmy looked at the woman who sat facing him. How could she understand what he was saying? How could she know how important a guy's friends were? The truth was, Jimmy had spent a long, lonely childhood. If anyone thought it was fun being an only child, they had their heads screwed on backwards! HUH! What's fun about playing by yourself, coming home from school by yourself, doing the chores by yourself? It wasn't until Jimmy had started high school that he had fallen in with Ernie, Chuck, and the others. Man, what a difference that had made! At last there had been someone to gripe with, plan with, waste time with, share dreams with . . .

Bette *responded to the content* of Jimmy's statement. "So you're saying you can understand your father's feelings. And you like some parts of the work here in school. But when the chips are down, you'd rather be with your friends."

"Uh huh. But see, it gets all mixed up. I mean, should I decide to live the way my father wants me to? Or the way my friends want me to? Or — or some other way that's just for me?" Jimmy shook his head uncertainly. The weird thing was, he knew his father was right in a lot of ways! School *was* cool in a lot of ways. But without Ernie and the others? . . . Damn! If only those clowns had stuck it out! Now it was Jimmy who was stuck. And he had a sneaking feeling that whatever decision he made, whatever road he chose, was going to make a lot of difference in the long run. God, just thinking about a whole life spent working for old Dick Morris was spooky!

Bette *responded to the meaning* of his statements. "You mean that the question is pretty basic to your whole life-style."

"Yeah, right! Like I don't even know how to make a decision, much less what decision I'm supposed to make."

Bette *responded to his feeling.* "It's pretty confusing, huh."

"Yeah." Jimmy looked down at the floor. "I think about it a lot. I don't know where to start or what to do."

"You feel pretty mixed-up about the whole thing."

"More than mixed-up. It just screws everything up. I can't get my mind going on anything else."

"So you feel really torn apart, and it keeps you from functioning in any other area of your life."

"Uh huh." Ms. Simmons was really kind of sharp. "I really get depressed about the whole thing. Really down. I just wish someone'd come up to me and say 'Hey, here's what you oughta do!'"

Finally, Bette *responded to the reasons* Jimmy saw for his feelings. "So you feel pretty miserable and low because no one is able to set you on the right track."

"Yeah, that's it exactly." It was really strange, Jimmy thought, the way Ms. Simmons seemed like she was right there with him. Not like his father, just laying his own trip on Jimmy all the time. And not like that clown Harry, the college boy, either. Ms. Simmons was a whole other thing. Maybe she really *could* help him after all!

In this exchange — only a part of the longer dialogue between Bette and Jimmy — we can see the exploratory

HELPER   **HELPEE**

Skilled
Approach   U-A

                                        EXPLORATION

Responding to feelings ⟶ Explores immediate
  plus reasons   reasons for feelings
Responding to feelings ⟶ Explores immediate feelings
Responding to meaning ⟶ Explores immediate meaning
Responding to content ⟶ Explores immediate situation

I

Figure 3-2: *Responsive skills used by helper to promote full*
helpee exploration.

movement that takes Jimmy from defensiveness to gradual openness and self-discovery. He is able to be specific about his immediate situation. He articulates the meaning the situation has for him. He presents feelings. And he grapples with the reasons for those feelings. Bette is with him at every step, using her responding skills in order to promote further exploration and discovery. Her response to Jimmy's situational specificity helps him to recognize the inherent meaning that this situation has for him. Her early response to feeling is modified by Jimmy's reaction: "More than confused. It just screws everything up." In the end, Jimmy recognizes that he feels miserable because no one has been able to help him out — a recognition far removed from his original angry defensiveness.

Jimmy's voyage of self-discovery could not have resulted from the well-intentioned yet inept attempts at help made by Harry, our educated yet largely unskilled college student in chapter one. Someone like Bette is needed. Someone who can go beyond good intentions and put to use a functional battery of real helping skills. Someone who can, at this stage, respond to Jimmy at the level at which he is experiencing the world. Someone who knows that helping is for better or worse — and who has the practical tools needed to ensure that her helping, at least, will be for better!

The Research Background

Most major theoretical orientations to counseling and psychotherapy have recognized the importance of the patient talking about what is troubling him or her. In particular, Freud (1924) popularized a "talking cure" for emotional problems while Rogers, Gendlin, Kiesler, & Truax (1967) strongly stressed the necessity of helpee self-exploration. In addition to these theoretical emphases, a great deal of research has been amassed that indicates a significant positive relationship between the degree of helpee self-exploration and therapeutic outcome. That is, those helpees who talk in greater detail about their unique problems and situation are more apt to improve over the course of helping.

One of the reasons for the increasing number of studies on helpee self-exploration has been the development of reliable and observable rating scales by means of which the dimension of self-exploration can be analyzed. The most widely used scale of self-exploration, upon which countless numbers of research investigations have been carried out, can be found in Robert R. Carkhuff's *Helping and Human Relations*, Volume 2 (1969).

Effects of Helper Responding Skills on Helpee Exploration

Perhaps one of the most significant scientific discoveries in therapeutic research is that certain skills the helper uses directly influence the degree to which a helpee will explore personally relevant material (Carkhuff, 1969; Rogers et al., 1967; Truax & Carkhuff, 1967). These helper skills, once referred to as the facilitative conditions of empathy, respect, and genuineness, are now operationalized in the helper skill of responding. A series of experimental studies has found that a helper can deliberately increase and decrease the helpee's depth of self-exploration by directly changing the level of the helper's responding skills (Cannon & Pierce, 1968; Holder, Carkhuff, & Berenson, 1967; Piaget et al., 1967; Truax & Carkhuff, 1965). The research results show that when the helpers were most responsive, the helpees' self-exploration was much more personally relevant; when these same helpers became less responsive, the helpees' exploration became less personal. In addition, the effects on helpee self-exploration of relatively unskilled helpers were also studied. Investigators discovered that the helper who is unskilled in responding will, over time, decrease her or his helpees level of self-exploration.

This is not to say that the helpee does not have a role to play in how willing he or she is to explore personally relevant material. Some helpees are certainly more willing to explore themselves than are other helpees. However, the research supports the belief that, irrespective of the helpees' own ability and willingness to explore, the responding skills of the helper can directly influence helpee self-exploration; and helpees who have helpers unskilled in responding will gradually introduce less and less personally relevant material into the helping interaction.

Although a helper can certainly do more than just use her or his responding skills (as will be seen in the remaining chapters), responsive skills in and of themselves can at times have a differential effect on helpee outcome.

Several experimental studies have demonstrated that the experimenters' responding skills can influence the effectiveness of a verbal conditioning or verbal reinforcement program. The outcome of a conditioning or a reinforcement program was found to be, in part, a function of the level of responding skills exhibited by the experimenter/helper (Mickelson & Stevic, 1971; Murphy & Rowe, 1977; Vitalo, 1970).

Undoubtedly the most significant and meaningful finding with respect to the relationship between responding skills and helping outcome has been made, not in the field of helping per se, but in the field of education. Over the past decade, one finding has consistently emerged from educational research: a positive relationship exists between the teacher's responding skills and various measures of student achievement and education outcome (Aspy, 1973, Aspy and Roebuck 1977; Carkhuff, 1971; Carkhuff & Berenson, 1976; Truax & Carkhuff, 1967). Thus a teacher's ability to respond to her students will affect how much her students learn. More recent studies have shown that a teacher's responding skills are not only positively related to educational outcome criteria but also to criteria that have primarily been the goals of guidance counselors and other mental health professionals — criteria like improved student self-concept and decreased student absenteeism.

Rogers and his associates (Gendlin, 1962; Rogers, 1951, 1954; Rogers & Dyamond, 1954; Rogers et al., 1967) more than any other group emphasized the empathic responsiveness of the helper to the helpee. Helper responsiveness facilitated the helpees' involvement in the first phase of helping — the exploration of themselves in relation to their worlds. This exclusive emphasis upon helper responsiveness and helpee exploration placed a severe limitation upon the client-centered approach. More recently this approach has begun to emphasize techniques that increase the participation of the helper in the exploration process. These helper techniques have, however, been limited to the promotion of the helper "genuineness". The helper shares his own reactions to the client as further information for client exploration (Rogers, 1974; Friedman, 1976; Wexler & Rice, 1974). 'Beyond the initial phases of therapeutic encounters, the technique of client-centered therapy appears to make no significant contributions to constructive changes over and above that change accounted for by the central core of facilitative conditions' (Carkhuff & Berenson, 1977, p. 74).

In summary, the skilled helper, regardless of his or her theoretical orientation, has much to gain by using responding skills. First, the use of responding skills will directly influence the amount of personally relevant material the helpee will express to the helper. Second, helpers who are trying to get their helpees to learn certain skills or follow a certain program will improve the outcomes of their helping programs if they are able to respond skillfully to the helpee's experience.

References

Aspy, D.N. *Toward a technology for humanizing education.* Champaign, Ill.: Research Press, 1973.

Aspy, D.N., & Roebuck, F. *KIDS don't learn from people they don't like.* Amherst, Mass.: Human Resource Development Press, 1977.

Cannon, J.R., & Pierce, R.M. Order effects in the experimental manipulation of therapeutic conditions. *Journal of Clinical Psychology,* 1958, *24,* 242-244.

Carkhuff, R.R. *Helping and human relations* (Vol. 2). New York: Holt, Rinehart & Winston, 1969.

Carkhuff, R.R. *The development of human resources.* New York: Holt, Rinehart & Winston, 1971.

Carkhuff, R.R., & Berenson, B.G. *Beyond counseling and therapy.* New York: Holt, Rinehart & Winston, 1967, 1977.

Carkhuff, R.R., & Berenson, B.G. *Teaching as treatment.* Amherst, Mass.: Human Resource Development Press, 1976.

Freud, S. *Collected papers.* London: Hogarth and The Institute of Psycho-Analysis, 1924.

Friedman, N. From the experiential in therapy to experiential therapy: A history. *Psychotherapy: Theory, Research and Practice,* 1976, *13*(3), 236-243.

Gendlin, E.T. Client-centered developments and work with schizophrenics. *Journal of Counseling Psychology,* 1962, *9,* 205-211.

Holder, B.T., Carkhuff, R.R., & Berenson, B.G. The differential effects of the manipulation of therapeutic conditions upon high and low functioning clients. *Journal of Counseling Psychology,* 1967, *14,* 63-66.

Mickelson, D.J., & Stevic, R.R. Differential effects of facilitative and nonfacilitative behavioral counselors. *Journal of Counseling Psychology*, 1971, *18*, 314-317.

Murphy, H.B., & Rowe, W. Effects of counselor facilitative level on client suggestibility. *Journal of Counseling Psychology*, 1977, *24*, 6-9.

Piaget, G., Berenson, B.G., & Carkhuff, R.R. The differential effects of the manipulation of therapeutic conditions by high and low functioning counselors upon high and low functioning clients. *Journal of Consulting Psychology*, 1967, *31*, 481-486.

Rogers, C.R. *Client-centered therapy.* Boston: Houghton Mifflin, 1951.

Rogers, C.R. *On becoming a person.* Boston: Houghton Mifflin, 1954.

Rogers, C.R. In retrospect: 46 years. *American Psychologist*, 1974, *29*, 115-123.

Rogers, C.R., & Dyamond, R.F. *Psychotherapy and personality change.* Chicago: University of Chicago Press, 1954.

Rogers, C.R., Gendlin, E.T., Kiesler, D., & Truax, C.B. *The therapeutic relationship and its impact.* Madison, Wisc.: University of Wisconsin Press, 1967.

Truax, C.B., & Carkhuff, R.R. The experimental manipulation of therapeutic conditions. *Journal of Consulting Psychology*, 1965, *29*, 119-124.

Truax, C.B., & Carkhuff, R.R. *Toward effective counseling and psychotherapy.* Chicago: Aldine Press, 1967, chapter 5.

Vitalo, R. The effects of facilitative interpersonal functioning in a conditioning paradigm. *Journal of Counseling Psychology*, 1970, *17*, 141-144.

Wexler, D., & Rice, L. *Innovations in client-centered therapy.* New York: Wiley & Sons, 1974.

What is this chapter all about?

This chapter focuses on the critically important stages of helpee exploration and on the specific responding skills that the helper can and should employ to promote and sustain such exploration.

Where does this fit in the overall helping model?

The overall model specifies four primary phases of helpee activity. The first of these — helpee involvement — was treated in the last chapter as an essential prehelping area of concern. Helpee *exploration* is the second of our four primary phases but the first within the actual helping (as opposed to prehelping) process itself.

PREHELPING   **HELPING**

ACTION

UNDERSTANDING

EXPLORATION   Explores immediate reasons for feelings
Explores immediate feelings
Explores immediate meaning
Explores immediate situation

♦ INVOLVEMENT

Why is helpee exploration important?

Helpees will quite often begin a counseling or helping session convinced that they know exactly what the problem is. An alcoholic getting help through an outpatient clinic may blame his drinking on his family life. A couple involved in marital counseling may see their children as the major cause of their own present difficulties. In the overwhelming majority of cases, however, thorough exploration of the immediate situation, the meaning of this situation, the feelings aroused in helpees, and the reasons for these feelings allow the helpees to gain a great deal of insight into "where they really are" in terms of the outside world; at the same time, of course, such exploration enables the counselor or helper to see the helpees and their world through the helpees' own eyes. At each level of exploration, the individual helpee is saying, in effect, "Here's what it's like to be me." And many of these statements will reflect not previous convictions and beliefs but new awareness and insights.

Who must do what during helpee exploration?

The helper's continued use of basic attending, observing, and listening skills take the helpee beyond full involvement to the point where he or she is able to talk about the *immediate situation*. Having come to preliminary terms with the helpee's frame of reference or mental set, the helper *responds to the content* of the helpee's situationally specific statements, often using the format, "You're saying that _____." Encouraged to continue exploration, the helpee elaborates upon the situation until he or she is able to communicate the *immediate meaning* that this situation has for him or her. The helper *responds* to the meaning that is expressed or implied by the helpee's words, employing a format along the lines of, "You mean _____," or "So this means that _____." Next the helpee explores the *immediate feelings* aroused by the situation, and the helper responds to these feelings by using the format, "You feel _____," where the blank space is filled in with a specific "feeling" word or phrase reflecting the helpee's own frame of reference. Finally, the helpee explores the immediate *reasons* he or she finds for each feeling. The helper *responds to each feeling plus reason* by making use of the format, "You feel _____ because _____."

When should helpee exploration begin?

As indicated earlier, all of the phases of helpee activity represent a developmental process. The helpee signals her or his full involvement in this process by expressing personally relevant material. Such expressions often blend at once into an exploratory discussion of the immediate situation, at which point the helper can begin responding to content. If the helpee does not focus on the situation of immediate concern, the helper can employ some gentle questions involving the basic interrogatives (Who, What, When, Where,

Why, How), making sure that he or she responds to each of the helpee's answers in turn.

How can you practice the skills involved in responding?

The various responsive formats outlined in this chapter may at first seem arbitrary and artificial to you. Nevertheless, these formats represent the simplest, most accurate, and most effective ways in which a helper can begin to promote helpee exploration. Learn the formats and practice using them in your conversations with others. Note how each format makes it possible for you to reflect your awareness of the other person's frame of reference; the format, "You feel _____," for example, is quite different from, "You feel that _____," in that the former allows you to capture the individual's own feeling while the latter forces you to substitute an abstract idea or indirect statement for such feeling. Each time you respond accurately to another person, you are saying, "I'm with you, I hear you, I know where you are." And you are doing so not with the patronizing officiousness often associated with such statements but with genuine interest and understanding. Once you have mastered and put to practical use the several responsive formats outlined in this chapter, you may be ready to develop new and individual formats on your own.

Overview

1. Helpee involvement and exploration prepare the helpee to achieve a personalized *understanding* of where he or she wants or needs to be.

2. The helper promotes helpee understanding by using specific *personalizing skills.*

3. The first phase of helpee understanding requires that the helpee recognize the *personalized meaning* in her or his situation.

4. At this level the helper lays a responsive base and then *personalizes the meaning* implicit in the helpee's statements.

5. The second phase of helpee understanding requires that the helpee recognize and accept the *personalized problem* or deficit that is at the base of the situation.

6. Here the helper *personalizes the problem* in terms that specify the helpee's limitations.

7. The third phase of helpee understanding involves the helpee's recognition of new and *personalized feelings* that flow from her or his acceptance of the deficit.

8. The helper initiates with the helpee at this level by *personalizing the implicit feelings* in the helpee's recent statements.

9. The final phase of helpee understanding is reached when the helpee recognizes and accepts the *personal goal* indicating where he or she really wants to be.

10. The helper *personalizes the goal,* which is the "flip side" of the helpee's deficit or problem.

11. The helpee's new and personalized understanding makes it possible for the helpee to take control of the situation by *"owning" her or his role in the situation.*

12. The helper may, if appropriate, use the additional skills involving *immediacy* and *confrontation* in order to move the helpee toward greater understanding.

Before a helper can accomplish anything of real and lasting value, the helpee or helpees must be drawn into full *involvement* in the counseling or helping session. Thus, as we have seen, involvement is an essential prehelping dimension facilitated by the helper's use of basic *attending skills.* Once helpees are involved, the helper must employ the results of effective positioning, observing, and listening in order to respond to these helpees. Accurate and meaningful *responses* are the chief tools the helper uses to facilitate helpee *exploration.* And such exploration — characterized by an expanding awareness of all those factors and feelings flowing from the basic situation — is essential if each helpee is to come to terms with her or his own problems.

Chapter two dealt with the ways in which the skills of positioning, observing, and listening should be used to promote helpee involvement. Chapter three focused on the ways in which effective helper responses can and must facilitate helpee exploration. But it is not enough for a helpee to recognize, through exploration, where he or she is. The helpee must go beyond this by learning to *understand* his or her present position in the light of where she or he wants to be. Thus if helpee involvement characterizes the prehelping stage and helpee exploration characterizes the first phase of the actual helping process, then *helpee understanding* is the goal during the second of these phases. Here in chapter four, then, we will take up those specific skills that the effective helper must be able to use in order to promote helpee understanding in terms that are both personal and meaningful. Up to now, the skills covered have been primarily *responsive* in nature; they have reflected ways in which the helper can absorb information and give it back to the helpee in the form of responses that mirror the helpee's own state. Now, however, we must shift our focus to skills that are primarily *interpretive* in nature — skills that enable the helper to provide each helpee with new and more constructive direction. As before, we shall begin with a brief account of a familiar counseling situation.

"Ms. Torrens — Darla, I mean — you said yourself you didn't have any kids. If you did, you'd know yourself what they can do to a marriage. Honest to God, sometimes they just drive me straight up the wall!" Marge Kenney sat back in her chair and looked around at the other members of the group for some sign of support. She did not have to worry. They were all right with her.

"Marge is right," Bill Kenney chimed in on his wife's behalf. "Listen, I work a long day. And then I come home really beat, just wanting to relax a little, and what do I get?"

Ted Deems cut him off. "Same thing I get, Bill," he said. "A couple of snot-nosed, whining kids climbing all over me, wanting me to buy 'em something or do something or — or — all kinds of crazy stuff!"

"Listen, by the time you get home I've been taking care of those kids for ten hours!" Ted's wife, Sue, spoke up. The quick anger in her voice changed to a subtle pleading tone as she shifted heavily in her seat and looked at Darla. "See, it's not like I don't love my kids. 'Course I do! But like Marge said, after a while they can just drive you up a wall!" She looked over at the Deemses and the Porters, the third couple in the group. "I don't know about you all, but Ted and me, we had a beautiful relationship, just beautiful, until we started having kids. But now —" she shrugged helplessly — "now it seems like the kids just need so much attention all the time that we don't have any time or anything to spend with each other!"

"Sure, that's exactly it!" Simmie Porter leaned forward and pushed a wisp of hair back behind one ear. "Our kids are the same way — 'Do this, do that, help me, stop him' all day long, and all night, too!"

"So you all feel really hassled because your kids come between you and your spouses," Darla responded. And six simultaneous, almost enthusiastic nods testified to the accuracy of her response. Somehow the swift unanimity of this reaction did little to raise Darla's spirits. She could not seem to rid herself of the feeling that her six clients — these three couples who had come to her for help — had somehow managed to put her just where they wanted her. Nothing with relief that their 90-minute session was just about over, she brought the discussion to a close.

"It was really strange," she told Jim, her husband, later that night. "I mean, this was our third meeting since they first came to the clinic. And I still don't have the feeling that we've done more than scratch the surface. Yet they all seem eager as anything to keep going."

"Well . . ." Jim sipped his glass of wine and looked at his feet stretched out on the coffee table. "From what you've said, they must find you a pretty responsive person. And who doesn't enjoy spilling his life story to someone who's a good listener and responder?"

Darla noded. "Yeah, I'm sure that's got a lot to do with it. But look — these people all got referred to the clinic for family counseling because their marriages were in trouble. And as far as I can tell, they're *still* in trouble! I mean, Bill Kenney told me he's been sleeping on a cot in his workshop in the garage for a month now! And one of the men at the clinic told me he's a neighbor of the Porters and that the police had to come just night before last because they were fighting so loud it was disturbing the peace! But when they're with me, all they do is sit around and blame everything on their kids!"

"Well, if you feel like you're not getting anywhere, you ought to shake things up a bit," Jim commented.

"Uh huh . . ." Darla ran a hand back through her hair. "That's exactly what I'm going to try to do. I told them today that I'm going to be meeting with the husbands and wives separately next time."

"You think maybe getting them apart like that will help them to focus on other things besides their kids?"

"Got it in one." Darla nodded vigorously. "In fact, I'm counting on it."

Darla's new strategy worked — but only up to a point. She spent the first 45 minutes of her next counseling session working with Marge Kenney, Sue Deems, and Simmie Porter. Sure enough, they were soon able to move beyond talk of their children and fix the blame for their marital problems where they felt it really belonged: on their husbands.

"Oh, sure, the kid's are a hassle," Simmie said. "But they wouldn't be so bad if Sam'd just try to help them out. But no, he comes home as grumpy as a bear and doesn't have a good word for anyone — me, the kids, not anyone. He even yells at the stupid dog!"

"Yeah," Sue chimed in. "Ted used to be a great guy — you know, always joking, doing things, a whole lot of fun to be with. And these days, what with acting like a den mother to a couple of screaming savages all day, I could sure do with some fun when he gets home. Hah! Fat chance! I'm lucky if he even says hello on his way out to the front porch with his first can of beer!"

Darla responded to all of this, of course. As her husband had noted, she was good at being responsive. She listened well. She paid attention to people. She really cared about what was happening in their lives. And because she cared, she could often pick up feelings that less attentive, less observant helpers might have missed. But deep down inside, she was becoming increasingly aware that being responsive was not enough. Although she had done some individual counseling at the clinic before, this was her first experience at group marriage counseling. And she had an awful feeling that she was not making it as a helper.

This feeling was reinforced by her subsequent 45-minute session with the three husbands. Like their wives, they readily abandoned their characterizations of their children as the main source of their marital problems. The real problem, it turned out, was their wives.

"Honest to God, Darla!" Ted Deems leaned forward. "The other day I come home from work and what do I find? The kids are beating each other black and blue over what TV program they want to watch. There's a big pile of dogsh— dog manure in the hall. And when I go looking for Sue, she's laying on the bed upstairs reading a magazine or something. I mean, I know she probably worked hard and all — but there was still a lot of stuff that hadn't got done!"

"How'd she look?" Sam asked.

"Huh?" Ted seemed to find the question confusing. Sam didn't wait but plowed right ahead.

"Like some nights I come home and find out Simmie's spent all day fixing herself up. I know she does it to make herself look good for me. And I appreciate that. But — but — well, it doesn't give me any choice but to go out of my way to pay a whole lot of attention to her. And believe it or not, a lot of days I get home from work so tired I don't want to have to pay attention to anybody!"

"I know what you mean," Bill Kenney agreed. "Listen, one of Marge's crazy friends hooked her into taking some of those — what are they, 'Complete Woman' classes? Well, all right, I can understand that. Like you said about Simmie, Marge is probably just trying to please me. But to me it just seems like — oh, I don't know — like she's taking off time unnecessarily to impress me when I'd really rather she just took care of business." Bill sighed. "Besides, Marge's friend convinced her to buy all these sexy new clothes. And — well, on her they just look—"

"A mess!" Darla exclaimed later, once again at home with Jim. "That's what he said. And that's what the whole thing is turning into! I just don't feel like we're making any progress at all."

"I know you must feel pretty frustrated," Jim responded. "Where do you go from here?"

"Well, I was thinking that I'd split our next session up into six fifteen-minute segments and try talking to each of them individually. I've just got to get them beyond blaming their kids and each other!"

Again Darla's strategy was only minimally successful. Given the chance to talk privately with Darla, each of her six helpees managed to pick up on Darla's own feeling of frustration and go on to explain why they were not getting more results.

"It's this whole group idea," Marge announced. "You just can't say what you want to when there are other people around."

"The sessions are too long," Bill commented. "You get tired of sitting around and talking and then nothing gets done."

"The sessions are too short," Sue declared. "We ought to try an all-day thing — maybe some Saturday. I could send the kids to Ted's mother's."

"The problem is, we need to have everyone here who's involved," Ted said. "Like the kids. And my mother. And Sue's parents, too, if you could talk them into getting off their butts and helping!"

"Nothing personal," Simmie told her, "but it might be better if we had a man working with us. You know, maybe that neat-looking guy we always run into in the office outside?"

"Nothing personal," Sam told her. "I mean, I think you understand us real well. But — well, I'm just not sure you can really help us." He shrugged and looked down. "I'm not sure anyone can."

Like some of the people considered in earlier chapters, Darla is a conscientious helper. She cares about her people. She wants to make a difference in their lives. And she is far from unskilled. Yet her arsenal of skills, as she was fast discovering in the situation just presented, is by no means adequate. She was able to be quite responsive, and this is important. But it is not enough. It was not enough for the three couples whose marriages were disintegrating. And it is not enough for the vast majority of people with whom most helpers work.

Helpees need to find responsiveness in their helpers. It is this quality of responsiveness that helps them to get involved. It is this responsiveness that, by communicating the helper's own interest, concern, and understanding, promotes helpee exploration. But there comes a time, as we see in Darla's situation, where simple responsiveness is no longer sufficient. More specifically, responsiveness alone cannot get the helpee over that "hump" that separates immediate, external problems from personal, internal participation.

Consider what happened with Darla's helpees. They blamed their marital problems on their children. Then they blamed the same problems on one another. Finally, they blamed the lack of progress in the session on a wide range of things, many of them contradictory. At no time did they begin to "own" the problems by putting themselves into the equation. *And all effective helping requires that the helpee learn to understand or "own" his or her personal stake — the degree of her or his personal control and responsibility,*

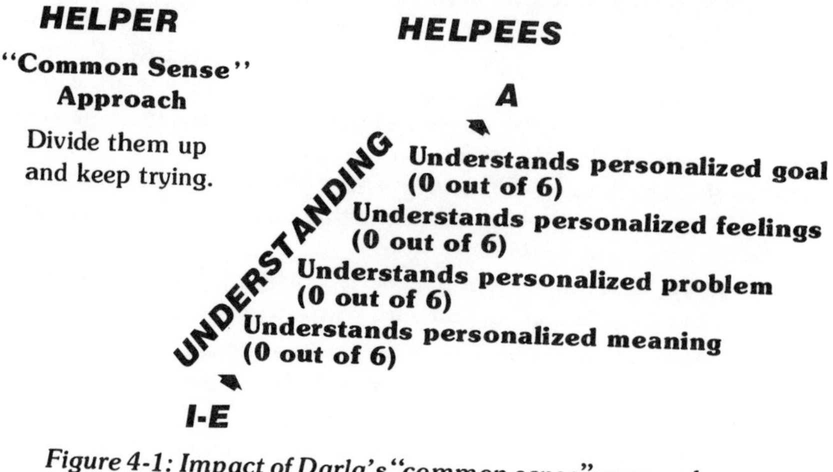

HELPER

"Common Sense" Approach

Divide them up and keep trying.

HELPEES

A

UNDERSTANDING

Understands personalized goal
(0 out of 6)

Understands personalized feelings
(0 out of 6)

Understands personalized problem
(0 out of 6)

Understands personalized meaning
(0 out of 6)

I-E

Figure 4-1: Impact of Darla's "common sense" approach on helpee understanding.

personal shortcoming — *before that helpee can set and achieve meaningful goals!*

Darla's approach to the problems posed by her helpees was once again what might be termed a "common sense" approach. Finding her helpees in a rut, she decided to isolate them from one another: first by sex, than as individuals in one-to-one sessions with her. Alas, neither approach worked — and with good reason. For no matter how a counselor may shift her or his helpees around, that counselor must always be limited by the number of concrete and functional skills available for use. Thus all of Darla's efforts were doomed from the start. She took her helpees as far as her existing skills allowed. Then, lacking those personalizing skills that would have enabled her to promote her helpees' understanding, she faced a dead end.

The tendency to blame other people or other forces outside ourselves for our problems seems to be as natural as it is widespread. Which of us has not muttered something along the lines of "Those miserable _____! It's all their fault!" Yet if we are mature and rational people, we recognize that few if any things are ever "all their fault." The unemployed man who blames his situation on callous and uncaring employers may be a sympathetic character; yet he would be a lot closer to finding work if he could understand the ways in which his own actions and capabilites — and the flaws in both — contribute to his situation. By the same token, the woman who blames her husband for stifling her own career plans might be able to revive those plans if she comes to understand how she herself has contributed to the problem from the start.

None of this is meant to start a round of heavy breast-beating — "Oh my God, it's all my fault!" Rather, the point is that no one can change a situation that is totally external. But anyone — and this specifically includes any helpee — can change a situation in which he or she has come to recognize and understand a personal, internal role. For example, the statement "I get asthma because the air where I live is polluted" reflects the hopelessness of a person confronting a wholly external situation. But consider a couple of alternative statements: "I get asthma because I can't figure a way to move to a town where there's less pollution"; or "I get asthma because I can't figure a way to get the factory near my house to cut down on its air pollution." Each of these statements reflects a way in which the individual may "own" a more personalized understanding of the problem. In each, the individual is put back into the situation by her or his understanding of a personal role in the problem itself.

Helpee understanding means helpee recognition and acceptance of *personalized meanings, personalized problems, personalized feelings,* and *personalized goals.* Only such understanding enables the helpee to continue movement through the several stages of helping. And only such understanding delivers to the helpee an awareness of her or his own ability to take control of and responsibility for the problematic aspects of personal experience. To promote such understanding, the effective helper must move beyond responsive skills and begin to initiate with the helpee. In this chapter, then, we will focus on the specific skills that the helper must be able to use in order to facilitate helpee understanding.

Personalize
the
Meaning

Helpee Goal:

To understand how he or she is involved in the reasons for his or her feelings.

During the final phase of exploration, the helpee focuses on a number of experiential reasons for her or his own immediate feelings. These reasons are invariably expressed in terms of external agents or causes.

"I get frustrated *because the kids keep coming between us in our marriage.*"

"I feel pretty angry *because my wife doesn't understand how hard I work.*"

"I get to feeling really down *because my husband never pays any attention to me.*"

Statements like these may sound quite familiar. They could have been uttered by any of the six people with whom Darla was working. Indeed, they could have been spoken by almost anyone at almost any time. Seen as the culmination of helpee exploration, such statements are perfectly valid. Yet they are severely limited in value because they fail to go beyond external or immediate causes. Stalled at this level — as Darla's helpees seemed to be stalled — no client can see himself or herself as anything more than the helpless victim of a wholly external, impersonal, and uncaring situation.

The helpee goal that overcomes this limitation involves translating immediate (external) reasons into personalized (internal) meanings. Although the helpee's feelings themselves may not change — at least not yet — the whole situation assumes a deeper and more personal quality of meaning.

"I get frustrated because the kids keep coming between us in our marriage" becomes "I get frustrated *because I don't have enough time to spend with my wife.*"

"I feel pretty angry because my husband doesn't understand how hard I work" becomes "I feel pretty angry *because all my work isn't appreciated.*"

"I get to feeling really down because my family never pays any attention to me" becomes "I get to feeling pretty down *because I need more attention from my family than I get.*"

Perhaps this shift from immediate reasons to personalized meaning seems slight. However, this is far from the case. The helpee's understanding of personalized meanings reflect her or his first real attempt to see a problem or situation in terms over which he or she has some control. This is a crucial — and major — step in the overall helping process.

Helper Skills:
Personalizing the helpee's meaning by using a format along the lines of, "You feel _____ because you _____."

The question now, of course, is: How can the counselor or helper facilitate each helpee's understanding of personalized meaning? To answer this question, we must focus on two closely related skill-areas.

First, the helper must *lay an adequate base for personalizing.* This means that the helper must continue to respond to the immediate reasons expressed by the helpee until the helpee's expressions at this level appear self-sustaining. As indicated in the previous chapter, the simplest format the helper can use in responding to immediate reasons is, "You feel _____ because _____." The helper will know that such a response is truly interchangeable with the helpee's own feelings and reasons if the helpee shows agreement and goes on to express a modified version of feeling/reason.

> Helpee: "I get mad a lot because none of the employers I go to will give me the time of day."

Helper: "You feel angry because they ignore you." *(interchangeable response)*

Helpee: "Yeah. I mean, you'd think they'd at least have the courtesy to listen"

Helper: "You feel pretty frustrated because they don't even treat you with simple decency." *(interchangeable response)*

The helper seeking to lay a base for personalizing should continue to respond at this level, all the while attempting to identify some major recurrent theme in the helpee's expressions. Invariably, this major theme is one to which the helpee keeps returning: for example, a person who seems to pose a primary obstacle, or a specific situation that consumes all the helpee's attention. Having isolated such a theme, the helper can respond directly to it.

Helpee: "The worst part is knowing how old I am and how there are so many young guys I have to compete with for jobs. That's really a bad feeling, seeing how much younger they are."

Helper: "It's pretty frightening, seeing yourself in the same position as these other guys but knowing you're twenty years older. That's a pretty major thing." *(interchangeable response to main theme)*

Helpee: "I'll say! Listen, these guys can afford to be patient. But me — I just can't waste any time, that's all. I just can't."

Helper: "You feel pretty desperate because the competition really seems to have time on their side." *(interchangeable response to main theme)*

If the helper has indeed focused on the major theme — and if she or he continues to respond to this theme in order to lay an adequate base — the helpee will react by elaborating upon this theme with little or no prompting from the helper. Such self-sustained elaboration is a signal to the helper that a base has been laid and that he or she can begin to initiate greater understanding with the helpee.

Now the helper must *initiate at a new level* by responding to the as-yet-unexpressed personalized meaning implicit in the helpee's statements. To do this, the helper translates the helpee's comments on those external reasons underlying the main theme into a statement reflecting personalized meaning. Here the simplest format for the helper to use is, "You feel _____ because you _____."

> Helpee: "Time. Yeah, that's the main thing, all right. It's really bad when I think about how much of an edge these young guys have just because of age. I mean, here I am, I'm forty-three, and these guys are maybe in their twenties. And maybe they've only got a couple of years experience compared to the twenty years I've got. But the employer looks at them and he knows he can get them for a lot less money than I'd need. And even if they don't get jobs, well, they can just hang around for a year or so and wait for something. But me, I don't have that kind of time. It's really bad.
>
> I get to thinking about it and — well, it's just spooky, that's all . . ." *(helpee self-sustained expression of major theme)*

> Helper: "You feel pretty frightened because you know you've got to be at your very best to overcome the age disadvantage." *(initiative response to implicit personalized meaning)*

Having personalized with the helpee at this new level, the helper must, of course, make sure that the helpee sees this new response as interchangeable with his or her own feelings and perception. Thus the helper looks and listens very carefully in order to assess the helpee's reaction. If the helpee should be uncomfortable with his or her new personalized role in the situation — "You feel _____ because *you* _____" — the helper can recognize this discomfort in negative behaviors like head-shaking or negative statements like, "No, that's not it . . ." In such a case, the helper must go back to the last level at which the helpee accepted an interchangeable response and continue to lay a base. It may be that the helper has mistaken a subordinate concern for the helpee's major theme. Or it may be that the helper's choice of terms has been inappropriate. In either case, the helper must make a renewed effort to lay a good base of interchangeable responses and to isolate the main theme before trying again to personalize with the helpee by responding to the implicit personalized meaning.

If the helper's interpretive response to personalized meaning is acceptable to the helpee, on the other hand —

"Yeah, that's just how it is!" — or if the helpee goes on to explore her or himself further, then the helper should continue to respond interchangeably at this new level. To do so, he or she can continue to employ variations on the basic "You feel _____ because you _____" theme. After exchanging perhaps six interchangeable responses with the helpee, the helper can initiate on a new level — that of the *personalized problem*.

Personalizing the Problem

Helpee Goal:

To understand what his or her unique problem is.

By accepting the helper's initial statement of personalized meaning, the helpee signals an understanding of the basic implications of the situation for him or her in personal terms. For the first time, the helpee is viewing the situation in terms of its internal rather than external significance. But he or she still has not grappled with the ways in which personal behavior or attributes may be contributing to this situation. For example, we saw the shift from terminal exploration to initial understanding in an earlier illustration:

"I get frustrated because the kids keep coming between us in our marriage." *(feeling and reason)*

became

"I get frustrated because I spend so much time taking care of the kids." *(personalized meaning)*

Although this statement of personalized meaning does reflect the helpee's understanding of the way in which the situation affects her personally, the statement does not indicate how the helpee's own behavior may be responsible for her situation and negative feelings. The next goal for the helpee, then, must be to "own" the problem by viewing it in terms of a personal deficit or area of limited capability. Needless to say, this is often an extremely difficult step for a helpee to take. One of the nicest things about blaming the rest of the world for our problems is that we can see ourselves as blameless individuals for whom no corrective action is either necessary or possible. By the same token, the recognition of a personalized problem or individual deficit means an acceptance of personal responsibility — and the need for personal action.

Helpees use an infinite number of strategies to avoid accepting their own personal responsibility. These strategies are often referred to as defense mechanisms. Most textbooks of abnormal psychology list some of the more common defense mechanisms (e.g., projection, rationalization, denial, displacement). In the helping model presented in this text these defense mechanisms are viewed as functional behaviors that prevent helpees from acknowledging that they must change their behavior. A helpee may or may not be aware that he or she is being defensive.

Some examples of helpee defenses against personalizing are:

1. An employee who *displaces* his anger at his boss onto his co-workers and then gets fired because his co-workers can't get along with him.

2. A student who *projects* his or her own distrust and disrespect of teachers onto the teachers and then leaves school because the teachers don't care for her or him as a person but just as an ID number.

3. An unemployed worker who, lacking the skills necessary to look for a job, *rationalizes* that it is hopeless for her or him to look because the economy is so bad.

4. A halfway house resident who, fearing that he or she will not be able to communicate with his wife or her husband on his or her return home, *denies* that he or she really wants to return home and has to be readmitted to a hospital.

Despite the helpee's defenses against accepting one's responsibility, however, this step is essential for any helpee who is to acquire new and more constructive behaviors and the new and more fulfilling life that such behaviors entail. Thus the goal for the helpee at this stage must be to recognize a new level of personal involvement. Personalized meaning ("I get frustrated because I spend so much time taking care of the kids.") must be expanded to incorporate the deficit expressed in a statement of the personalized problem ("I get frustrated *because I can't* arrange my time well enough to attend to both the kids and my husband.").

Helper Skills:
To personalize the helpee's problem or deficit by using a

format along the lines of, "You feel ＿＿＿＿＿＿＿＿＿ because you can't ＿＿＿＿＿＿＿＿＿."

Needless to say, few if any helpees will achieve the level of understanding that includes a personalized statement of the problem without help. To facilitate the helpee's understanding on this level, the helper must *identify the deficit theme* and then *initiate with the helpee by responding to this implicit theme in order to personalize the problem.*

The simplest way in which the helper can begin to identify the deficit theme is to ask and answer the question, "What is the helpee doing or failing to do that contributes most directly to this problem?" If it should turn out that the deficit theme centers on something the helpee is doing (drinking too much, for example), the helper should translate this action into negative terms implying a behavioral deficit: "He's contributing to the problem because he can't control his drinking," rather than, "He's contributing to the problem because he drinks too much." Such a translation into behaviorally negative terms is necessary because the helpee's personalized goal will eventually be stated in terms of the positive behavior desired: "He wants to control his drinking."

During the time that the helper has sought to identify the deficit theme, he or she must continue to respond interchangeably to the helpee's personalized meaning. Once the deficit has been identified, the helper can initiate by formulating a response that incorporates this deficit. Here the simplest format for the helper to use is, "You feel ＿＿＿＿＿＿＿＿＿ because you can't ＿＿＿＿＿＿＿＿＿."

> Helpee: "Yeah, I get really depressed because I know I've got a lot less time to really make it in a job than the young guys coming up." *(personalized meaning implying the deficit theme)*

The helper listens and asks, "What is it that he can't do that is causing the problem?" The answer is, of course, that the helpee can't figure out how to make the best possible use of his time. Now the helper responds to this deficit in terms of personalized problem.

> Helper: "So you get pretty down because you can't figure out how to use your time to maximum advantage."

As at earlier levels, the helper must check the validity of this initiative response in terms of the helpee's subsequent behavior and verbal reaction. Does the helpee seem to agree

108

with this new statement? Is he nodding his head? Is his next statement an affirmation of the helper's initiative response to a personal deficit? If not, the helper will need to go back to the previous level, continuing to respond interchangeably and to personalize meaning while seeking to identify the true deficit theme and determine how this theme may be expressed in terms that the helpee can accept from his own frame of reference.

If the helpee signals her or his understanding of the personalized problem, a giant step has been taken. The helper should continue to respond interchangeably at this new level, paving the way for an initiative response to *personalized feelings*.

Personalizing the Feelings

Helpee Goal:
To understand how he or she feels about him or herself.

Up to this point, the helpee's feelings concerning the main theme have remained relatively consistent. Or, he or she may have shifted from "depressed" to "frightened" to "sad" to "down." For the most part, however, the helpee has probably continued to express those immediate feelings first articulated during his or her period of exploration. Now, however, the helpee has come to understand the entire situation on a far deeper, more personalized level. And more often than not, this new level of understanding will give rise to new feelings. For example, the man who feels angry because his wife's new job consumes all her time may discover a whole new level of feeling after coming to terms with personalized meaning and the personalized problem.

"I feel angry because my wife spends all her time at her new job." *(feeling and reason)*

becomes

"I feel angry because I don't get to spend enough time with my wife." *(personalized meaning)*

becomes

"I get angry because I can't figure out how to get to spend more time with my wife." *(personalized problem)*

which may now become

"I feel *lonely* because I can't figure out how to spend more time with my wife."

Here the feeling word "lonely" is more consistent in terms of the helpee's expression of a personalized problem or deficit. In other words, the helpee understands that, though "angry" described his feelings accurately when he was blaming things on his wife, "lonely" is a more accurate description of his feelings about his own deficit or incapability.

The helpee's understanding and expression of new and more personalized feelings is extremely important. Such understanding confirms the helpee's own acceptance of the deficit and reflects her or his increasing "ownership" of the entire situation.

Helper Skills:

To personalize the new feelings the helpee may have as the result of recognizing the personal deficit by using a format along the lines of, "You feel *(new feeling term)* because you can't _____."

Here again, the helper cannot expect a client or helpee to understand and express new and more personalized feelings on her or his own. The helper must actively seek to facilitate such understanding by *identifying new feelings* implicit in the helpee's statement and by then *responding to these implicit and personalized feelings.*

The helper or counselor can begin to identify the helpee's personalized feelings by asking and answering the question, "What is the helpee doing or saying that might reflect a new type of feeling?" Perhaps a helpee has been sitting erect and expressing considerable anger; and perhaps the same helpee, now having come to terms with the personalized meaning and the personalized problem, is slumped in his chair with his eyes downcast. Any such dramatic shift in posture reflects an equally dramatic shift in feeling akin to our sample helpee's shift from "angry" to "lonely." We can see, then, that the effective helper uses all of her or his skills cumulatively — in particular, never failing to attend, observe, and listen with maximum care.

Having focused on certain new behaviors or expressions, the helper can now ask, "Given these specific shifts in the helpee's actions and expressions, how is he or she probably feeling?" As we have seen, "angry" may have given way to "lonely"; or "lonely" may have yielded to "dumb"; or "discouraged" may have turned into "frustrated." Whatever the shift in feeling, it will be implicit in everything that the helpee does and says following recognition of the now-personalized problem. The helper must be able to use her or his attending, observing, and listening skills in order to identify this shift.

Once the helpee's new feelings are clear to the helper, he or she should respond directly to these feelings by using the format, "You feel _____(new word)_____ because you can't _____."

> Helpee: "It's really pretty silly. I mean, maybe these young guys competing for jobs really are sharper than me. You'd think I'd be able to figure out how to make the best use of my time instead of just going around in circles." *(expression of personalized problem implying new feelings)*

> Helper: "You feel kind of stupid because you can't figure out how to put your time and energy to better use." *(initiative response to new and personalized feelings)*

The helper has asked and answered the two questions outlined above and has decided that the helpee probably feels pretty "stupid" for not handling his time better. Having responded at this new level, the helper must check to see if the helpee's reaction reflects acceptance or rejection of the personalized feelings. Although they are not as much of a stumbling block as personalized problems, a helpee may still reject new and more deeply personal expressions of feeling: "No, why should I feel stupid?" Here, as before, the skilled helper must backtrack to the last level of clearly interchangeable responses and continue to respond at this previous level until he or she feels the helpee is ready to move on. Alternatively, it might develop that the helper has identified the general quality of the helpee's new feeling but has not used a term that the helpee can readily recognize and accept. In such a case, the helper's vocabulary of "feeling" words and phrases comes in quite handy. He or she can select related or analogous terms until one is found that fits in with the helpee's new frame of reference.

Finally, of course, the helper may determine by the helpee's reaction that the latter recognizes and accepts the new level of personalized feeling. If this is the case, the helper can continue to respond interchangeably at this level until he or she is ready to initiate by helping to *personalize the helpee's goal.*

Personalizing
the
Goal

Helpee Goal:

To understand where he or she want to go.

At this stage in the overall helping process, the helpee has managed to translate immediate or external meaning, feelings, and reasons into personalized or internal terms. He or she has really learned how the situation can be "owned" in a way that promises the possibility of a solution. It now remains for the helpee to understand how this new awareness of meaning, problems, and feelings can be expanded in order to include a statement of personalized goals.

Here we can see why it is important for the helper to personalize the problem of a negative behavior or deficit. The helpee is now able to view her or his situation in terms of something that, at present at least, cannot be done.

"I feel weak because *I can't* seem to make decisions for myself."

"I feel bad because *I can't* figure out how to spend more time with my wife."

"I feel stupid because *I can't* arrange my time more effectively."

Given this level of understanding, the helpee is now ready to move on to a consideration of the personalized goal that flows from her or his previous statements. This goal is clearly implied by the statement of deficit or personalized problem. It is, in fact, the "flip side" of this problem. In other words, the helpee's eventual expression of a personalized goal will entail behavior that corrects the understood deficit.

"I feel weak because I can't seem to make decisions for myself *and I really want to be able to stand on my own two feet.*"

"I feel lonely because I can't figure out how to spend more time with my wife *and I want us to share more things together.*"

"I feel stupid because I can't arrange my time more effectively *and I'd like to make the best possible use of my time.*"

Helper Skills:

To personalize the helpee's goal by using a format along the lines of, "You feel _____ because you can't

_____ and you want _____."

Helping an individual to understand a personalized goal is usually far easier than helping to personalize meaning, problems, and new feelings. The helpee who has come to understand and accept her or his own role in a situation is usually eager to pinpoint a goal that will lead to a resolution of the situation. Nevertheless, the effective helper must continue to use specific skills in promoting greater understanding. The helper must begin by *identifying the goal* that is implicit in the helpee's own expressions. He or she must then go on to initiate greater understanding by *responding to this implicit and personalized goal.*

As noted, the helpee's goal is invariable the "flip side" of the personalized problem or deficit. What the helpee cannot do, in other words, is usually just what he or she wants to be able to do. Thus the helper can identify the goal by asking and answering the questions, "What is it that the helpee cannot do and wants to do?" and "Will the ability to do this help to resolve the helpee's problem?" This second question represents a type of last-minute check. By asking whether achievement of the potential goal will solve the helpee's problem, the helper can make sure that no crucial steps or pieces of information have been left out and that the understood deficit or problem is really at the heart of the helpee's situation. For example, one helpee might express an understanding of the personalized problem by saying, "I get really depressed because I can't seem to make friends." The effective helper tentatively identifies the goal as "wanting to make friends." Then the helper checks out the value and validity of such a goal by asking, "Will making friends help this person to overcome his feelings of depression?" If the answer is yes, the helper knows that the goal is valid. In those rare cases where the answer is no or even "not sure," however, the helper will see that the expressed deficit is not itself the heart of the helpee's true problem. In such cases, the helper should backtrack to determine the level at which he or she last responded with complete accuracy to the helpee.

Having identified the helpee's goal, the helper can go on to respond with initiative at this new level by employing the format, "You feel _____ because you can't _____ and you want _____."

"You feel sad and lonely because you can't make friends and you really would like to make some friends."

"You feel pretty scared because you can't figure out how

to ensure your job when so many of your co-workers are getting laid off and you really would like some job security."

"You feel pretty unhappy with yourself because you can't seem to forget about your handicap enough to function in the community and you really want to live a full and useful life."

Here again, the helper must assess the helpee's reactions in order to make sure that the latter understands and accepts this personalized statement of goal. Since the entire process of initiating personalized responses is cumulative, the effective helper knows that helpee understanding of the goal reemphasizes and reinforces helpee understanding of the personalized meaning, problem, and feelings.

Once the helpee has indicated acceptance of the personalized goal, the helper should begin preparations for the third stage of the overall helping process — the stage where helpee exploration and understanding yield to effective helpee *action*. We will focus on the skills needed to promote such action in the next few chapters. Before we move on, however, there are two additional skill-areas that must be dealt with here.

Communicating with Immediacy

At every stage of the prehelping and helping processes, it is critically important for the helper to be "right there" with each helpee, communicating that "hovering attentiveness" mentioned in an earlier chapter. There are times, however, when the helper may want to communicate the immediacy of her or his attention and concern in a more explicit way. Such immediacy of expression serves two purposes. First, the immediacy response assists the helpee in personalizing the helper-helpee relationship. Thus the helpee's understanding is made more real because it embraces an understanding of what is happening then and there with the helper. A second purpose is that the helpee learns something about effective communication by being presented with a model of one person, the helper, who is able to communicate fully and accurately.

The skilled helper can formulate a response with immediacy by asking and answering several specific questions. "How does what this helpee is saying about the problem relate to what is going on between us right now?" In other words, how do the helpee's words reflect upon his or her relationship with the helper? "Is the helpee acting out her or his own part in the problem?" This is probably the single most common situation calling for a response with immediacy. "Does the helpee perceive me (the helper) as doing things that he or she has described others as doing?" "How does the helpee feel about what I'm doing or saying right now?" "Is the helpee acting out a problem with another person by taking that person's part?"

Once the skilled helper has identified the helpee's present feelings and focused on specific verbal or behavioral cues, he or she can respond with immediacy by using some variation of the basic format, "Right now with me you feel _____ because ___you (can't)___." For example, one helpee might express her understanding of a personalized problem by saying, "I feel pretty lonely because I can't seem to get people to like me." At the same time, this helpee might be slumped down in her seat, looking away from the helper with the corners of her mouth turned down in a mournful expression. Responding with immediacy, the helper might say, "I can see that. Even here with me, you feel pretty miserable because you don't think I want to be your friend." A response with immediacy along these lines may well promote greater understanding by helping the girl or woman to see how her feelings and situation are reflected in her every word and action. She may also realize that the helper is indeed "right there" with her all the time — and that her or his concern is a genuine as it is immediate.

Responding with immediacy is also one way in which the helper can promote further exploration or greater understanding on the part of a helpee who seems stalled.

Helper: "You feel pretty miserable because you can't seem to really trust anyone — not even the people in your own family." *(response to a personalized problem that the helpee has already accepted)*

Helpee: "Yeah, I guess so." *(long pause as the helpee looks down at her hands clasped in her lap)*

Helper: "You're really unhappy because you can't accept people in the way they present themselves to you." *(interchangeable response to the personalized problem.)*

Helpee: "Uh huh." *(long silence)*

Helper: "Right now you feel miserable because you can't even trust me when I seem to understand you." *(response with immediacy)*

Helpee: "Yeah, I guess that's true, I mean, how can I trust you — or anyone? I just get let down all the time." *(The helpee recognizes the accuracy of the helper's new response with immediacy.)*

Helper: "Uh huh. It's a desperate feeling when you can't let your defenses down with anyone."

Using
Confrontations

Responding with immediacy may be employed by the skilled helper at almost any point. It poses little threat to the helpee and can do a lot to facilitate greater understanding. Confrontations, however, are a different story. The effective helper may decide at some point that he or she can help the client personalize his or her responsibility only through confrontation. But this decision can never be made lightly. In the past, far too many helpers have made frequent and often harmful use of confrontation. They have sought to "jolt" their helpees into recognizing problems or situations. Yet a review of the literature shows that *confrontation is neither a necessary nor a sufficient condition of helping!* At most, it is a tool that the skilled helper uses cautiously, if at all.

Confrontations may take a number of forms and be prompted by any one of several helper perceptions. The goal is increased helpee self-understanding. The helper may find that a given helpee is unwilling to abandon defensive "smoke screens" of some sort. The helper may see a significant discrepancy between what a helpee is saying and what he or she is doing. Or the helper may perceive another discrepancy between how the helpee acts and how she or he wants to act.

There are, as noted, many ways of confronting a helpee. In general, however, these break down into two basic categories: mild confrontations and strong confrontations.

In the first, the helper often employs a format along the lines of, "On the one hand you say/feel/do _____, and on the other hand you say/feel/do _____." Any helper considering confrontation should begin by employing this sort of mild approach — and one that, moreover, focuses on the situation from the helpee's own frame of reference.

"On the one hand you say that you're looking forward to getting out of the hospital, and on the other hand you say you're nervous about being at home with your family again."

A mild confrontation of this sort is only minimally threatening to the helpee. Yes, it does focus on a discrepancy or element of contrast. But it does so in terms that come entirely from the helpee's own frame of reference.

In many cases, the accuracy of the helper's interchangeable responses at any given level make confrontation unnecessary and undesirable. In other cases, mild confrontation may be all that's needed to promote greater understanding on the helpee's part. In a few cases, however, the helper may need to confront a helpee directly. Rather than limiting itself solely to the helpee's own frame of reference, such a direct confrontation stresses external and observable data. Here the format is usually a variation on, "You say/feel/do _____, but it looks to me like you say/feel/do _____." In confronting a helpee directly like this, an effective helper must have paved the way by laying a thorough base of interchangeable responses and by initially using a series of mild confrontations. Moreover, the helper will use the technique of direct confrontation only when he or she has ample observational data to back up any statement. No skilled helper, for example, would confront a helpee by saying, "You say you feel confident but that's baloney. You're really pretty unsure of yourself." Besides being threatening in the extreme, such a statement reflects arrogant opinion rather than helpful observational fact.

"You say you feel confident, but you look to me as though you're sort of nervous." Here the helper has arrived at an understanding of the helpee's state by observing his constant shifts of position, his erratic eye movements, and his fingers that have been plucking at the arms of his chair.

The most common approach to confrontation might involve a helper who has given interchangeable responses to several incongruous or contradictory helpee expressions.

Helpee: "I just don't think I can make it in school this

year." *(The helpee has consistently earned good grades and strong teacher recommendations.)*

Helper: "You're really scared because you don't feel you can handle the load." *(interchangeable response)*

Helpee: "I need a lot of help. All the time."

Helper: "You feel pretty helpless on your own." *(interchangeable response)*

Here there is an obvious incongruity between the helpee's expression of anticipated failure and the objective evidence pointing to high capability and achievement. After continuing to respond at this level to lay an adequate base, the helper decides to try a mild or tentative confrontation:

Helper: "On the one hand you're worried about failing in school, but on the other hand all your teachers say you're doing top work for them." *(using a mild confrontation)*

Helpee: "I know that's how they feel. And I guess I have been doing OK so far. But — but it's just luck! I just know the bottom's going to drop out one day and I'll be lucky to end up with Ds!"

This mild confrontation by the helper has not really changed things for the helpee. The helper continues to respond interchangeably and tries several other forms of mild confrontation with the same result. Finally she decides to try confronting the helpee directly:

Helper: "You say you're bound to fail but all the evidence points the other way. It sounds to me as if you can't generate any real confidence in your own ability." *(using a direct confrontation)*

Helpee: "T-that's true, I guess. I've never had a whole lot of confidence in myself. It — well, it always seemed to make more sense to me to prepare for the worst. That way, I wouldn't ever be taken by surprise if the worst actually happened."

Helper: "So you're afraid to accept your own capability because you can't deal with even the remotest chance that you'll be let down." *(interchangeable response to a new level of helpee insight)*

Here a direct confrontation has paid off for both helper and helpee. The helper chose to use such a confrontation because neither interchangeable responses nor mild confrontations seemed to work. Had any other approach suggested itself, the helper would certainly have chosen it over this type of direct — and risky — confrontation.

In the end, skilled helpers always keep in mind those principles that guide and control the use of confrontation. *No helper confronts a helpee when there is an alternative approach that promises helpee gains; and no helper confronts a helpee directly when a mild confrontation might work as well.*

Personalizing the helpee's meaning; personalizing the problem; personalizing new feelings; and personalizing the goal — these are the skills every effective helper must have in order to facilitate helpee growth and understanding. Together with responses with immediacy and techniques of confrontation, these skills enable the effective helper to move beyond simple responsiveness and begin to make interpretations with respect to the helpee's own role in the situation. The helper who possesses such initiative skills will not, like Darla, leave her people stalled, stuck, unable to see beyond the external and antagonistic world that seems responsible for all their woes. Rather, the skilled helper will function like Bette in our continuing story — personalizing with each helpee in order to help him or her to understand and control the vast and often confusing realm of personal existence.

Bette and Jimmy

As was evident in the last several chapters, Bette was able to work with Jimmy Bessom in ways that her unskilled predecessors — Jimmy's father and Harry the college wonder — were not. Bette knew how to get Jimmy *involved* in the overall helping process; not by berating him or by playing the know-it-all but by showing Jimmy how her help could make his life a whole lot more enjoyable! She knew, too, how to facilitate Jimmy's *exploration* of his present situation: by attending, observing, and listening, and by responding to his own expressions concerning his immediate situation, the meaning this situation had, the feeling it aroused in him, and the external reasons for those feelings.

Bette did not lack common sense. But she also knew from her own past experience that common sense was not enough. What made the difference was skills. And fortunately for Jimmy, she possessed these skills in full measure.

"So you feel pretty bummed out because there's no one around who can straighten your life out for you." Bette continued to respond to the external reasons that Jimmy saw for his feelings.

"You got it," Jimmy agreed. He sat a little straighter in his chair now. Damn! This woman really was different. She didn't sound anything like the old man with his 'Whadya wanna be, a bum?' line. And she sure was an improvement over old Mr. Cool, that guy Harry that the old man had sicced on him. "Yeah. Boy, I never knew how good I had it when I was a kid! No hassles, no pressure, just good times."

"You remember how good it felt, how easy it was when no one expected anything from you." Bette continued to respond interchangeably to Jimmy as she regarded him. He was sitting straighter, no longer so afraid to look her in the eyes. His expression, one of cynicism tinged with sullen defensiveness when he first came in, had now relaxed into something approaching a grin.

"Uh huh." Jimmy agreed. "But now — what with my father pulling me in one direction and my friends in another — heck, what's a guy supposed to do?"

"You really feel pretty torn because you're stuck between two different ideas, two different directions." Having laid what she felt was an adequate base, *Bette made an interpretation by responding at the level of personalized meaning* implied by his words.

"Yeah." Jimmy did not even hesitate. As far as he was concerned, Ms. Simmons' last statement was as accurate a summary of his situation as any of the earlier statements. Then he thought about it a moment longer. "Yeah. Yeah, I guess I'm sort of stuck, huh?"

Noting his dawning awareness, Bette responded a few more times at this level and then *interpreted again by personalizing what she felt sure was Jimmy's problem or deficit.*

"You feel really down because you can't figure out a plan all your own that would still let you get along with your father and friends at the same time."

"Huh?" Jimmy's eyes widened. "God, that's what I need all right. Some way I could do my own thing without turning everyone else off! Man, that'd be perfect." Then his shoulders slumped and his eyes sought the floor. "But how can I do that? There's no way. I just can't, that's all." Then he recited in a tone of mock gruffness and contempt, "Only a damned fool thinks he can get everything he wants!"

Bette's response was one that incorporated *immediacy:* "Now you sound like your father explaining why you can't do something."

Her aim was accurate. Jimmy raised his eyes and grinned ruefully. "Yeah, I guess I was." Then he shook his head. "I don't know. Maybe some smart guy could figure it out — you know, how to have my own way and please the rest at the same time. But I just can't see it."

"You feel pretty dumb because you can't figure out a plan that will get you what you want and keep the others on your side." Now *Bette's interpretive response articulated Jimmy's new feelings,* clearly implied in his last statement. And again, her aim was accurate.

"Yeah, I guess it is kinda dumb, huh?" Jimmy responded. Man! This woman was something else. She was right — he did feel dumb! And after all, wasn't it pretty dumb to let a bunch of other people run your life? Hell, if a lot of guys together could figure out how to send a space probe to Mars, one guy by himself ought to be able to figure out how to make a simple decision and then make it work out!

Bette's next response helped Jimmy to personalize his goal: "So you feel pretty dumb because you can't figure out how to get what you want and still keep the others with you, and you really want a plan that'll let you have both."

"Oh, man — if only I could!" Jimmy's expression of longing was mute testimony to the extent to which he understood, accepted, even leaped at Bette's personalization of the goal. "If only I could . . ."

Here we can clearly see the effects of that shift from helpee exploration to helpee understanding. Jimmy began by exploring his situation. His father wanted him to remain in college. His friends — and they meant a lot to Jimmy — wanted him to drop out and come to work with them. Jimmy's own feelings — largely ones of anger and frustration —

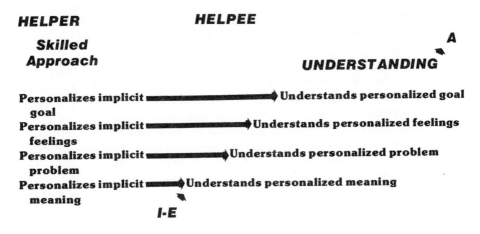

Figure 4-2: Initiative skills used by helper to promote full helpee understanding.

tended to shift their focus back and forth. First it was his father's fault. Then his friends' fault. Finally, however, Bette helped Jimmy to see that the problem was his own. At the deepest level, his negative feelings stemmed from his own inability to come up with a plan of action that would let him do what he wanted without costing him his father or his friends.

The helpee growth reflected in the above figure (4-2) is in sharp contrast to those "stalled" helpees whom we saw at the beginning of this chapter. There, all of Darla's fine intentions and good common sense were inadequate when it came to promoting helpee understanding. Her helpees were stalled precisely because they could not view their situation from a perspective that allowed them any hope of action or control. Blaming everything on some external "them," Darla's helpees could do no more than spend endless time exploring — and exploring — and exploring.

Working with a skilled helper, Jimmy Bessom was able to move beyond exploration and come to meaningful terms with the ways in which he himself could "own" his situation. In her interaction with Jimmy, Bette showed quite clearly the difference between herself and Darla. Although the latter was limited by her skills and could do no more than respond to her helpees, the former possessed the skills needed to go on and personalize with her helpee. It is as simple as that. Without interpretive skills, the best counselor or helper in the world cannot add to any helpee's understanding of himself or herself. And without greater insight and understanding, no helpee in the world can resolve a problem or situation.

Preparing, positioning, observing, listening; responding to content, to meaning, to feelings, to reasons — all these are essential responsive skills. To them we must now add the interpretive skills covered in this chapter: personalizing the meaning, personalizing the problem, personalizing the feelings, personalizing the goal; yes, and the additional interpretive skills involving immediacy and confrontation. Taken together, all of these specific responsive and interpretive skills enable the helper to move helpees through the several stages of exploration and understanding. They enable the helper to promote real and tangible helpee growth. They enable the helper to make a real difference.

But not enough of a difference. For until a helpee can take *action*, the helping process and its outcome are still in doubt. And in order to facilitate such action, the effective helper needs a new battery of skills. These skills are the focal point of the next several chapters.

The
Research
Background

Research has shown that there are skills beyond responding that a helper can use to assist the helpee to develop insights into his or her unique situation (Carkhuff, 1969, 1971; Carkhuff & Berenson, 1977; Truax & Carkhuff, 1967). In other words, the skills of responding are *usually* necessary but *rarely* sufficient. It is typically not enough for the helper to see the world only through the helpee's eyes. The helpee is often unable to develop the necessary insights by herself or himself; at these times, the helper must use interpretive skills to go beyond what the helpee alone can do.

What is needed is a transitional stage between helpee exploration and helpee action. That stage is understanding. It is a stage in which the helpee comes to personalize his or her problems and their goals. The helper's task during the understanding phase is to personalize the helpee's understanding of his or her problems and goals (Carkhuff & Berenson, 1977). This personalized understanding relates the helpee's exploration to the helpee's action programs. It helps the helpee to have a programmatically developed insight into his or her problems and goals before embarking upon an action course.

It is important to remember that the use of personalizing skills to make interpretations of client deficits and goals is tied to no single theory of psychotherapy. The existence of many theories of psychotherapy, with new theories being developed every year, is perhaps the clearest indication that no one theory is capable of organizing and explaining all human behavior. The current proliferation of psychotherapeutic theories is a direct reflection of the inability of any one theory of counseling to prove itself universally correct and useful. Thus, the use of personalizing skills is not a function of what theory the helper espouses but, rather, of how skillful the helper has been in understanding and dealing with each client's situation.

The importance of the particular theoretical base of knowledge adhered to by the helper has been called into question by several research studies (Anthony & Carkhuff,

1970; Carkhuff, Kratochvil, & Friel, 1968). These studies suggest that, although graduate students in the helping profession improved over training in their ability to *know* what a helpful response is, there was no corresponding improvement in their ability to actually *make* a helpful response within a counseling interaction. Thus it may be surmised that what counselors have learned about counseling theory does not necessarily translate into what they *do* in a counseling interaction.

Further support for this assumption was provided by a rather ingenious study that examined the relationship between a therapist's theoretical orientation and the level of responding skills that he/she demonstrates in a counseling interview. The study divided the professional therapists (all M.D.'s and Ph.D.'s) into three major theoretical orientations — psychodynamic, behavioristic, and humanistic — based on the therapists' own stated preferences. Each therapist tape recorded an actual interview with a pseudoclient. Ratings of the therapists' responding skills evidenced no significant differences between therapists of any of the three theoretical orientations, even though theoretically one would expect their levels of responding skills to differ (Fischer, Pavenza, Kickertz, Hubbard, & Grayston, 1975).

These research studies, as well as the current plethora of counseling theories, have a fairly straightforward implication for the development of counselor personalizing skills. That is, it would certainly be premature to make interpretations based exclusively on any one theory of psychotherapy. It would appear that at the present state of our research and theoretical knowledge, it would be most effective to assume an eclectic theoretical stance, that is, using any theory that is appropriate when it is appropriate. The "appropriateness" of the theory is a function of how well the theoretical perspective allows the helper to make personalized responses to the helpee — a personalized response to which the helpee can understand and agree — which in turn sets the stage for helpee action, which is the next phase of the helping process.

One series of studies, *The Effects of Personalizing upon Helpee Understanding,* was undertaken to assess whether counselors who were able to demonstrate their responsive and interpretive skills with a client were different in any other ways from helpers whose best responses demonstrated only attending, listening, and/or responding skills (Anthony, 1971). To ensure that counselors in the study would be functioning at interpersonal skill levels greater than the average counselor, this study used counselors who had just received a 30-hour interpersonal skills training experience. Each counselor conducted a 30-to-40-minute interview with the same physically disabled client. Comparisons between counselors who were rated as functioning at relatively higher levels of interpersonal skills versus those counselors who were functioning at slightly lower levels indicated that the higher-level counselors outperformed their relatively lower-level functioning counterparts on four other indices: (1) client's depth of self-exploration; (2) counselor's level of immediacy after confrontations by the client; (3) counselor's use of experiential confrontation; and (4) counselor's score on a test reflecting the favorability of the counselor's attitude toward physically disabled persons. The results of this study suggest that meaningful differences exist between those counselors who possess both responding and interpretive skills and those who do not. Particularly significant is the fact that the high-functioning group of counselors had a greater effect on a client-process measure related to counseling outcome (client self-exploration) and was significantly different from the lower group on an entirely independent measure of one's ability to function with this type of client (attitude score).

Another series of experimental studies investigated one such instance when it is necessary for the helper to become additive in his understanding, that is, when the helpee becomes reluctant to engage in any further self-exploration (Alexik & Carkhuff, 1967; Carkhuff & Alexik, 1967). In these research studies the client, unknown to the therapists involved, was given a mental set to explore herself deeply during the first third of an interview, to talk only about irrelevant and impersonal details during the middle third, and to explore herself deeply again during the final third of the interview. The research data indicated that in the middle third of the session, when the client began to "run away" from the therapeutic encounter, the most responsive therapists began to become initiative — that is, they became more interpretive, more immediate, and more confronting; overall, more personalized in their understanding of the helpee's immediate problems.

In this context, the skill of confrontation is a therapeutic technique that can be one of the most potent (albeit one of the most abused) interpretive skills. Berenson and Mitchell (1974) have comprehensively researched and analyzed the unique contributions of the interpretive helping skills and, in particular, the skill of confrontation. Their pathfinding efforts in this area have led to many specific conclusions including the facts that: (a) helpers who have a higher level of responsive skills confront in a different and more effective manner than helpers who possess low levels of responsive skills; (b) there are different types of confrontation that can be used most effectively in a certain sequence; and (c) confrontation, in and of itself, is never a sufficient therapeutic skill.

A number of approaches to counseling and psychotherapy emphasize the understanding phase of helping. Best known, of course, are the psychoanalytic and neo-analytic positions (Adler, 1927; Brill, 1938; Freud, 1924, 1933; Fromm, 1947; Horney, 1945; Jones, 1953; Jung, 1939; Mullahy, 1948; Rank, 1929; Sullivan, 1948).

Most modern psychoanalysts and psychiatrists, whose predominant technique is psychoanalysis, recognize that, although the theory may have contributed to the beginnings of an understanding of human thoughts and feelings, the techniques and assumptions of classical analysis are no longer adequate (Lorand, 1972; Freund, 1972; Conn, 1973; Friedman, 1975; McLaughlin, 1978; Older, 1977). From the beginning, although there was controversy over specifics, analysts felt strongest about their ability to provide a *description* of what they saw as "man in relation to his environment" (Lowenstein, 1954). As Morgenstern (1976) said in an address to the American Psychoanalytic Association, current concepts of psychoanalysis emphasize "character analysis" less than the treatment of illness, in an effort to move from the less observable "id" to the more evident processes of the "ego" (Silverman, Bronstein, & Mendelsohn, 1976). Present psychoanalytic discussion is turning more directly to the problems of empirically validating their beliefs (Anchor, 1977; Silverman, Bronstein, & Mendelsohn, 1976; Jaffe & Pulver, 1978). Severe criticisms have shaken the analysts' views about themselves and their approach (Jaffe & Pulver, 1978; McLaughlin, 1978). Perhaps, over the years Freud's own words had been forgotten: "The future may teach us how to exercise direct influence . . . (By means of . . . chemical substances). . . . *For the moment* we have nothing better at our disposal than the technique of psychoanalysis and for *that reason, in spite of its limitations,* it is not to be ignored" (quoted by Freund, 1972).

Unfortunately, psychoanalysts seem to have been so

burdened by their Freudian dogma that it was its limitations that were for so long ignored. With their basic assumption concerning the evil nature of humankind, these positions emphasized analyzing away the destructiveness. The final irony is that ". . . after peeling back the trappings and exposing the undergarments of an ugly world, Freud found no alternatives" (Carkhuff & Berenson, 1967, p. 107). The psychoanalytic positions had no real constructive alternatives to offer.

Some of the existential approaches to therapy attempted to fill this void by offering their working cosmologies as alternatives to the pathological assumptions of the helpees (Binswanger, 1956; Boss, 1963; Heidegger, 1962; May, 1961). Unfortunately, in the process of maximizing the emphasis upon honest encounter in the exchange of cosmologies, the existential approaches minimized the role definition of the helper. Thus, paradoxically, they failed to define the skills that are part and parcel of any effective cosmology (Carkhuff & Berenson, 1977).

In summary, the effective helper may draw from a variety of systems in helping to personalize the understanding of the helpee. Unfortunately, the study of counseling systems alone does not translate readily to skills that benefit the helpee. The danger of simply exchanging one cosmology for another is that the helpers are asking the helpees to fit their models of functioning rather than to develop the models to fit the helpees. Personalizing skills offer helpers an opportunity to work with helpees to overcome personalized problems and achieve personalized goals in their lives.

References

Adler, A. *Understanding human nature.* New York: Wolfe & Greenberg Publishers, 1927.

Alexik, M., & Carkhuff, R.R. The effects of the manipulation of client self-exploration upon high and low functioning counselors. *Journal of Clinical Psychology*, 1967, *23*, 210-212.

Anchor, K. Personal integration and successful outcome in individual psychotherapy. *Journal of Clinical Psychology*, 1977, *33*.

Anthony, W.A. A methodological investigation of the "minimally facilitative level of interpersonal function." *Journal of Clinical Psychology*, 1971, *27*, 156-157.

Anthony, W.A., & Carkhuff, R.R. The effects of rehabilitation counselor training upon trainee functioning. *Rehabilitation Counseling Bulletin*, 1970, *13*, 333-342.

Berenson, B.G., & Mitchell, K.M. *Confrontation: for better or worse*. Amherst, Mass.: Human Resource Development Press, 1974.

Binswanger, L. Existential analysis and psychotherapy. In F. Fromm-Reichman and J.L. Moreno (Eds.). *Progress in psychotherapy*. New York: Grune & Stratton, 1956.

Boss, M. *Daseinanalyses and psychoanalysis*. New York: Basic Books, 1963.

Brill, A.A. *The basic writings of Sigmund Freud*. New York: Random House, 1938.

Carkhuff, R.R. *Helping and human relations*. New York: Holt, Rinehart & Winston, 1969.

Carkhuff, R.R. *The development of human resources*. New York: Holt, Rinehart & Winston, 1971.

Carkhuff, R.R., & Alexik, M. The differential effects of the manipulation of client self-exploration upon high and low functioning counselors. *Journal of Counseling Psychology*, 1967, *14*, 350-355.

Carkhuff, R.R. & Berenson, B.G. *Beyond counseling and therapy, 1st ed.* New York: Holt, Rinehart & Winston, 1967.

Carkhuff, R.R., & Berenson, B.G. *Beyond counseling and therapy, 2nd ed.* New York: Holt, Rinehart & Winston, 1977.

Carkhuff, R.R., Kratochvil, D., & Friel, T. The effects of professional training: The communication and discrimination of the facilitative conditions. *Journal of Counseling Psychology*, 1968, *15*, 68-74.

Conn, J. The rise and decline of psychoanalysis. *Psychiatric Opinion*, 1973, *10*(5), 34-38.

Fischer, J., Pavenza, G.J., Kickertz, N.S., Hubbard, L.J., & Grayston, S.B. The relationship between theoretical orientation and therapist's empathy, warmth and genuineness. *Journal of Counseling Psychology*, 1975, *22*, 399-403.

Freud, S. *Collected papers*. London: Hogarth and the Institute of Psycho-analysis, 1924.

Freud, S. *New introductory lectures*. New York: Norton, 1933.

Freund, J. Psychoanalysis: Uses and abuses. *Psychosomatics,* 1972, *13*(6), 377-379.

Friedman, L. The struggle in psychotherapy: Its influence on some theories. *Psychoanalytic Review,* 1975, *62,* 453-462.

Fromm, E. *Man and himself.* New York: Holt, Rinehart & Winston, 1947.

Heidegger, M. *Being and time.* London: SCM Press, 1962.

Horney, K. *Our inner conflicts.* New York: Norton, 1945.

Jaffe, D., & Pulver, S. A survey of psychoanalytic practice: Trends, implications. *Journal of American Psychoanalytic Association,* 1978, *26*(3), 615-632.

Jones, E. *The life and work of Sigmund Freud.* New York: Basic Books, 1953.

Jung, C.G. *The integration of the personality.* New York: Holt, Rinehart & Winston, 1939.

Lorand, S. Historical aspects and changing trends in psychoanalytic therapy. *Psychoanalytic Review,* 1972-73, *59*(4), 497.

Lowenstein, R. Some remarks on defenses, autonomous ego and psychoanalytic techniques. *International Journal of Psychoanalysis,* 1954, *35,* 188-193.

May, R. (Ed.). *Existential psychology.* New York: Random House, 1961.

McLaughlin, F. Some perspectives on psychoanalysis today. *Journal of American Psychoanalytic Association,* 1978, *26*(1), 3-20.

Morgenstern, S. Current concepts of psychoanalytic process. *Journal of American Psychoanalytic Process,* 1976, *24*(1), 181-195.

Mullahy, P. *Oedipus: Myth and complex, a review of psychoanalytic theory.* New York: Grove, 1948.

Older, J. Four taboos that may limit the success of psychotherapy. *Psychiatry,* 1977, *40,* 197-203.

Rank, O. *The trauma of birth.* New York: Harcourt, 1929.

Silverman, L., Bronstein, A., & Mendelsohn, E. The further use of the subliminal psychodynamic activation method for the experimental study of the clinical theory of psychoanalysis: On the specificity of the relationship between symptoms and unconscious conflicts. *Psychotherapy: Theory, research and practice,* 1976, *13*(1), 2-16.

Sullivan, H.S. The meaning of anxiety in psychiatry and life. *Psychiatry*. 1948, *11* (1).

Truax, C.B. & Carkhuff, R.R. *Toward effective counseling and psychotherapy*. Chicago: Aldine, 1967.

What is this chapter all about?

The primary concern of this chapter is with the acquisition by the helpee of a real degree of *personalized understanding* and with the *interpretive skills* that the helper must use to promote such understanding.

Where does this fit in the overall helping model?

The first two phases of helpee activity in the prehelping/helping process are involvement and exploration. *Understanding* represents the third major phase of helpee activity. Helpees who have explored where they are must understand where they want or need to be before they can act to get there.

PREHELPING | **HELPING**

ACTION

UNDERSTANDING
Understands personalized goal
Understands personalized feelings
Understands personalized problem
Understands personalized meaning

EXPLORATION

INVOLVEMENT

Why is helpee understanding important?

Like the rest of us, helpees often view their problems initially as the result of outside forces or agencies: the "me versus them" perspective. By working for and achieving a real degree of personalized understanding, the helpees can put themselves back into the picture. Instead of blaming everything on some external force, they can understand how they themselves have a role in the overall situation — and, more specifically, how their own actions and limitations have contributed to their problems in the past. Once helpees have achieved such understanding, they can set personalized goals for themselves — the necessary prelude to taking action to reach these goals.

Who must do what in achieving helpee understanding?

During the primary phases of helpee involvement and helpee exploration, the helper has been both attentive and responsive. Now, however, the helper must go beyond this and *be interpretive* with the helpee in a directionful manner. In particular, the helper must, after laying an adequate base, interpret by *personalizing the meaning, the deficit or problem, the new feelings, and the goal,* which are implicit in the helpee's own statements. As in chapter three, the personalizing or interpretive skills outlined for the helper here involve certain simple formats. The format "You feel _____ because you _____" personalizes the meaning; "You feel _____ because you can't _____" personalizes the problem; "You feel _____ (new feeling term) because you can't _____" personalizes the helpee's new feelings; and "You feel _____ because you can't _____ and you want _____" personalizes the goal. If necessary and appropriate, the helper may also employ the interpretive skills that involve *responding with immediacy* and *confrontation* — although this last technique should be employed only by a skilled helper who has determined that no other approach will yield constructive results in terms of helpee understanding.

When should the helper begin to personalize with the helpee?

The helpee signals the culmination of his or her exploring by continuing to present material related to immediate feelings and the reasons for these feelings without any additional prompting from the helper. In other words, the helpee's exploration at last becomes self-sustaining. This is the point at which the helper should begin to be interpretive with the helpee — at first, by endeavoring to personalize the meaning implicit in the helpee's statements. At no time should a helper attempt to personalize on a new level with a helpee until that helpee has signalled, verbally and nonverbally, her or his recognition of the last level of personalized understanding.

132

How can you practice your personalizing skills?

Although you might be able to try out your personalizing skills during ordinary conversations with friends or family members, you will run less risk of making harmful mis-
takes if you confine your practice to a more formal setting.
Arrange with someone else to do some role-playing. The
other person should decide on a situation of real (but not
major) import. He or she should then act as helpee while you
practice all of the skills you have acquired up to this point —
the skills any helper needs to get helpees to become involved, to promote their self-exploration, and to translate the
terms of this exploration into those of a more personalized
understanding. If possible, you can arrange to have a third
party act as uninvolved observer. When you have finished
your interaction, you can get feedback on your skills from
both the observer and the "helpee" with whom you have
been working.

helping people define goals and select courses of action: INITIATING SKILLS I

5

Overview

1. The first two steps in the helpee's efforts to take constructive *action* require that the helpee *define the goal* and *choose the optimum course of action* leading to that goal.

2. The effective helper promotes the helpee's completion of these initial action-steps by using specific *goal-development* and *problem-solving skills.*

3. The helpee begins this phase of activity by defining her or his personalized goal in terms that are *meaningful, measurable,* and *realistic.*

4. At this state the helper uses a *combination of responsive and initiative skills,* the latter involving questions of the *5WH* type.

5. Next the helpee *explores all those alternative courses of action* that might lead to attainment of his or her particular goal.

6. The helper promotes exploration through *continued responsiveness* and also *focuses the helpee's attention on relevant and constructive alternatives* until all such alternatives have been listed.

7. The helpee then *develops all those personal values* that might be affected in any way by one or more of the alternative courses of action already listed.

8. The helper promotes the helpee's full development of values by *outlining a favorability scale* and *assigning a specific numerical weight to each value.*

9. Finally, the helpee combines alternatives and personal values in order to *make a decision* as to which alternative is the *best possible course of action.*

10. The helper assists at this level by *outlining a single decision-making matrix* that makes it possible for the helpee to choose a course of action in a systematic and effective manner.

11. In summary, the basic activities of the helpee at this

stage involve *operationalizing the goal* and *making decisions* in a clear and systematic fashion.

12. In summary, the helper uses *goal-development* skills to enable the helpee to operationalize or define the goal and *problem-solving* skills to enable the helpee to make decisions.

The aim of all helping is to promote real, fundamental, and constructive change in a given client's or helpee's pattern of behavior. Individuals usually become involved in a helping situation because they are encountering some sort of difficulty they cannot resolve on their own. This difficulty may be mild or severe, immediate or remote. The individuals may come to the helping or counseling situation voluntarily or at the request of some other agency or person; the helper's attending skills promote and sustain helpee involvement. None of this alters the basic dynamics of effective helping. Each individual must always begin by *exploring* the external ramifications of her or his situation: "What's going on? What does it mean to me? Whose actions are affecting me? How do I feel about things? Why do I feel this way?" Exploration, promoted by the helper's responding skills, allows the helpee to find out where he or she is at the present moment. The helpee must then go on to *understand* the implications of where he or she is in terms of where she or he needs or wants to be. In this context, understanding means grasping the personal and internal ramifications of the situation: "What am I doing or failing to do that contributes to the problem? How do I feel about my own shortcomings? What is it that I really want to do?" The helper uses personalizing skills to promote helpee understanding.

As we have seen, the final phase of helpee understanding leads to the formulation of a general personalized goal. Given the helper's guidance in taking the helpee through the cumulative phases of exploration and understanding, this goal will always entail a resolution of the helpee's personalized problem. "You feel ashamed because you can't get passing grades and you really want to succeed in school . . ." But to point to a general goal and to attain a specific goal are two totally different things. To achieve any goal, a helpee must *act*. And to ensure that the goal to be achieved is both functional and real, the helpee must begin his or her sequence of activity by defining this goal. As the following account shows quite clearly, this is a step that all too many people overlook entirely.

Competition is fierce for teaching jobs today — especially in humanities areas like English. While this situation makes it tough for many recent college graduates looking for teaching positions, there is at least one major benefit for the schools: They can be reasonably assured of getting the pick of the crop, the best of all those applicants who apply.

Ernie Varoz was indeed one of the best — and Hilltown High School grabbed him to fill a last-minute vacancy in the English department.

The grandson of Mexican immigrants who had waded the Rio Grande one long-ago night, drawn by the promise of Yankee dollars (which turned out to be more elusive than the mythical desert snipe), Ernie had come up the hard way. Forbidden to converse in his own Spanish with friends at school, he had determined to beat his new countrymen at their own game. So he learned English. He read everything he could lay his hands on. He absorbed the new language like a cactus drawing up water. For Ernie saw, sooner than most of his friends, that English was quickly becoming the common tongue of a dozen disaffected minorities in the U.S. Black people were bending and shaping the language into a vehicle capable of expressing their own unique experiences and needs. Chicanos were using English to express themselves to a wider group than that represented by the Spanish-speaking community. Native Americans, young Asians, and many others were quickly turning English into an exciting and flexible lingua franca capable of communicating and, at the same time, transcending ethnic individuality.

Ernie worked, in school and out of it. At one point while attending the local branch of the State University, he held no fewer than three part-time jobs. Nor did he stop working when the time neared for him to graduate. Months prior to graduation, while most of his classmates were whiling away leisure hours with beer, dope, dates, and endless bull-sessions about the condition of the world, Ernie was already contacting prospective employers. By February of his senior year, carrying a 3.6 academic average and a raft of recommendations, Ernie was ready to sign a contract to teach English at a local high school.

He stayed there for two years until something told him it was time to explore the world beyond the southwest corner of the United States. By now his job-hunting skills had been honed and his file of recommendations was even stronger. The application he submitted to faraway Hilltown High was only one of over 100 similar applications. But Hilltown's offer sounded the best. And Ernie, packing his few things in two battered suitcases, took a last lingering look at the arc of impossibly blue sky, the ragged line of buttes that marched along the horizon, and headed east.

From the outset, Hilltown High confronted Ernie with a whole new set of educational problems. The overwhelming majority of students at his first school had been highly motivated. Like Ernie before them, they had begun to see education as a means of taking control of their own lives. They had struggled to succeed. They had worked hard. But Ernie's new students already felt they were in control. Most of them the sons and daughters of established business people, merchants, professionals, they seemed to believe that the world would provide whatever they really needed when the time came. Until then, they were content to follow the path of least resistance. In Ernie's English classes, this meant that although a few worked hard and did well and a few refused to work at all and courted outright failure, the vast majority simply went along doing as little as possible for a passing grade.

Their writing was shot through with careless errors. Many had trouble spelling any word more complicated than "I." They read little and seemed to understand less. In short, they were a frustrating and depressing group with which to work.

After a month in his new post, Ernie cornered the English department chairperson and tried to outline his concern. The chairperson, an overworked woman who seemed to sit on every faculty committee at the school, listened sympathetically.

"You're right, of course," she agreed when Ernie had finished. "Our entire school is a haven for the underachiever. Believe me, I've been struggling with the same problem for years." Here she paused and smiled at Ernie. "You know, one reason we asked you to come work with us at Hilltown was this very problem. If anyone can begin to reach these disaffected children, it will have to be a person with all the energy, youth, and enthusiasm in the world. We're hoping you'll be just such a person."

Ernie smiled back uncertainly. This was all quite flattering, of course, but a bit disconcerting. He had come to the chairperson for advice and leadership — not to be told in so many words that the problem was one that only he could solve.

Things gradually got worse instead of better. Fighting a rearguard action against educational erosion, Ernie set a number of baseline requirements in his courses. The only result was a substantial increase in the number of failures at the next marking period. The students' concern seemed to decrease in direct proportion to Ernie's mounting frustration. Finally one afternoon, following up a tip from a fellow teacher, Ernie stopped by after school at the office of the school's counselor, Brenda Vacarro. He had met Brenda at the start of the academic year and had been impressed with her directness and apparent honesty. Now he hoped that she might be able to lead him out of the academic swamp in which he seemed to be mired.

"Do you have a few minutes?" he inquired, finding Brenda at her desk.

"Of course." Brenda smiled. "Mr. — Varoz, isn't it?"

"Just Ernie's good enough," Ernie said. He slumped down in a seat dejectedly. Brenda sat forward in her chair and regarded him.

"You look pretty down, Ernie," she commented, responding to the clear evidence of his posture, his expression, his tone of voice. And Ernie, without quite knowing why, began to relax. At the very least, Brenda seemed like someone he could talk to.

So Ernie talked — about his experiences at his first school; about the enthusiasm he felt when teaching highly motivated students; about the problems he was encountering with his own students at Hilltown High; about his own gathering depression and the reasons for it. And Brenda attended to him. She observed him. She listened to him. And she responded to him in terms of his own frame of reference.

"So you feel really frustrated, even angry at times, because most of your students just don't care about developing skills in your courses." Brenda's responses at this level captured and reflected Ernie's own feelings about the immediate, external situation.

"Yeah," he found himself answering. "Uh huh, that's just how it is — I really get angry with them almost every day."

Gradually, Brenda began to respond in increasingly personalized ways. She helped Ernie to personalize the manner in which his own limitations, his own deficits, were contributing to the situation: "You feel frustrated because you can't figure a way to get these kids motivated and working." She helped him to identify and understand the new feelings that arose as a result of internalizing the problem: "You feel angry with yourself because you can't find a way to get through to them." Finally, she helped him to develop a personalized goal: "You feel angry with yourself because you can't get across to them and you really want to get them working at their optimum level."

"Exactly!" Ernie agreed. "I can see that. The problem is at least as much mine as it is theirs. I mean, these kids have been encouraged to hang out and do as little as possible. Now it's up to me to turn them around, at least in terms of my own classes. But how can I do that?"

Alas, Brenda's interpersonal-skills repertoire did not extend that far. She could attend to people. She could respond to them. She could help them to grapple with a personalized understanding of feelings, problems, goals. But she had still not developed the skills she needed to help people move toward their goals. Thus she had to fall back on our now-familiar "common sense" approach.

"Well, look," she said. "You know where you are — frustrated about your own limitations. And you know where you want to get to — the point where your kids are really working. Now it seems to me that there are a number of ways in which you could try to achieve this sort of a goal. For example, you could take a hard-line approach and schedule a full period test for every class period you spend on specific material. That way, there wouldn't be any interval for the kids between learning and using."

Ernie nodded slowly. "Uh huh. Sure, there are several alternatives. I could go to the opposite extreme and really lower my standards to the point where I know I'm getting each kid to learn at least one solid thing, however trivial, every day. Like spending a whole day on spelling "ie" and "ei" words." He looked at Brenda. "OK, so I map out a bunch of alternative approaches. But how do I know which one is best?"

"Well, I think you're going to have to make that decision on the basis of your own personal values. I mean, what do you feel is the most important thing for your kids to have?"

Ernie didn't even have to think about this. His memory flashed back to the classes and students he had taught at his first school. "Enthusiasm," he told Brenda. "If the approach I take gets supported enthusiastically by the kids, I'm almost there! What's killing me now is this 'blah, ho-hum' attitude about everything we do."

Brenda smiled and leaned back. "There you are, then," she said. "Choose the approach that you feel will generate the most enthusiasm from your students and you should be headed toward your goal."

Grinning, Ernie thanked Brenda and left to do some planning. What she had said made sense. Pick the teaching method designed to generate maximum enthusiasm. This was not really a new thought for Ernie. But Brenda's responsiveness and helpful concern had helped him to focus his own thoughts. Enthusiasm — surely that was the top priority!

Ernie was right — Brenda's advice did make sense. And yet, as the next few weeks were to demonstrate, enthusiasm was by no means equal to excellence in performance — or even to learning.

The alternative Ernie chose involved setting up a wide range of individualized projects with his students. Given student enthusiasm as a top priority, Ernie decided to let each kid choose and develop an extended project related in some way to his course content. Sure enough, this new-found freedom prompted a great deal of enthusiams from the previously jaded students. "That Mr. Varoz, he's really all right," the kids told one another. "Yeah, he's a good guy — no hassles like we get from the rest of the fascists around here!"

No hassles. And also, Ernie discovered, no real improvement. Some students wrote enthusiastic but almost illegible papers on favorite poets or songwriters. Some students developed enthusiastic but incompetent research projects that omitted data that, though perhaps relevant, was of little personal interest. Some students initiated and staged enthusiastic debates that consistently failed to reach any conclusion or teach anything about the uses of logical argument. Some students enthusiastically embarked upon creative writing projects that ended up on Ernie's desk as a welter of scribbled verse or prose with little or no relevance for anyone beside the original writers.

And Ernie, surveying the ranks of enthusiastic and unhassled students who now grinned at him from every seat, could only grin back hollowly, all the while wondering, "Where did I go wrong? Where oh where oh where . . ."

Once again we are faced with a situation in which a helper, possessed of functional and concrete skills up to a point, still does not deliver the quantity and quality of real help needed. As noted earlier, exploration and understanding are necessary but by no means sufficient conditions of effective helping. By themselves, they cannot promote these constructive changes in helpee behavior that are the only real proof that help has actually been given and received.

Brenda Vacarro, like some of our earlier helpers, fell back on a "common sense" approach to helping. Yes, her responsiveness enabled Ernie to continue his exploration of the whole situation. And yes, her interpretive skills enabled him to arrive at a more personalized understanding of his feelings, his problem, and his goal. Yet without a program of action, Ernie's past exploration and understanding were as useless as cans of fine food would be to a starving man who did not have a can opener!

Brenda's common sense was sufficient to show that Ernie must develop alternative ways of reaching his goal. This development of alternative approaches is indeed one element in the process of developing and implementing a program of action — as we shall see later in this chapter. But before any helpee can choose a course of action, a specific approach to a goal, *he or she must define that goal in concrete terms!* How else will the helpee know exactly what he or she is striving toward? Yet Brenda did not possess the skills needed to help Ernie define the goal she had personalized for him.

By the same token, Brenda encouraged Ernie to decide on a course of action based on "what was most important" yet failed to help him explore and prioritize the many values that he and all of us have. Making an important decision based on only the single helpee value that is most immediate, obvious, and accessible is perhaps the most common mistake helpees make. Ernie made his decision based on "enthusiasm" as his highest priority — and thereby completely overlooked such values as student outcome, his own time, and so on.

Up to this point we have treated a major phase of helpee activity in each chapter. Thus chapter two focused on helpee *involvement,* chapter three on helpee *exploration,* and chapter four on helpee *understanding.* The last of our four major phases of helpee activity, of course, is helpee *action.* Due to the complexity of those skills required by the helper to promote and assure the success of such action, we will modify our format somewhat and focus in this chapter on only the first two steps the helpee must complete in developing and implementing a program of action. These two steps are, of course, *defining the goal* and *choosing a course of action*. Figure 5-1 shows us what happens when a helper like Brenda Vacarro lacks the skills to promote a helpee's completion of these important steps.

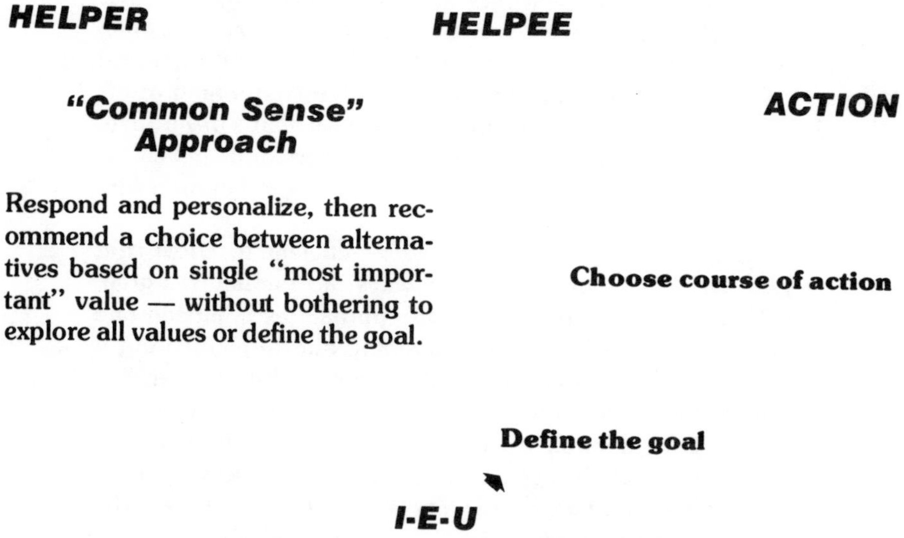

HELPER   **HELPEE**

"Common Sense"   **ACTION**
Approach

Respond and personalize, then recommend a choice between alterna-
tives based on single "most impor-   **Choose course of action**
tant" value — without bothering to
explore all values or define the goal.

Define the goal

I-E-U

Figure 5-1. Impact of Brenda's "common sense" approach on Ernie's attempt to complete first two action-steps.

In the pages that follow we will focus on the specific helpee activities required for completion of the first two action-steps: *defining the goal, developing alternatives, developing values, and making the decision about which course of action is best.* In promoting these helpee activities, the helper must make use of *goal-development* and *problem-solving* skills. (In rare instances, a helper may not need to use problem-solving skills because there is clearly only one possible course of action open to a helpee. We should remember, however, that there are almost always a number of different ways to reach any goal. The existence of even two possible courses of action open to a helpee is sufficient to require the helper's application of problem-solving techniques.)

Defining
the
Goal

Helpee Goal:

To have a precise and constructive objective.

In the majority of cases, helpees initially state their personalized goals in terms that are general and even vague. "I feel miserable because I can't seem to study effectively and *I really want to do well in school.*" Or in the case of Ernie — "I feel pretty angry with myself because I can't seem to reach my students and *I really want to get to them and help them master English.*" Such statements of goals, though both valid and valuable, cannot provide helpees with the focus they need to work toward something concrete and meaningful. Equally important, such statements provide helpees with no way of knowing if or when they have actually reached their goals. What does "doing well in school" really mean? Does it mean just good grades? Strong recommendations from teachers? Admission to a good college or graduate school? All of these? Something different? And how can a teacher know when his or her students are really being "reached"? When they do better on tests? When the quality of their writing improves? When they hang around after class to talk with one another and with the teacher?

The first thing any helpee must do in beginning a program of action is to *define the goal in terms that are meaningful, measurable, and realistic.* In this context, *meaningful* means fully relevant to the original problem. Thus a helpee having trouble in, for example, a Russian language course in college should not treat her reading of Tolstoy's epic *War and Peace* in translation as meaningful proof that she is acquiring new skills in Russian. Yet the same reading might be quite meaningful to the helpee whose personalized goal involves acquiring a broader understanding of world literature.

Helpee definitions of goals must also be stated in *measurable* terms. A married couple encountering difficulties might personalize their common goal as "to get on better with each other." Such a goal becomes far more tangible and constructive when stated in terms that involve "at least eight hours a week of shared activities with no major arguments." And this latter definition of a common goal is improved even more when the phrase "no major arguments" is understood to mean no exchange of personal criticism or insults. Given such a definition of goal, the couple has something quite tangible to work toward — and will be able to tell when they reach it.

Finally, a helpee's definition of the goal must be stated in *realistic* terms. This means, in essense, that the goal must be one the helpee can realistically expect to achieve once he or she has developed and implemented an effective program of action. For example, one young helpee might have stated his personalized goal in the following terms: "I really want to earn the respect of my parents and friends." It would not be realistic for this helpee to define the goal as "earning the respect of parents and friends as measured by their asking for my opinion before they made any decision." No one can reasonably expect to be consulted by others prior to every decision. Assuming that the helpee's original problem involved his inability to get parents and friends to share their thoughts on important matters with him, a far more realistic goal might be defined as "earning the respect of parents and friends as measured by having at least one 20-minute conversation with each individual each week on a topic of importance to him or her."

Helper Skills:

Initiating with the helpee so that he or she can define the personalized goal in terms that are meaningful, measurable, and realistic.

To facilitate the helpee's definition of her or his goal, the helper must employ a combination of responsive and initiative skills. The responsive skills required here are those already treated in the chapters preceding this one. By continuing to position, observe, and listen, the helper can make sure that the helpee is maintaining focus on the personalized problem — the deficit — and the personalized goal already formulated. Should the helpee lose sight of these critical elements, the helper's skills in responding to meaning, feelings, and problems will get the helpee back on track.

But the helper must do more than respond. He or she must also initiate in order to promote the helpee's definition of the goal in meaningful, measurable, and replicable terms. One of the simplest and yet most effective ways to accomplish this is to ask questions — usually variations on what has been termed the "5WH" format: Who, What, Where, When, Why and How. For example, one helpee might have arrived at the following understanding of a personalized goal: "I feel stupid because I can't figure out how to show people I'm a capable person and *I really want to prove myself to others.*" The helper might ask some or all of the questions below in order to facilitate the helpee's definition of the goal in effective terms.

"Who do you really want to prove youself to?" (Wife, husband, children, parents, teachers, employer?)

"What area of capability do you really want to demonstrate?" (Study skills, home maintenance, budgeting, work skills?)

"Where can you best demonstrate your capability?" (Home, school, work some other place?)

"When do you need to do this by?" (Next week, next month, a year from now?)

"Why do you want to prove yourself?" (To feel better? To earn someone else's respect? To gain some material reward?)

"How can you best demonstrate your capability?" (By getting good grades, saving money, making more sales, having fewer absences?)

Questions of this sort enable the helpee to focus on the specific ingredients of her or his goal. Once the helper feels that the helpee has focused on the critical ingredients, he or she can initiate with the helpee by suggesting one version of an effectively defined goal employing the simple format, "So your goal is _____ as measured by _____." Thus for the helpee above, the goal might be defined in the following way: "Your goal is to prove your capability to your boss as measured by your ability to double your number of actual sales within the next three months." While measurability is the only one of our three criteria that is explicit in the above format, the other two criteria — meaningfulness and achievability — are clearly implied. For this helpee, doubling the number of sales is clearly relevant to his personalized goal; and since his current level of sales is so low, doubling it is a realistic goal.

Defining the goal allows both helper and helpee to move beyond the stage of personalized, yet often general, concerns. But a definition of the goal only specifies the helpee's destination; it does not specify how he or she can reach that destination. The helper and helpee must therefore go on to the next step and *choose the course of action that is best suited to the helpee.* In order to choose the best method to achieve the helpee's goal, the helper must assist the helpee by using the skills of problem solving. The key to effective problem solving involves the helper's initiation of the three major problem-solving steps. First, the helper explores with the helpee all possible alternative ways of achieving his or her goal. Next, the helper assists the helpee in identifying those helpee values that might be affected by the selection of any one of the alternative courses of action. Lastly, the helper aids the helpee in using the previously identified values to make a decision about which course of action will be most satisfying to the helpee's values.

Exploring Alternatives

Helpee Goal:

To explore a number of ways to reach the goal.

During the first major phase of the actual helping process, the helpee or client explores the external elements of her or his situation; as we saw, this exploration is an expansive process. Now, in developing alternative ways to reach the goal, the helpee once again uses exploration as an expanding "tool" in order to consider as many possibilities as he or she can. In a sense, what the helpee does here is take the "How" element in the definition of the goal and open it up in order to see how many small "hows" may be involved.

Since exploration of this sort is, as noted, an expanding rather than a narrowing process, the helpee need not be concerned with questions of practicability, relevancy, simplicity, or the like — at least not at this moment. He or she should simply try to come up with a number of different ways in which the goal might be reached — no matter how "far out" some of these may seem.

By way of example, one helpee might have defined her goal as follows: "I want to gain my independence from my parents by making enough money in the next three months to get my own apartment." Such a definition is meaningful (getting own apartment equals independence); it is measurable (enough money for rent within a predetermined period of time); and it involves realistic activities (it is achievable — a reasonable amount of money). Now the helpee explores some possible ways of reaching this goal.

"I could get the money by borrowing it."

"I could get the money by robbing a bank."

"I could get the money by finding a job."

"I could get the money by creating some product or service and selling it."

Quite obviously, not all of these four possibilities or alternatives are equally constructive. Yet had she not been given a relatively free rein, this helpee might have come up with only one possibility: the traditional "get a job." As it is, she let her imagination run loose and was thus able to develop another real possibility: a product or service she might create and sell.

Helper Skills:

Initiating with the helpee to ensure that she or he does not overlook any viable approach to the goal.

The helper can facilitate the helpee's exploration of alternative courses of action by continuing to attend and respond and, when appropriate, by making concrete suggestions. Ideally, of course, the helpee will be able to come up with any number of possible approaches to the goal. Yet this is frequently not the case. It is the helper's primary aim here to keep the momentum of helpee exploration going. Thus if the helpee comes up with only one or two possibilities and then seems stalled — shaking his head, shrugging her shoulders, or the like — the helper can respond to this new feeling: perhaps, "You feel frustrated because there don't seem to be many ways to get where you want to go." If the helper sees other possible courses of action, he or she can then suggest one or more of them: "Another way to get there might be to _____."

By making concrete suggestions, the helper does more than maintain the momentum of helpee exploration. He or she is also showing a continuation of real involvement and concern —the opposite of the "now it's up to you" approach. Each suggestion, in turn, may also serve to promote renewed helpee exploration and understanding.

As noted, the helpee should be encouraged to explore all possible approaches to the goal. The helper should impose no initial check on this helpee "brainstorming." However, the helper should keep in mind that any course of action must be *workable* to be considered a viable alternative. Thus when the time comes for the helpee and helper to work together on a list of alternative courses of action, the helper can recommend eliminating any that are vague ("working harder," "doing better," etc.) as well as any that are either irrelevant to the goal or simply not doable. Needless to say, all helper critiques of this sort must be accompanied by an explanation that meets the helpee's needs. Should a helpee continue to wonder why a particular course of action is not workable, the helper must respond to this uncertainty, re-cycling the processes of helpee exploration and understand-ing until the confusion is cleared up.

In essense, then, the helper initiates with the helpee at this level by making concrete suggestions and, later, by helping to focus mutual concern on those alternative courses of action that are workable and that would realistically lead to the helpee's goal. The final list of alternatives should not omit any viable possibility — and should not include any possibility that is not viable.

Developing Values

Helpee Goal:

To understand how personal values may be affected by alternative courses of action.

At this stage, the helpee has defined the goal and has explored and isolated a number of alternative ways of reach-ing this goal. Before attempting to choose between these alternatives, however, the helpee must come to terms with the ways in which her or his personal values may be affected by such a choice. Thus the phrase "developing values" does not mean that the helpee creates new values but, rather, that he or she must achieve a concrete understanding of relevant existing values. The process involved has four main phases: *exploring existing values; defining those related to any of the alternative courses of action; developing a "favorability scale" for each value;* and *weighting all values numerically.* The end result is that the helpee, far from making a decision based on vague notions, is able to choose that alternative course of action best suited to her or his clearly understood personal values.

Expansion and exploration of personal values really in-volves the helpee's asking and answering the question, "What things are important to me?" All of us have a wide range of personal values in any number of different areas: our family lives, our career activities, our hopes for the future, and so on. As the helpee begins to explore these personal values, he or she should simply try to note as many value "headings" as possible; "family," "friends," "financial security," "comfort," and "independence" are only a few possible examples. We may see this process more clearly by considering one helpee whose problem and goal is expressed in the following statement: "I really feel weak because I can't give my kids six weeks at an overnight camp this summer and I really want to do that for them." This helpee has listed a number of alternative ways of reaching his goal. He could borrow the necessary money. He could seek a new and better-paying job. Or he could look for a parttime job for a temporary period that would earn the required amount of money for his children's summer camp. Here is how he has layed out the three alternatives:

Alternative A: Borrow money

Alternative B: New job

Alternative C: Parttime job

Now the helpee explores his personal values. Many of these values are not relevant to any of his alternative courses of action (his love of sports, for example). Other values that he explores, however, are clearly relevant. One such value is *finances*. This helpee is a person who hates the whole idea of being in debt. Where another person might accept the idea of going into debt with a grin and a shrug, this helpee places a high value on remaining debt-free. This obviously has implications in terms of his "borrowing money" alternative.

After exploring a number of other personal values, the helpee lists two additional values that are both important and relevant: *family* and *friendship*. The helpee values the time he can spend with his family very highly. He also values the friendships he has formed over the years with co-workers at his present place of employment. Again, these values have clear implications for his alternative courses of action.

In the end, then, the helpee explores many values and lists all those that seem to be relevant to the alternative ways in which the goal can be reached. Our sample helpee lists his values in the order in which he explored them:

Value A: Finances

Value B: Family

Value C: Friendship

Once a helpee has expanded and explored her or his personal values and listed all those relevant to the present situation, the helpee must go on to define each of the listed values. All too often we are aware of vague values that influence our actions yet never really try to understand what these values are all about. What is "independence," for example? For one person it may come down to self-employment while for another it may mean living alone.

To define her or his values, the helpee must be able to describe them in objective and measurable terms. We have already noted that, for our sample helpee, "finances" can be measured by the number of dollars in debt he is. "Family" means the number of hours each week that he is able to spend with his wife and two children. And "friendship" means the number of hours he can spend with his present co-workers each week. Thus this helpee can complete the next phase of value-development by defining his values in objective, measurable terms.

Value	**Definition**
Finances	Number of dollars in debt
Family	Hours each week spent with family
Friendship	Hours each week spent with present co-workers

A helpee's definition of personal values lays the groundwork for her or his development of an individualized "favorability scale." Such a scale is simply a systematic design for determining in advance the sorts of things that will have a positive or negative effect upon any given value. Let us say one helpee considers "income" to be of great personal value. A job paying $15,000 a year, then, will be far more favorable than a second job that, while equal in every other way, pays only $12,500 a year. Not all values are as easy to deal with as "income," of course — yet once defined in objective terms, all values do lend themselves to a simple rating in terms of favorability. The scale helpees can use most easily is the one shown below:

++   Most favorable

+   Favorable

+/−   Acceptable

−   Unfavorable

−−   Most unfavorable

Thus our sample helpee might explore his three relevant values and decide what things would be most favorable, favorable, acceptable, unfavorable or most unfavorable in relation to each — again, sticking to terms that are concrete and measurable. The results of his use of the favorability scale might look like this:

Value	Definition	Scale	
Finances	Number of dollars in debt	++	$0
		+	$100 - 500
		+/−	$500 - 1,000
		−	$1,000 - 1,500
		− −	over $1,500
Family	Hours together each week	++	21-28 waking hours
		+	14-20 waking hours
		+/−	10-13 waking hours
		−	7- 9 waking hours
		− −	0- 6 waking hours
Friends	Hours together each week (counting work)	++	Over 34 hours
		+	Over 26 hours
		+/−	Over 20 hours
		−	Between 15 and 20 hours
		− −	Fewer than 15 hours

Once a helpee has explored and defined all relevant values and has developed a favorability scale for each of these values, he or she is ready to assign a numerical weight to each value. Up to this point, the helpee may have been treating all the values as if they were of more-or-less equal importance. This is rarely the case, however. Some of our personal values are clearly of far greater importance to us than others. Nor will a simple rank-ordering serve our purposes; for one value that we place ahead of another may be many times more important than that other value. Thus the helpee may choose to begin with a simple rank-ordering —

Value 1: Most important

Value 2: Important

Value 3: Least important

— but should go on to assign a numerical weight to each of these values in order to achieve at least a rough understanding of their absolute as opposed to their merely relative importance. Our helpee who wishes to send his children to camp, for example, uses a 1-to-10 scale where 1 refers to his

151

least important value relevant to his present problem and 10 to the most important relevant value. He then begins by rank-ordering his three values—

> *Value* 1: Family (most important)
>
> *Value* 2: Friendship (important)
>
> *Value* 3: Finances (least important)

— and then goes on to assign his specific numerical weights. His "family" value rates a 10 on the 1-to-10 scale while his "finances" value gets a 1. His "friendship" value is slightly less important than "family" but considerably more important than "finances." Thus he decides to assign his "friendship" value on a 7 on the 1-to-10 scale.

> *Value* 1: Family (10)
>
> *Value* 2: Friendship (7)
>
> *Value* 3: Finances (1)

Once a helpee has explored and defined her or his values, applied the favorability scale, and assigned each value a specific numerical weight, the helpee is ready to choose that alternative course of action that is demonstrably most appropriate.

Helper Skills:

Initiating with the helpee by assisting him or her to identify, define, and prioritize personal values relevant to any viable approach to the goal.

Just as the helper promoted the helpee's exploration and expansion of alternative courses of action, so he or she aids in developing the helpee's personal values. The effective helper knows only too well that a decision that disregards helpee values — or one that, like Ernie Varoz's, takes only a single value into consideration — will rarely if ever succeed in getting the helpee to the goal.

During the helpee's period of value development, the helper can draw upon all the understanding gained through previous and present use of basic attending and responding skills. By now, the helper should have a good idea about what the helpee's real personal values are: the things he or she hates, loves, fears, worries about, hopes for, and so on. Indeed, many helpees' initial problems may reveal themselves as the results of conflict between personal values. Thus the helper who has worked effectively up to this point is usually in a good position to promote helpee exploration of values. In addition to continued use of attending and responding skills, the helper can ask questions of the 5WH type:

"*What* other things are really important to you?"

"*Who* are the people that really count in your life?"

"*Where* do you want to be spending your time?"

"*When* do you want to do these things by?"

"*Why* does this alternative look good to you?"

"*How* do you feel about this value?"

Once the helpee has explored and isolated relevant values, the helper can suggest ways in which each of these values might be defined. The helpee must understand that defining values is simply one way of anticipating the relationship between these values and personal action. A value that is vague and ill-defined is a value that may cause problems — or, alternatively, be overlooked — in a helpee's personal life. A clearly defined value, on the other hand, is one that can be lived fully and freely.

The key ingredients of value definition of which the helper must be aware are *amount* and *time*. The question here is, "What does this value mean to the helpee in terms of the number of things done in a particular time period?" Thus the helper working with our sample helpee promoted the man's translation of his "family" value into the number of hours each week spent with his family. Such a definition provides a basis for using the favorability scale to determine what things will be favorable and unfavorable in terms of a given value.

The helper will almost certainly have to lead the helpee through the favorability scale. He or she can use a simple Tell/Show/Do format: *telling* the helpee about the scale, *showing* him or her a sample scale (like the one presented earlier), and then aiding the helpee as he or she *does* a personal scale. Simple questions are often a good way to promote development of a personal favorability scale: "You say that the value of your family life for you lies in the number of hours each week you spend with your family. About how many hours do you feel would be really great, really the best? What amount of time would make you feel worst? What would be just an OK amount of time each week — not great but not terrible either?" The helper can then assign a "most favorable" (+ +) rating to the helpee's optimum amount of time, a "most unfavorable" $(--)$ rating to the minimum amount of time, an "acceptable" $(+-)$ to the "just OK" amount of time, and can go on to explore the "favorable" $(+)$ and "unfavorable" $(-)$ time frames with the helpee.

Having facilitated the helpee's use of the favorability scale, the helper must go on to work out a system of weighting helpee values numerically. As indicated, a good first step may be to rank-order all values in terms of their relative importance. The helper can then say something along the lines of "OK, you say 'family' is your most important value. We'll give it a ten. And 'finances' is least important to you — although it's certainly still significant — so we'll give it a one. Now, what about 'friendship'? Is it close to 'family' in importance? Closer to 'finances'? How would you rate it on your one-to-ten scale?"

By the end of the value-development phase, both helper and helpee should have a clear understanding of exactly what values are important to the helpee — and how important each is in relative terms. Now the stage is set for the helpee's choice between alternative courses of action.

Making
the
Decision

Helpee Goal:

To select the course of action most consistent with her or his personal values.

All of the alternatives previously outlined by the helpee have been shown to lead to achievement of the helpee's goal. The choice the helpee now makes will be that course of action that fits most effectively with the personal values developed.

The process here is a simple mechanical one involving the construction of a matrix. The helpee begins by outlining her or his alternatives in vertical rows. We will use the case of our sample helpee by way of illustration.

Alternatives

Borrow Money	Change Jobs	Get Part-time Job

The helpee then adds all relevant personal values along with the numerical weights assigned to each.

Values &　　　　　　　　　　**Alternatives**
Weights

	Borrow Money	Change Jobs	Get Part-time Job
Family (10)			
Friendship (7)			
Finances (1)			

Now the helpee can consider each point of intersection of a specific alternative with a specific value and, using the favorability scale, ask and answer the question, "Would this alternative have a most favorable, a favorable, an acceptable, an unfavorable, or a most unfavorable effect upon this value?"

The first cell in our sample helpee's matrix involves the interaction of borrowing money (the alternative) and spending time with family (the value). The helpee realizes that, though borrowing money would not increase his time with his family (which would be "most favorable"), this action would at least allow him to spend the same 12 hours a week with his family as he now spends. Since this is a "favorable" interaction, he can rate the interaction +.

Borrow Money

Family　　(10)　　| + |

Moving down the first column, the helpee considers the impact of borrowing money on his "friendship" value. Here again, the action would not enable him to spend more time with his friends from work but would allow him to maintain these same friendships as he has in the past; here again, he decides that the interaction is "favorable" and rates it +.

Borrow Money

Family   (10 | + |

Friends   (7) | + |

Finally, he reaches the last cell in this row and considers the impact upon his finances of borrowing money. As will be remembered, this helpee strongly dislikes indebtedness. Borrowing enough money for his children's camp would put him in debt for at least $2,000. Thus he decides to rate this interaction as "most unfavorable" or − −.

Borrow Money

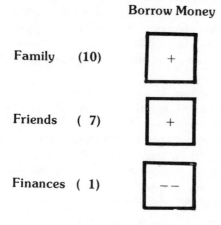

Family   (10) | + |

Friends   (7) | + |

Finances (1) | − − |

Our sample helpee can go on in this manner, judging the interaction of value and alternative in each cell and assigning it a rating anywhere from "most favorable" (+ +) to "most unfavorable" (− −) according to the precise definitions outlined in his favorability scale. Here is how this helpee's matrix looks when he has completed this step.

Values & Weights	Borrow Money	Change Jobs	Get Part-time Job
Family (10)	+	+ −	− −
Friends (7)	+	− −	+ −
Finances (1)	− −	+	+ +

Now the helpee can complete the matrix by using his or her numerical weights for personal values. The process involves multiplying the numerical weight by the favorability rating in each cell: here + + equals 2; + equals 1; + − equals 0; − equals −1; and − − equals −2. Thus a sample value weighted at 7, say, would be affected by the favorability scale as follows:

Weight of Value	Multiplied by	Favorability Rating		Equals
7	X	+ +	=	+14
7	X	+	=	+ 7
7	X	+ −	=	0
7	X	−	=	− 7
7	X	− −	=	−14

Below we can see how our sample helpee completed his matrix.

Values & Weights	Alternatives		
	Borrow Money	Change Jobs	Parttime Job
Family (10)	+10	0	−20
Friends (7)	+7	−14	0
Finances (1)	−2	+1	+2
Totals	+15	−13	−18

Once the helpee has integrated values and alternatives and has made use of the favorability scale and the previously assigned numerical weights for values, he or she need only see which alternative achieves the highest total of points. This will be the optimum course of action for reaching the goal without infringing on relevant personal values. In the case of our sample helpee, the optimum course indicated is "borrow money."

Helper Skills:

Initiating with the helpee by outlining a matrix that will allow the helpee to rate in numerical terms the interaction of alternatives and values and thus choose an optimum course of action.

Needless to say, few if any helpees will be able to construct a decision-making matrix without specific assistance from a skilled helper. Thus the helper must guide his or her helpee at every step and must make sure that no steps are left out. Once again, perhaps the best approach for the helper to take here involves a Tell/Show/Do format:

Tell the helpee what the matrix is;

Show the helpee by constructing a sample matrix; and

Have the helpee *do* what is necessary to create a matrix.

Remembering that the decision-making matrix is a way of reaching a purely human decision, the helper must be alert for ways in which different alternatives can be combined. The problem-solving skills we have outlined here are systematic, which is good; but they are also flexible, as they must be in order to deal with real human problems and situations. Thus the best solution is not always the one that receives the highest score *as it is presently defined;* instead, the best solution may ultimately be one that combines several different alternatives that have received high scores.

Again, we can see this process best by returning to our sample helpee. The alternative that received the highest score involved borrowing money. Yet even this alternative had a "most unfavorable" rating $(--)$ at the level of financial values; this value was impacted "most favorably," however, by the alternative involving a parttime job, since such a job might add even more to the family coffers than was needed for the kids' summer camp.

The helper considers this situation and suggests a way in which to consolidate the best features of both alternatives. "How about borrowing the money now on a short-term basis, waiting until your kids are away in camp, and then getting a parttime job while they are away to repay the loan? In this way, your indebtedness wouldn't last nearly so long and you would only be working extra hours while your children were away from home." They decide to chart this new possibility on the matrix and find that it is far more favorable in terms of the helpee's personal values than any of the other three alternatives.

Defining the goal; exploring alternative courses of action; developing personal values; choosing the preferred course of action — each of these involves specific helpee or client behaviors and equally specific helper skills. And each is a critical ingredient of the overall process with which this chapter has been concerned: helping people develop goals through problem solving. For the skills that the helper uses to move the helpee through the stages of goal development and problem solving are the same skills needed to resolve any problem. And for the helpee, pinning down the goal and figuring out exactly how to get there are nothing if not problems! Only when these problems are resolved can the helpee move on to the next action-phase: developing programs of activity to reach desired goals.

Before we move on, let us take another look to see how Bette has made out with her young helpee, Jimmy.

Bette and Jimmy

As will be remembered from the last chapter, Bette was able to help Jimmy Bessom come to an understanding of a personalized goal that focused on his own limitations rather than those of his father or his friends: "I really want to figure out a plan that will let me do what I want without messing things up with either my old man or my friends."

Bette's next job is to help Jimmy develop this goal. And the first phase of this goal development involves defining the goal in meaningful, measurable, and realistic terms.

"All right," Bette said. "You've got a general idea of what you want. But how will you know when you've got it? How will you be able to tell when you're 'not messing up' with the people you care about?"

"Well . . ." Jimmy thought about this for a minute. "I guess I'd know things were all right with the old man if I didn't have any more arguments with him. Man, I hate hassling like that!"

"Fine," Bette responded. "But what about your friends? How will you know if you're hanging on to them?"

"Oh, I'll know!" Jimmy said. "As long as we keep hanging around together, everything's OK."

"Yeah, but how much 'hanging around' time do you have in mind?" Bette asked. She really wanted Jimmy to pin things down in a concrete way.

"Oh —" Jimmy considered this. "I don't know — I guess if I spend a couple hours with them every day, that's probably good."

"All right," Bette said. "Let's call it three hours to be on the safe side." Now she could articulate a clearer definition of Jimmy's goal: "So you'll know you're reaching your goal of doing what you want if you can do it without having arguments with your father and at the same time keep seeing your friends at least three hours a day. Right?" Jimmy nodded vigorously: "Sure, that'd be just great. Too bad I'm not Houdini or something."

"You still feel pretty discouraged about the fix you're in," Bette said, responding to Jimmy's feelings. Then she moved on. "All right, then, the next thing we've got to do is figure out some different ways to reach your goal."

For the next 10 minutes she and Jimmy explored alternative ways of reaching his goal. In the end, they narrowed their list to three:

Alternative A: Stay in school and see friends at night.

Alternative B: Drop out and go to work fulltime, using new income to get a room away from home.

Alternative C: Switch some classes to nights and take parttime job with friends during the day.

Each of these alternatives had some apparent strong and weak points. True, Jimmy could see his friends at night; but he knew they wouldn't have the same close relationship because they wouldn't be sharing many of the same experiences. On the other hand, getting a room away from home would allow

Jimmy to avoid hassles with his father but only by keeping a safe distance between the two. Finally, switching to night classes for some of his courses would be a royal pain; by popular vote, most night classes were far too long and boring.

Jimmy was skeptical. "Yeah, I can see how each of these things would get me where I want to go — sort of. But I still can't tell which one to choose!"

"You should probably choose the one that best fits in with your personal values," Bette told him. And they turned their talk to consideration of these values. Predictably, Jimmy placed considerable and equal value on maintaining a good relationship with both his father and his friends.

"That's only to be expected," Bette told him. "After all, if your father were more important than your friends — or the other way around — you wouldn't be in this fix to begin with!"

Jimmy nodded. Damn! This woman really understood how his head worked, he thought. And not once had she tried to lay some private trip on him — like "You ought to do what your father wants" or some such stupid thing!

A third value that Jimmy expressed involved his career prospects for the future. "I really want to know that in — oh, say five years or so — I can get a good job. You know, one that's interesting and pays a decent salary at the same time." Both he and Bette were somewhat surprised to discover that after some exploration Jimmy himself gave this a slightly higher value than either his relationship with his father or that with his friends.

"OK," Bette said at last. "You've got three alternatives — stay in school, drop out, or get a parttime job. And you've got three values — your relationship with your father, your friends, and your future."

Once Jimmy had explored and isolated these personal values related to his alternative course of action, Bette helped him to define each in concrete and observable terms. Not surprisingly, those values of "relationship with father" and "friends" expressed in Jimmy's original goal could also be defined in terms reminiscent of that goal.

"I guess what's really important to me about my relationship with my old man is being able to be around him without having any fights," Jimmy said.

"Fine," Bette answered. "But you know what? That really means you have two separate values concerning your father. First, you want to spend time with him. And second, you want that time to be free of arguments about your school and work situation. We've already labeled the last one 'relationship with father.' How about calling the first 'time with father'?"

This made sense to Jimmy. Working with Bette, he managed to define each of the four personal values he now had. The first — "time with father" — they defined as "the amount of time spent each day with Jimmy's father." The second — "relationship with father" — they defined as "the number of arguments with Jimmy's father each day about Jimmy's school/work situation." The third value — "friends" — was defined as "the amount of time spent with friends each week." And the fourth — "the future" — they defined as "the amount of money Jimmy would be able to earn in five years."

Next Bette introduced Jimmy to the favorability scale — first telling him about it, then showing him a sample scale and finally helping him to do one for his own values. After some initial hesitation, Jimmy caught on and forged ahead. Here is how he applied the scale to his "time with father" value:

Value	Definition	Favorability Rating	
Time with father	Amount of time spent together each day	+ +	More than 3 hours per day
		+	From 1-3 hours each day
		+ −	From ½ to 1 hour each day
		−	Time less than ½ hour
		− −	No time at all

Using the favorability scale helped Jimmy to define and clarify his relevant values still further. Once he had described favorability ratings for each value, Bette helped him to assign numerical weights to these values. She started with a simple rank-ordering process.

"OK, let's explore these values some more to figure out how important each one is in relation to each other one." Once again, Jimmy's exploration showed that the "future" was really his most important value. He and Bette assigned it a 10 on the 1-to-10 scale. Jimmy then decided that, though "time with father" was an important value, it was probably the least important of the four values he had developed. They assigned this value a 1 on the 1-to-10 scale. Finally, they agreed that Jimmy's values of "relationship with father" and "friends" were of equal value and ranked only slightly below "future" in their order of importance. They finally settled on a rating of 8 for each of these two values.

The next step involved development of a simple decision-making matrix. Jimmy took to this like the proverbial duck to water. "Hey, this is kinda neat, huh?" Bette grinned and responded, "You feel pretty good about being able to lay out your situation in some sort of organized form. It's really a relief after floundering around for so long."

Staying in school, Jimmy decided, would be "most favorable" (+ +) in terms of his relationship with his father but generally "unfavorable" in terms of his friends (−). This same alternative would be "favorable" in terms of his future job prospects — but not "most favorable" since staying in school gave him no access to practical work experience. Finally, this alternative would be "favorable" in terms of Jimmy's "time with father" value.

Continuing to apply the favorability scale, Jimmy eventually completed his matrix. The final version looked like this:

	Alternatives		
Values & Weights	Stay in School	Drop Out, Leave Home, and Work	Switch and Work Parttime
Future (10)	+10	−10	+20
Friends (8)	− 8	+16	+ 8
Relationship with Father (8)	+16	− 8	+ 8
Time with Father (1)	+ 2	− 2	0
Totals	+20	− 4	+36

Looking at the results, Jimmy could hardly believe his eyes. "Wow, I thought staying in and dropping out were like neck and neck," he said. "How come there's such a gap there? How come I was even thinking about dropping out? Minus 4 — damn!"

Bette grinned. "It's pretty exciting how these things turn out sometimes," she told him. "I think what happened was largely the result of your finding that your future job prospects were actually more important than your time and relationship with your father and your relationship with your friends — and then realizing the implications for this value if you dropped out and went to work for Morris fulltime. The experience you can get working parttime is one thing — but committing yourself to a job like that fulltime is like — oh — putting all your hopes for the future in one place and then praying that the wind doesn't blow them away!"

"Yeah," Jimmy murmured softly, still fascinated by the matrix. "Wow, it's so clear now! I oughta switch around my schedule and take some night classes so I can work with my friends during the day!"

"That looks like the best way," Bette agreed. "Which means you know where you're going and you know the basic approach you're going to use to get there. Now it's just a question of working out a program to actually get you there."

Jimmy felt as though a set of weights had been removed from his scrawny shoulders. For the first time in weeks, he had a direction and a goal. He knew where he was going — and that made all the difference!

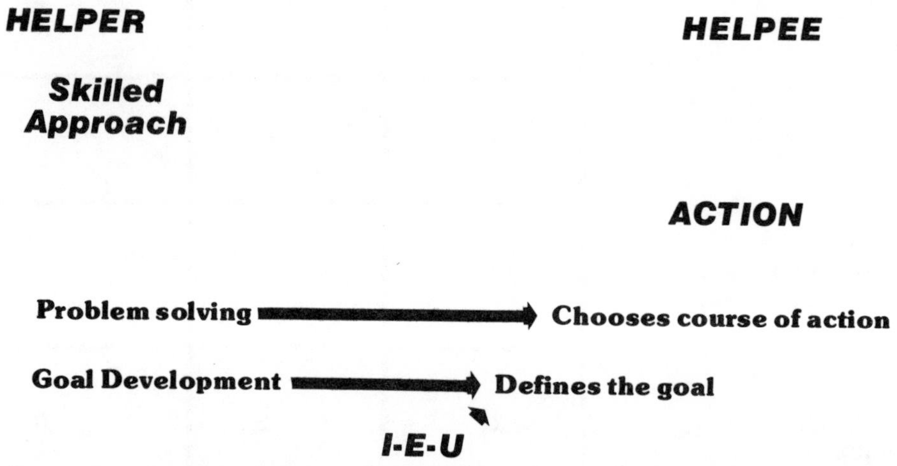

HELPER   **HELPEE**

Skilled
Approach

ACTION

Problem solving ━━━━━━━━━▶ Chooses course of action

Goal Development ━━━━━▶ Defines the goal

I-E-U

Figure 5-2: Problem solving and goal development skills used by helper to promote helpee's completion of first two action-steps.

Once again we can see the difference between a skilled and an unskilled approach to helping. Rather than letting Jimmy make an important decision based on little or no data, Bette helped the young man to explore his alternatives and personal values and the ways in which they might interact. In the process, both Bette and Jimmy learned something.

There is more that Jimmy must do, of course. But like the overwhelming majority of clients or helpees, one of the most critical problems he faced was bound up in the choice between different ways to approach a poorly understood goal. By helping Jimmy to define his goal and then go on to explore alternatives and values in a systematic way, Bette enabled Jimmy to reach the best decision possible. And having made this decision, Jimmy's own feelings of vast relief reinforce his intention to go on, to go ahead, to keep working with Bette. She has, like all skilled helpers, made a difference in his life. Now, by helping him to move closer to his goal, she will continue to make a difference.

The
Research
Background

One of the reasons why the continual challenges to the efficacy of counseling and psychotherapy cannot be completely answered is that therapists have typically not defined their goals in observable terms. For example, helpers often describe helpees as needing to become more motivated, adjusted, self-actualized, self-accepting, congruent, insightful, and so on. These goals certainly do not describe an observable activity; as a result, their achievement would be difficult to document and verify. Thus, even if counseling were having a positive impact on its helpees, the adherents of psychotherapy would still be unable to demonstrate the capabilities of their methods without first defining their goals in observable terms. The critics of psychotherapy have not claimed that psychotherapy is *ineffective;* rather, they have pointed out that the evidence that does exist has failed to indicate that psychotherapy *IS EFFECTIVE* (Eysenck, 1972). In other words, the burden of proof is on the provider of the service; and until therapeutic goals are defined in a more observable and meaningful manner, therapeutic effectiveness will be difficult to document.

Defining Goals Can Get Results

The ability to define or operationalize goals, then, is the key to the effective action-steps that the helpee must take (Carkhuff, 1969). A goal is defined in terms of the operations required to achieve it. A goal is, therefore, observable, measurable, and achievable (Carkhuff, 1974).

Perhaps one of the most intriguing findings with respect to the skill of goal definition is that simply requiring the therapist to set observable goals seems to improve therapeutic outcome in and of itself. In an experimental study of the benefits of goal definition (1976), Smith had one group of adolescent helpees counseled by professional therapists in their own style with one notable exception: The therapists had been instructed in how to define observable goals for their helpees. Another group of therapists counseled their helpees without receiving prior training in defining observable helpee goals. At the end of eight counseling sessions, the group of helpees aided by counselors who had defined observable goals showed significantly greater improvement on a variety of counseling outcome indices. In an entirely different study, client satisfaction and subsequent prediction of recidivism has been found to be related to client goal-attainment (Willer & Miller, 1978).

Walker (1972) has studied the importance of goal definition based on his interest in developing evaluative procedures within the helping professions. In studying an agency designed to rehabilitate the hardcore unemployed, Walker found that, when feedback to the helpers about how well their helpees were achieving observable rehabilitation goals was experimentally withdrawn, the number of helpees rehabilitated decreased; likewise, when the helpers were once again provided feedback as to how well their helpers were achieving their goals, the helping outcome improved once again. In other words, the setting of observable helpee goals combined with feedback to the helpers in terms of how well the helpees are achieving these goals can, in and of itself, improve an agency's helping outcome. Other researchers have reported similar positive effects of goal-setting training in improving general job performance (Latham & Rinne, 1974).

In areas as diverse as the world of work and conservation programming, goal-setting manipulations have been used to increase performance (Bucker, 1978; Erez, 1977). Administrative decision making can also be improved through the operationalization of goals (Alden, 1978). Unfortunately, mental health professionals have had a more difficult time in adopting goal-setting as a regular part of their practice (Holroyd & Goldenberg, 1978). Yet some researchers believe the setting of clear goals to be one of the most potent ingredients in successful skill training (Flowers, 1978; Flowers & Goldman, 1976).

The Many Applications of Problem-Solving Skills

One of the most impressive aspects of problem-solving skills is the applicability of problem-solving skills to a wide variety of settings and situations (D'Zurilla & Goldfried, 1971; Heppner, 1978). Hill (1975) has adapted the problem-solving process for the purpose of helping to clarify counseling goals for helpees who, after attempts at proceeding through the understanding phase of counseling, still remain rather vague and ambiguous with respect to the goals that are most important to them. At this point, use of problem-solving skills by helpers can assist such helpees to more systematically and observably identify and rank-order a number of alternative counseling goals based on their own values.

Further use of problem-solving-skills training has been made in the rehabilitation of alcoholics. Problem-solving skills were found to be significantly related to social competency and the ability of the client to plan ahead for possible future problem behaviors. One study reported on the training of 64 VA alcoholic patients in problem-solving skills. Results of this study found increased clients' skill levels which were generalized from training into real-life problem situations after discharge (Intagliata, 1978).

Other applications of problem-solving skills have been made in the areas of health care (Anthony & Carkhuff, 1976) and career education (Friel & Carkhuff, 1974). In the field of health care, patients are being allowed and/or are demanding to have more input into decisions regarding their own courses of treatment. Problem-solving skills can enable patients to better understand and organize the suggestions and information they receive and thus to see more clearly why they might prefer one course of action over another.

In terms of career development, fewer than one-quarter of young people make decisions by weighing the alternatives carefully. Most career decision-making stances can be summarized under the term "accidental." Chance rather than systematic planning is typically the determining influence. Yet problem-solving skills are uniquely suited to career decision-making; results attesting to this applicability have been well documented (Carkhuff & Berenson, 1976).

The major counseling approach to emphasize the problem and goal definition has been the trait-and-factor approach — an approach that received prominence in the 1950s (Caplow, 1954; Darley & Hagenah, 1955; Ginzburg, Ginzburg, Axelrod, & Herma, 1951; Holland, 1962; Hoppock, 1957; Roe, 1956; Shartle, 1946; Strong, 1955; Super, 1957; Super & Bohn, 1970; Tiedeman, O'Hara, & Baruch, 1963; Tyler, 1953). Beginning with Parsons (1909), adherents of this approach have facilitated educational and vocational choice and development by operationalizing the dimensions of both the helpees and the situations they are considering. The trait-and-factor approach has been successful to a limited degree in developing strategies to achieve substantive goals with the following formula: goal achievement = information + client values + success probabilities. Unfortunately, it has limited its own sources of information by developing fairly conventional and narrow goals. Nevertheless, it is worthwhile studying as a source of application and transfer (Carkhuff & Berenson, 1977).

In summary, flowing from the helpee's extensive exploration of where he or she is, the helping process converges in the helpee's understanding of the goals for where he or she wants or needs to be. The ability to achieve this goal is a function of the ability to define or operationalize the goal. Given the time and the resources, any goal that can be operationalized can be achieved.

References

Alden, J. Evaluation in focus. *Training and Development Journal*, Oct. 1978, 46-50.

Anthony, W.A., & Carkhuff, R.R. *The art of health care.* Amherst, Mass.: Human Resource Development Press, 1976.

Bucker, L. Joint effect of feedback and goal setting on performance: A field study of residential energy conservation. *Journal of Applied Psychology*, 1978, *63*, 428-433.

Caplow, T. *The sociology of work.* Minneapolis: University of Minnesota Press, 1954.

Carkhuff, R.R. *Helping and human relations.* New York: Holt, Rinehart & Winston, 1969.

Carkhuff, R.R. *The art of problem-solving.* Amherst, Mass.: Human Resource Development Press, 1974.

Carkhuff, R.R., & Berenson, B.G. *Teaching as treatment.* Amherst, Mass.: Human Resource Development Press, 1976.

Carkhuff, R.R., & Berenson, B.G. *Beyond counseling and therapy.* New York: Holt, Rinehart & Winston, 1977.

Darley, J.G., & Hagenah, T. *Vocational interest measurement: Theory and practice.* Minneapolis: University of Minnesota Press, 1955.

D'Zurilla, T., & Goldfried, M.R. Problem solving and behaviour modification. *Journal of Abnormal Psychology*, 1971, *78*, 107-126.

Erez, M. Feedback: A necessary condition for the goal-setting performance relationship. *Journal of Applied Psychology*, 1977, *62*, 624-627.

Eysenck, H.J. New approaches to mental illness: The failure of a tradition. In H. Gottesfeld (Eds.), *The critical issues of community mental health.* New York: Behavioral Publications, 1972.

Flowers, J. Goal clarity as a component of assertive behavior and a result of assertion training. *Journal of Clinical Psychology,* 1978, *34,* 744-747.

Flowers, J., & Goldman, R. Assertion training for mental health paraprofessionals. *Journal of Counseling Psychiatry,* 1976, *23,* 147-150.

Friel, T., & Carkhuff, R.R. *The art of developing a career: A helper's guide.* Amherst, Mass.: Human Resource Development Press, 1974.

Ginzberg, E., Ginzburg, S.W., Axelrod, S., & Herma, J.L. *Occupational choice.* New York: Columbia University Press, 1951.

Heppner, P. A review of problem-solving literature and its relationship to counseling process. *Journal of Counseling Psychology,* 1978, *25,* 366-375.

Hill, C. A process approach for establishing counseling goals and outcomes. *Personnel and Guidance Journal,* 1975, *53,* 571-576.

Holland, J.L. Some explorations of a theory of vocational choice: I. One- and two-year longitudinal summaries. *Psychological Monographs,* 1962, *76* (26), (whole no. 545).

Holroyd, J., & Goldenberg, I. The use of goal attainment scaling to evaluate a ward treatment program for disturbed children. *Journal of Clinical Psychology,* 1978, *34,* 732-739.

Hoppock, R. *Occupational information.* New York: McGraw-Hill, 1957.

Intagliata, J. Increasing the interpersonal problem-solving skills of an alcoholic population. *Journal of Consulting and Clinical Psychology,* 1978, *46,* 489-498.

Latham, G., & Rinne, S. Improving job performance through training in goal setting. *Journal of Applied Psychology,* 1974, *59,* 187-191.

Parsons, F. *Choosing a vocation.* Boston: Houghton Mifflin, 1909.

Roe, A. *The psychology of occupations.* New York: Wiley, 1956.

Shartle, C.L. *Occupation information.* New York: Prentice-Hall, 1946.

Smith, D.L. Goal attainment scaling as an adjunct to counseling. *Journal of Counseling Psychology,* 1976, *23,* 22-27.

Strong, E.K., Jr. *Vocational interests eighteen years after college.* Minneapolis, Minnesota: University of Minnesota Press, 1955.

Super, D.E. *The psychology of careers*. New York: Harper & Row, 1957.

Super, D.C., & Bohn, M.J. *Occupational psychology*. Belmont, Calif.: Wadsworth, 1970.

Tiedeman, D.V., O'Hara, R.P., & Baruch, R.W. *Career development: Choice and adjustment*. Princeton, N.J.: College Entrance Examination Board, 1963.

Tyler, L. *The work of the counselor*. New York: Appleton, 1953.

Walker, R.A. The ninth panacea: Program evaluation. *Evaluation*, 1972, *1* (1), 45-53.

Willer, B., & Miller, G. On the relationship of client satisfaction to client characteristics and outcome of treatment. *Journal of Clinical Psychology*, 1978, *34*, 157-160.

What is this chapter all about?

This chapter focuses on the helpee's need to *define the personalized goal* and *choose an optimum course of action* and on the skills of *goal development* and *problem solving*, which the helper must employ to facilitate these helpee activities.

Where does this fit in the overall helping model?

Earlier chapters dealt with the major phases of helpee *involvement,* helpee *exploration,* and helpee *understanding.* This chapter focuses on defining the goal and choosing the course of action as the first two steps within the primary phase of helpee *action.*

PREHELPING ‖ **HELPING**

UNDERSTANDING   **ACTION**

Choosing course of action

Defining the goal

EXPLORATION

INVOLVEMENT

Why is it important for helpees to define goals and choose courses of action?

Once a helpee has managed to reach an understanding of a personalized deficit and goal, he or she has a good general idea of where to go. But a general idea is by no means enough to ensure success. The helpee must define the goal in concrete terms so that he or she knows precisely where to go — and can tell when this goal has been reached. Moreover, the helpee must be able to choose that course of action that will lead to goal attainment without conflicting with important personal values.

171

Who must do what during the initial stages of helpee action?

As with personalizing, it is the helper's responsibility to take the initiative in defining the helpee's goal and choosing a course of action. As treated in this chapter, these processes involve four major areas of activity. First, the helper must work with the helpee to *define the goal* in meaningful, measurable, and realistic terms; in essence, this definition spells out the particular behaviors the helpee will be able to perform within a specific period of time. Next, the helper must use basic attending and responding skills to aid the helpee in *choosing the best alternative course of action*. This process involves three steps: First, exploring all alternative courses of action, the helper makes sure that the helpee overlooks no single way in which the goal might be effectively achieved. Second, the helper must aid in *developing the helpee's personal values;* this process involves exploring all important values, defining in objective terms all those relevant to the present situation, developing and using a favorability scale, and assigning a specific numerical weight to each value. Finally, the helper must aid the helpee in *making the decision about which course of action* is best; here the helpee constructs a simple decision-making matrix, judges and quantifies the interaction of each alternative with each personal value (making use of the favorability scale), and adds the resulting numbers in each column to determine which alternative earns the highest total. Here, too, the helper must be alert for any possible ways to combine positive aspects of two or more alternatives.

When should this phase of helpee action begin?

The helper should initiate the first stages of helpee action when he or she judges that a helpee has really understood and accepted a statement of a personalized goal that includes a summary of the personalized feeling and the personalized problem or helpee deficit. As noted in the chapter, in some few cases there may be one course of action that both helper and helpee immediately agree is the only realistic possibility; in such cases, the helper may not need to employ problem-solving skills. Such cases are unusual, however. Neither helpee nor helper will lose by answering the question, "Is there more than one way in which this goal might conceivably be approached?"

How can you practice the skills involved in goal development?

As we have seen before, the great majority of the skills treated in this text can and should be applied in a wide range of clinical and nonclinical settings. Yes, the skills of goal development are extremely effective when employed within a formal counselor/client relationship. But these same skills can be used with great effect in many informal situations, as well — with friends, family, or anyone else!

You can check out your own goal-development skills quite easily. Start by picking a real-life situation in which you have been involved in the last year or so — one that prompted you to do some serious thinking and to get some sort of goal for yourself. Perhaps you decided to return to school. Or to buy a car. Or to change jobs. Once you have selected a situation, go through the following steps.

1. Reflect on your own feelings and thoughts at the time this situation came up, focusing as much as possible on the problematic or negative aspects of these feelings and thoughts.

2. Recapture your own role in the situation in terms of personalized feeling, problem, and goal. Restate this role in the past tense by using the format, "I felt _____ because I couldn't _____ and I wanted to _____ ."

3. Define the personalized goal (what you wanted) in objective, measurable terms. Here you may use the format, "My goal at that time could/should have been stated as

_____ ."

4. Now explore to see how many alternative courses of action you can discover that would have led to attainment of your goal. (What you actually chose to do may or may not figure in this new list.) If the course of action you actually pursued did lead you to your goal, include this course of action; if it did not lead to your goal, omit it. Using a separate sheet of paper, list all of the realistic alternatives you come up with.

5. Now explore all those personal values you espoused at that time that were relevant to any one course of action on your list.

6. Define each value and develop a five-step favorability

scale for each. Then assign each value a numerical weight using a 1-to-10 scale in which 10 is the most important relevant value.

7.   Construct a matrix and chart the interaction of your alternatives and your values. Get totals for each alternative and consider ways in which positive features of different alternatives might be combined.

8.   Now ask yourself, "What was my best alternative? Did I take it? If so, how did it turn out? If not, how did my actual course of action turn out? WOULD I HAVE BENEFITED BY USING GOAL-DEVELOPMENT AND PROBLEM-SOLVING SKILLS?"

In the great majority of cases, you will find that the answer to this last question is an unqualified YES!

helping people develop programs to reach goals: INITIATING SKILLS II

6

Overview

1. During this phase of helpee *action*, the helpee designs *a systematic program of steps* to take her or him to the defined goal.

2. The helper uses *program development* skills to promote the helpee's design of an effective series of steps.

3. The helpee begins by designing the *primary action- or do-steps* leading from where he or she is to the goal itself.

4. The helper continues to *respond empathically to and initiate with the helpee* to ensure that there are no gaps in the primary-step program, that each step moves the helpee in a direct line toward the goal, and that each step is defined concretely in terms of the time involved and the number and type of helpee behaviors entailed.

5. Next, the helpee designs a series of *secondary action- or do-steps* leading to the completion of each primary step.

6. The helper promotes the helpee's development of secondary steps by *showing how each primary step can be treated as a separate goal in its own right* as well as by continuing to check for gaps in the program and for steps that may not have been defined by the helpee in concrete and measurable terms.

7. Finally, the helpee develops a series of *check- or think-steps* to support his or her performance of each primary and secondary action-steps.

8. The helper works with the helpee to make sure that check-steps are developed to monitor helpee progress *before, during, and after each primary and secondary action-step.*

9. The key to a program that will move the helpee successfully from where he or she is to the goal is a *systematic series of gradually incremental steps beginning with the*

simplest task and ending with the most complex, each step supported by check-steps that allow constant helpee-monitored feedback.

10. The key to effective program development on the helper's part is her or his ability to *control the nature and scope of the program* in such a way as to maximize the chances of helpee success at each consecutive level.

Most people become involved in counseling or helping sessions because they are having trouble dealing with some aspect of their personal lives. These helpees may begin with what they feel is a clear idea of the problem they are confronting. Alternatively, they may feel overwhelmed — or irritated or just mildly concerned — by the elusive complexities of the world in which they find themselves. Whatever the case, helpee *exploration* — promoted by the helper's responding skills — enables each helpee to come to terms with the specifics of his or her immediate situation: who is involved, what is really happening, and so on. At the next level of the helping process, each helpee can and must gain a personalized *understanding* of the way in which she or he is personally involved in and responsible for the situation; here the focus shifts from the "they won't" perspective of externalized fault-finding to the "I can't" perspective, which at last points the way to a meaningful goal for the helpee. The helper facilitates such understanding by using specific *personalizing skills.*

As we have seen, the ultimate product of helpee understanding is a statement of the personalized goal which, taking into account the helpee's own behavioral deficit, specifies where the helpee wants or needs to be. Having outlined this personalized goal, the helpee engages in real and constructive *action* for the first time by working to define the goal in concrete and measurable terms — aided by the helper's use of *goal-development* and *problem-solving* skills. At the end of that sequence of activities treated in the last chapter, the helper has defined the goal and has systematically selected the best approach to this goal in terms of both effectiveness and personal values. Having succeeded in getting a helpee or a group of helpees to this point, a helper may breathe a sigh of relief and decide that all is well. After all, once the goal has been set and the mode of approach has been determined, what more is needed?

As the following account shows quite clearly, a great deal more must be done — for the criterion of success in any helping situation is nothing less than the helpee's full achievement of the goal!

Andy Johnson had been a teacher. For five long years he had labored in an urban high school, trying to get through to the shifting, changing swarm of street-smart kids who made up his classes. Sometimes he thought he was beginning to accomplish something. More often, he felt as though he was doing little more than putting in his time. This latter notion was confirmed one blustery winter day when he came upon a group of his students pitching coins against a wall in a dimly lit hall outside the basement gymnasium. Surprised to find the students lingering after the school day was officially over — and even more surprised to discover that the group included several kids who rarely appeared in class — Andy had stopped to talk.

"How come you guys are still hangin' around?" he asked. "Don't tell me you finally found something good about school!"

Chickie, one of the older boys, looked up at him and grinned. "Oh, man, there's always been somethin' good about this place — 'specially in winter!"

"Yeah?" Andy grinned back. "What's that?"

"It's warm," one of the other boys said. He spoke without looking at Andy, his gaze intent upon the row of nickels that lay along the wall where they had been pitched. And suddenly, noting the way the boys were dressed, the way they hunched their shoulders and studiously avoided his gaze, Andy realized an awful truth: The biggest attraction the school held for them — perhaps the only attraction — was that it provided a sanctuary! Like the rest of their families, many of the kids lived a hand-to-mouth existence. As often as not, their homes were tiny, overcrowded apartments that went unheated in winter, unairconditioned in stifling summer. Their natural habitat was the street. Denied this surrogate "home" by icy temperatures and chilling winds, they were ready to settle for any dim area where the temperature might stay above freezing.

All this Andy had known before, of course. But his prior knowledge had been intellectual rather than visceral. Now, standing over the defensive huddle of youthful figures, he was struck for the first time by some of the blunt, inescapable facts of urban existence. These kids were not ready for education, for the niceties of classes and assignments and academic effort. How could they be ready for these things when they had to expend so much effort just to keep warm?

Andy's new career began that same wintry day. He decided on the spot that his commitment to working with kids could no longer be limited to the safe-yet-sterile classroom. Sure, he would keep teaching. And he would work harder to make his classes fit with the realities of life as understood by his students. At the same time, however, he would go beyond this and do something about meeting his students' real needs outside of class.

"You guys need a place to stay warm, huh?" he said. "OK, then. Why don't we work on that together?"

That was the start of what soon came to be called Project Open Door. Working on his own, Andy managed to locate an abandoned storefront near the school. Apprehensive at first, the owner finally agreed to let Andy and his kids have free use of the space in return for their promise to clean things up and keep them that way. Recent talk of demolishing the building had made it all but impossible for the landlord to rent the space. This way he was able to hedge his bets. If the building came down, the city would compensate him accordingly. If the building stayed up, he would get his storefront overhauled for nothing.

It took several weeks for Andy and the kids — now increased in number to about 20 — to make the place habitable. The small amount of money Andy chipped in was more than matched by the enthusiasm and hard work of the kids themselves. Making use of every bit of material they could beg or borrow, the group carried out a spree of cleaning, painting, and furnishing. Fortunately, the plumbing was still functional. One of the boy's uncles donated an old kerosene heater that he described as "kinda beat up, but safe." A battered refrigerator was rescued from a junk yard, as were several old chairs. Tables were constructed out of sheets of plywood that were too warped to be put to any other use. The last act was to paint the name on the plate glass window in front.

"Hey, man, how come this door won't shut right?" Chickie asked Andy, demonstrating by slamming the door, which promptly sagged open again.

"It just wants to be open, I guess," Andy said. "That way anyone who wants can come in. I guess you could say we got an 'open door' policy around here." And thus the name "Open Door" was agreed upon.

It was just as well Andy was single. He soon found that his commitment to Project Open Door meant the end of his free time. The storefront opened every weekday at 3:00 when Andy got through with his classes and stayed open until 10:00 or even later each night. Saturdays he was there all day. And on Sundays he slept late but always opened up by 1:00 or 2:00.

Needless to say, Andy was never lonely. Whatever the hour, the storefront was always full. Many of his own students took to spending time there, of course; and Andy noticed that these same students now tended to show up more regularly at his classes. The word got around and new faces started to appear.

At first, Andy's concern was simply to provide a place for kids to come and relax. Inevitably, however, he found that more, far more, was needed. The young people who milled about inside the "Open Door" needed things to do. They needed directions in which they could expend their energy. Most of all, they needed someone who could really give them help with the thousand-and-one problems that beset them. Andy did his best. So did Sue, another teacher who appeared in the storefront one day and announced her desire to "help work things out with the kids." Together, they even talked the school board into subsidizing some night classes in psychology and counseling, which they arranged to take on an alternating basis. But it was increasingly hard for the two teachers to stay on top of things. There were so many problems — a new one every day, it seemed. And there seemed so little that they could really do.

The crunch came when Mr. Williams, the landlord who owned the storefront, announced that he was going to look for a paying tenant.

"It's not like I don't appreciate what you and your kids have done," he told Andy one warm spring afternoon. "But see, I just found out they're not going to tear the building down after all. That means I'm going to have to keep paying taxes and all on the property. And *that* means I've got to get some money out of it."

After talking to Williams for over two hours, Andy finally got him to agree to let the group stay in residence if they could come up with $75 a month. At that, Andy figured the cost would be twice what the place was worth. But he was not ready to see the whole project go down the drain.

Several nights later Andy and Sue met with those kids who regularly spent time at the "Open Door" storefront. At first the kids were angry.

"That old skinflint," Chickie growled. "Why, he couldn't get anyone else to use this place even if he paid them! Seventy-five bucks a month — the man's got bricks in his brain!" Sully, Art, Debbie, and several others chimed in and agreed with Chickie. Fortunately, Andy and Sue had developed some new skills that came in handy. They were able to respond to the irritation of the kids and gradually move the talk in a constructive direction. Eventually, most of the kids were able to see things in a more personalized way.

"Man, it really gets me down sometimes," a heavyset boy named Sonny said. "I mean, we're so used to gettin' the short end of the stick that we don't even know how to take care of ourselves anymore. You know, unless some hassle can be fixed up by breakin' heads, we're just nowhere at all!"

Andy nodded. "You really get bummed out because you can't control things to get what you really want."

"That's it, man," Robert chimed in. "We got no control at all!"

Further talking — and some hard listening by Andy and Sue — revealed that what "having control" really came down to was having a regular and reliable place to get together: "Like this place," Chickie said. "Only now that old bastard wants to take it away because he knows how much better it looks once we put in our time on it!"

The goal was clear. At first, however, the way to reach this goal seemed less clear. The kids explored a number of possibilities, still trying to figure out how to get what they wanted without giving in to Williams's demand for regular rent.

"We could maybe find another place to fix up," Robert said.

"Yeah — or maybe find another place for less bread," Debbie put in.

"Hey, what about gettin' some money from, like, the welfare people?"

Chickie asked. "Don't they get into doin' stuff for poor undernourished kids like us?" He grinned broadly, his tone imitating the impersonal pity often expressed by welfare and other bureaucracies.

They wrestled with these and other options for over an hour. In the end, however, it was clear that paying Mr. Williams the $75 he wanted each month made the most sense. Even Chickie gave his grudging consent in the end.

"OK," Andy said at last. "You know what you want — to have a place you can count on every day of every week. A place that's really yours. And you know that you're going to have to come up with $75 each month to get it. There's no way Sue and I can help out with that kinda money — and I don't think it would be good even if we could. You people want to control what's going down your own selves — not take a handout from someone else. All right, then, how are you going to come up with the money?"

Both Andy and Sue were surprised at the response. For kids who never seemed to have a dime of their own, Chickie and the others seemed to have an incredible number of money-making schemes ready at hand. Even after eliminating the patently illegal ones, there were quite a few that sounded promising: individual parttime jobs, washing cars, making things to sell, and any number of other possibilities.

"All right," Andy laughed at last, overwhelmed by the unending flow of suggestions. "You people don't sound like you'll have any trouble making some bread. We've got until the first of the month to come up with the initial $75. That's almost three weeks. So why don't we say we'll have another meeting like this in — oh, two weeks — and make sure that things are going OK." He looked around the room, counting noses. "There's fifteen of you here. Why don't you agree that everyone has to come up with five dollars by the next meeting? That'll give us what we need for the first month. And at the meeting we can talk about some ways to regularize the whole thing so we don't have to get into a panic every month."

"Let's hear it for the Open Door," Chickie yelled. And the others, fired with enthusiasm, raised a yell that could be heard in the next block.

Not wanting to put pressure on the kids, Andy cooled it for the next two weeks. In point of fact, he had more than enough to keep him busy. And after all, raising five bucks apiece did not seem like the hardest thing in the world — especially given the motivation and enthusiasm the kids had already shown.

But that enthusiasm seemed strangely missing as the usual group wandered in on the evening scheduled for the next meeting. Even Chickie seemed listless and uninvolved. Andy looked at the group, then at Sue, then back at the group.

"You look really down," he said. "I take it we got some money problems."

Robert avoided his gaze. "Oh, man, people're just too tight! You know, I musta gone to about two hundred stores asking for some kinda work. *Any* kind! I mean, I didn't come on proud or anything like that." He shrugged. "They just didn't wanta know me, that's all."

Debbie nodded. "Me'n Sharrie was gonna wash cars, remember? We told people fifty cents. You know what they say? 'Damn, why should I pay you that fifty cents; I c'n just go down the street there and do it my own self inna car wash for a quarter!'" She sniffed. "Never seen sucha bunch of puckered-up people in my life, I swear!"

Everyone had the same story, it seemed. Lots of effort, little or no money. When Andy got them to pool their cash, the total amount was less than $18.

"What's the matter with you people?" Andy said at last, his voice betraying his angry frustration. "I mean, you know what's at stake here, right? All you had to do was come up with a lousy five bucks apiece! And instead, all I hear is this 'poor me' jive about how rotten everyone treated you! What is it with you, anyway? You knew what you had to do! Why couldn't you just do it?"

Why indeed? Andy Johnson's question is probably a familiar one for most of us. How many times have we seen people set out on what looks to us like a simple and sensible course of action, only to blow it before they are halfway to their goal? And how many times have we ourselves headed for a goal that seemed well within reach, only to wake up some time later with the goal still beckoning us and all our efforts gone for nothing?

As the account of Andy and Project Open Door illustrates, there is a considerable gap between goal development and goal attainment. It is not enough for any helpee simply to know where he or she wants to be. Nor is it enough for that same helpee to know the general way in which the goal should be approached. A helpee who attempts to reach a goal on the basis of this limited kind of knowledge will almost certainly fail — just as Andy's kids failed. And a

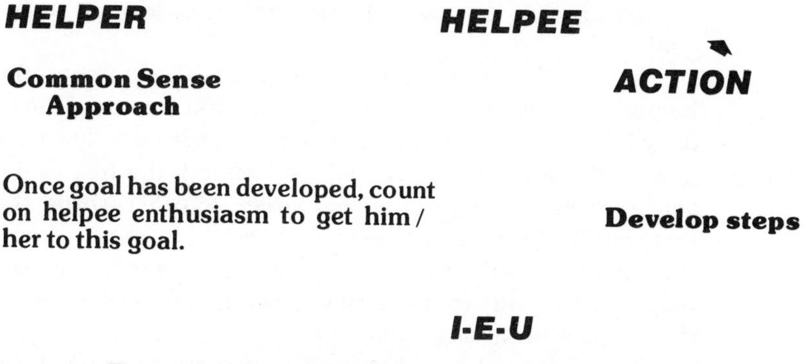

HELPER   **HELPEE**

Common Sense   **ACTION**
  Approach

Once goal has been developed, count
on helpee enthusiasm to get him /   **Develop steps**
her to this goal.

I-E-U

*Figure 6-1: Impact of Andy's "common sense" approach
on helpees' ability to act.*

helper who takes a "common sense" approach at this stage in the helping process can only promote helpee failure — just as Andy promoted such failure with his kids.

Once a helpee or group of helpees has developed a given goal, the helper must do far more than point the way toward that goal. Instead, the helper must work with each helpee to *develop a program* of activities that will allow the helpee to approach the goal in a systematic, sequential fashion. The key to effective program development is the charting of specific steps. The helpee must begin by developing a series of *primary steps* that bridge the gap between where he or she is and where he or she wants to be. Next, these primary steps are treated as new goals, each of which can be attained by the helpee who charts and takes a series of *secondary steps*. Finally, each primary and secondary action-step must be supported by a series of *check-* or *think-steps* that allow the helpee to monitor progress before, during, and immediately after each period of activity.

Effective program development begins once the helpee has defined the goal and selected the optimum approach to that goal. Effective program development ends as the helpee begins to implement the program. During the rest of this chapter we will focus on the specific helpee and helper activities that make up the process of program development. In doing so, we will see what was missing in Andy Johnson's "common sense" approach to helping.

Developing Primary Steps

Helpee Goal:
To develop the major behavioral steps leading to the goal.

During the initial phase of program development, the helpee develops two primary steps: the first step that she or he will take; and the last step, which leads directly to the goal itself. In practice, it is most effective if the helpee develops these two steps in reverse order. In other words, the first step that the helpee developed should be the final step that he or she will take to reach the goal. In this way, the helpee can be sure that the final program will lead to rather than bypass or miss the goal.

The helpee should begin the process of program development by asking and answering the question, "What is the last thing I must do in order to reach the goal I have set for myself?" The helpee's answer must involve a specific behavior that will lead directly to the goal. We can best see this process at work by looking at a sample situation.

Essie is a woman who has been helped to develop a personalized goal for herself. As she puts it, "I really feel frustrated because I've been stuck in a dead-end job for five years and I'd like to get a new job this year that pays better and offers some chance of promotion." In the process of developing this goal, Essie and her helper decided that her best course of action was to avoid employment agencies and, instead, work on her own job-hunting skills. Thus Essie knows where she wants to go and, moreover, knows the basic approach she is going to take to reach her goal. Now it is time for her to start developing her program.

"What's the last thing I have to do to reach the goal I have set for myself?" Essie decides that the last thing she will have to do is learn how to handle the personal interview that will inevitably precede any job offer. If she can control the interview in a positive and constructive manner, she will be able to get the job. Thus the final primary step in Essie's program will involve developing *interview* skills.

Once the helpee has determined the final step in the program, he or she should work to pinpoint the very first step in this program. Here the helpee can ask and answer the question, "What is the first thing I must do in order to start moving toward my goal?" Like the final primary step, the first primary step must lead directly toward the goal rather than allowing the helpee to go off on a tangent.

Essie already knows the specific type of job she wants. Were this not the case, her first step might involve expanding

Final Primary Step ⟶ **Goal**

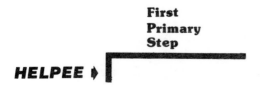

First Primary Step

HELPEE ▶

183

her career possibilities. As it is, she decides that her first step should be to develop a complete *job list* of prospective employers — individuals or companies that might be expected to hire people in Essie's field. In effect, she has pinpointed the first as well as the last thing she must do to reach her goal.

Once the helpee has developed the final primary step leading to the goal itself and the first primary step he or she must take, the helpee must develop additional primary steps to bridge the gap between these initial two.

There is no hard-and-fast rule concerning the total number of primary steps in an effective program of action. Rather, the helpee must begin by considering the first primary step and asking, "Where will I be when I have completed this step?" Having explored and answered this question, the helpee can go on to ask, "What should my next major step be?" Essie answers the first question by saying, "I'll have a list of prospective employers." After some thought, she decides that her next major step should be to develop the *application* materials that she will send to each of the people or companies on her list.

The helpee can use the same set of questions to develop additional primary steps. In other words, he or she can continue to explore each step and ask, "Where will I be when I have completed this step?" and "What should my next major step be?" Each new step, of course, should begin precisely where the previous step leaves off and should move the helpee in a direct line toward the overall goal. Using this approach, Essie charts two additional primary steps. Once she has developed her job list and her application materials, she must develop the *personal contact* materials that will form the basis of her cover letter and/or her telephone calls. Once she has completed this step, she will have to *get in touch* with each and every employer on her list in order to secure as many interviews as possible.

At the end of this phase of program development, the helpee should have a clear and specific outline of all those major steps leading from where he or she is at the moment to where he or she wants to be — the goal. This program of major or primary steps should be such that there are no significant gaps between steps. Essie's program at this point includes five primary steps laid out in a systematic manner. First, she will develop her *job list*. Next, she will develop her *application materials*. Next, she will develop her *personal contact materials*. Next, she will actually *get in touch* with her prospective employers in order to gain as many interviews as possible. Finally, she will develop her *interview skills* so that she can handle each job interview in the best possible manner.

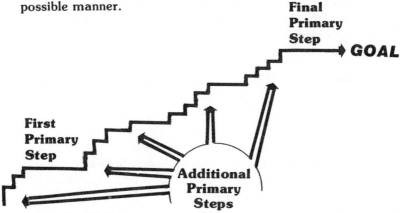

Helper Skills:

Initiating with the helpee to develop a program of primary steps leading to the goal.

During the initial phase of program development, the helper must make sure that the helpee handles each task in the appropriate sequence — final step first, then first step, then additional steps — and that all of the primary steps developed lead directly to the helpee's goal. The final primary step can usually be recognized by the effective helper as the most complex behavior flowing from the helpee's goal. In Essie's situation, for example, the personal interview will be more complex than any earlier phase of her program since it will involve her in face-to-face interaction with a prospective employer. Thus, if the helpee has trouble answering the question, "What's the last thing I must do to reach my goal?" the helper can determine the single most complex behavior required of the helpee and suggest this as the final primary step.

Once the final primary step has been set, of course, the helper must assist in developing the helpee's first primary step. Here the helper's attention should focus on the answers to two questions: "Will this helpee be able to take this first step successfully?" and "Does this first step lead directly toward the goal?" Unless the helper can answer yes to both of these questions, the first primary step under consideration is not satisfactory. The great majority of people who abandon programs do so because they find they are unable to complete the first step successfully. Failure to complete the first step must cast doubts on the value of the entire program. Conversely, successful completion of the first step invariably reinforces a helpee's determination to go on by promoting self-confidence. The importance of a positive answer to the helper's second question should be self-evident. A first step that does not move the helpee closer to the goal may jeopardize the entire program by leading the helpee far astray.

As we have seen, the entire helping process is characterized by the translation of personally relevant and accurate insights into measurable, concrete terms. This consideration is as important in program development as it has been in the earlier phases of helping. Thus the helper must continually strive to understand and present the helpee's insights in objective and functional terms. In Essie's case, for example, the helper responded to her thoughts on "developing a list of employers" by saying, "Good idea — a list is an important first step. Now let's try to figure out how long such a list has to be to maximize your chances of getting the kind of job you want." Based on Essie's career field and the geographic area in which she lived, they finally decided that an optimum size for her job list would be 100 prospective employers. A higher number would have been unrealistic while a lower number might have limited Essie's chances. Finally, the helper suggested a time frame that made sense to Essie: "Let's say that you'll finish developing your job list by the end of this week." Thus Essie was provided with far more than a vaguely defined primary step. She knew exactly how long it would take her to complete her first step — and what she would have when she had completed it.

Once the first and final primary steps have been set, the helper must continue to promote and support the helpee's development of additional primary steps. As before, the helper should make sure that each step is defined in specific, concrete, and measurable terms and that each step moves the helpee closer to the goal that has been developed.

There are many ways of translating a major or primary step into measurable terms. As noted, one criterion is *time*. The helper should aid the helpee in establishing a realistic time frame for each phase of the action-program. The purpose in so doing is not to put pressure on the helpee but, rather, to enable the helpee to know exactly when he or she should be performing a specific set of activities. Many helpees find it relatively easy to plan primary steps once the process has been begun; yet few if any will think to specify a particular period of time within which a given step should be completed. Unless the helper ensures that appropriate time frames are established, the helpee's initial enthusiasm and energy may dissipate. Conversely, the presence of clearly defined time limits gives the helpee something concrete to look forward to: a definite point in the future when one sequence of activities will be completed and another can begin.

A second way to concretize a primary step is to define it in terms of the *amount or number of things involved*. A helpee whose goal involves achieving better communication with his children, for example, may decide that one primary step will involve having more conversations with the kids. The helper can concretize this step by suggesting that the helpee define it as "having at least two half-hour conversations with each child during the next week on subjects the children find personally meaningful." (The helpee's ability here to discriminate "personally meaningful" material, of course, presupposes his acquisition of some basic interpersonal skills at an earlier primary step-level.) In the same fashion, the helper working with Essie makes sure that each of her additional primary steps are defined in terms of both the amount of time required by each and the number of specific things involved.

As indicated, the helper must continue to make sure that each primary step will move the helpee in a direct line toward the goal. In addition, the helper should keep an eye out for any significant gaps between primary steps. If there is a gap, the helpee will almost certainly fall into it! At the same time, the helper should check to see if any of the primary steps the helpee develops actually include too many activities. If this turns out to be the case, the helper can suggest that two or more primary steps be made of the one original step. For example, Essie originally lumped her second and third primary steps together when she said that, after developing her job list, she should "get the things together that should go to each possible employer." Her helper pointed out that every application would involve at least two basic elements: the résumé materials outlining Essie's work and educational background and the personal cover letter asking for an interview. "These two elements will actually have quite different aims," the helper explained. "Your letter will really be designed to get the employer to read your résumé; and your résumé will be designed to get you an interview. Perhaps you should think of the application and the personal letters as two separate steps." This made sense to Essie who then included "personal contact material" as a new primary step.

By the end of this phase of program development, the helper should have promoted the helpee's development of a full program of primary steps — each clearly and concretely defined — that lead from where the helpee is to where the helpee wants to be. Armed with this program of primary steps, the helpee will be ready to move.

Developing Secondary Steps

Helpee Goal:

To treat each primary step as a goal and develop a program of action to achieve it.

Each of the steps the helpee has developed up to this point is a primary step. As such, it will almost certainly entail a number of separate but related activities. For example, the acquisition of program-development skills is a primary step for any counselor who wishes to reach the overall goal of developing effective helping skills. And as this chapter itself demonstrates, developing such program-development skills requires the individual to take a number of secondary steps: learning to develop first and final primary steps; learning to develop additional primary steps; learning to develop secondary steps themselves; and (as we shall see) learning to develop effective check-steps.

Once the helpee has charted a complete sequence of primary steps, each leading directly to the next and the last one leading directly to the goal, he or she must determine exactly how each of these primary steps can be taken. Here the helpee can take each primary step in turn and then ask and answer the question, "What are the different things I must do in order to take this major step successfully?" This means that, in effect, the helpee transforms each primary step into a separate goal and then maps out a sequence of activity or pattern of secondary steps leading to the attainment of this goal.

We can see the manner in which secondary steps are developed by returning to Essie and her partially developed program. She has determined that her first primary step will involve listing at least 100 different employers in her area. Now she asks, "What do I have to do in order to take this step?" One obvious step will be to check the "Help Wanted" ads in local newspapers. But given today's job market, it is highly doubtful that Essie can gather a dozen names of possible employers in this way, never mind 100 such names! Aided by her helper, she outlines a sequence of other activities that will enable her to complete this first primary step and achieve the goal it now represents. She will visit the local branch of the state employment office and collect as many listings as possible. She will also visit the public library and, by using sources like the Yellow Pages in area telephone books and the "Service Directory" published in her state, will add to her list the names of local companies that may not be actively looking for applicants but that might still be convinced to hire Essie on the basis of her qualifications. Finally, Essie will fill out any incomplete entries on her list by calling companies to learn the name of the officer to whom she will send her application and any other pertinent information.

We can see, then, that Essie's first primary step — to develop her job list of prospective employers — involves at least three separate secondary steps: visit the state employment office; visit the public library; and call any companies whose entries on her list are incomplete in order to gain the necessary information. By taking each of these secondary steps in the proper order, Essie should have no trouble completing her first primary step. She can go on to treat each additional primary step as a goal and develop a set of secondary steps to reach it.

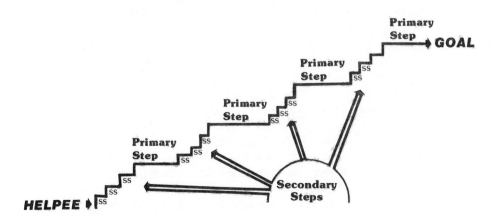

Helper Skills:

Initiating with the helpee to ensure that each primary step can be achieved through a sequence of secondary steps.

In promoting the helpee's development of effective secondary steps, the helper must keep in mind that the criterion governing program development is success. Thus, the question that the helper should continue to ask is, "What specific things must the helpee do in order to succeed at this level of her or his program?"

As there is no hard-and-fast rule concerning the number of primary steps a good program must have, so there can be no set number of secondary steps a helpee must take to complete one of these primary steps. The helper can begin by focusing the helpee's attention on the last thing that should be done in order to complete the primary step in question. Thus, in Essie's case, the helper suggests that the last secondary step leading to her development of an effective job list will be to get the information needed to complete each separate entry. As indicated, Essie can do this by contacting any companies for which she has only part of the data she needs. The helper can then go on to develop with the helpee the very first thing she or he must do — that is, the first of the secondary steps being developed. Once this has been done, the helper can continue to focus the helpee's attention on secondary steps that will bridge the gaps in the miniprogram leading to completion of the primary step in question.

It frequently turns out — especially with complex programs — that one of the secondary steps itself is quite demanding in terms of the number of separate activities involved. The helper should watch for this and should be ready to suggest to the helpee that this secondary step be treated as a new primary step. The step can then be treated as a goal in its own right and a new set of secondary steps can be developed leading up to it.

The nature of a given program will determine whether the helper needs to define each secondary step in terms of time limits and number or amount of things involved. Here again, the helper should remember that the real criterion of effectiveness is helpee success. Thus, he or she can ask, "Does this secondary step, as presently defined, give the helpee all the information he or she needs to complete the step successfully?" For example, Essie's helper felt that the overall time frame for taking her first primary step was adequate. At the same time, however, the helper knew that Essie would stand a far better chance of success if her secondary steps spelled out precisely what she would have to do. For this reason, the helper worked with Essie to outline the exact categories of information she would be looking for when she took her final secondary step of contacting companies to complete entries on her job list.

Whether the steps involved are primary or secondary ones, the effective helper continues to use basic attending and responding skills in order to keep track of where the helpee is at any given moment and to communicate lasting interest and understanding. Many helpees, confronted by what may at first seem a maze of steps and procedures, may become discouraged by the demands of effective program development. The helper must be able to recognize and respond to any helpee confusion: "You really feel confused by all this and wonder whether you're going to be able to handle it." The fact of the matter is that the helpee *can* handle program development quite well — but only if some skilled help is available!

Developing
Think-
Steps

Helpee Goal:

To develop steps to ensure that he or she is staying on track and moving toward the goal.

Up to this point, the helpee has been concerned with developing a series of primary and secondary steps. These steps have one major thing in common: They are both examples of *do*-steps. A do-step is just what it sounds like — a specific activity that a person can perform or *do*. But a program comprising only do-steps will not always ensure the helpee's attainment of her or his goal. The helpee needs to have a continuing series of reference or *check* points — ways of determining how things have gone up to now, how they are going at present, and how they can be expected to go during the next phase of activity. Thus, during the final stage of program development, the helpee should develop some specific check- or *think*-steps to support the do-steps already developed.

There are three areas of think-steps involved in all effective programs. *Before-think*-steps prepare the helpee for a given do-step. *During-think*-steps allow the helpee to keep track of progress while actually involved in the do-step activity. And *after-think*-steps make it possible for the helpee to consolidate learning and to make sure that the do-step has been completed satisfactorily. As the phrase itself indicates, think-steps really specify in advance the particular things the helpee should think about as he or she moves through the sequence of secondary and primary do-steps toward the goal.

Perhaps the simplest and most effective method of developing check- or think-steps involves the helpee laying out a series of questions for each do-step. To see this developmental process in action, let us look again at Essie's program — and at the secondary do-step with which she will begin her program. The first thing that Essie will actually do is start compiling her job list by going through the "Help Wanted" section in the local papers. The first check-steps she should develop, therefore, are those before-think-steps, which will let her know when she is set to start. So Essie outlines the following questions:

Before-think-steps:
"Do I have copies of all the local papers?"
"Do I have writing materials with which to begin my list?"
"Am I familiar with the various abbreviations that prospective employers may use in their ads?"
"Do I know exactly what information I'm looking for?"

Affirmative answers to these questions will confirm Essie's readiness to begin. One or more negative answers will signal an area or areas of inadequate preparation that Essie can then remedy.

Essie's development of additional think-steps continues in a similar manner. She goes on to outline the questions she should ask herself as she is performing the activity in the do-steps:

During-think-steps:
"Is this advertised job within my geographic area?"
"Could I qualify for this job?"
"Does this job deserve a place in my job list?"
"Do I have all the relevant information in the ad?"

Finally, Essie outlines the questions that she can ask and answer once she has completed the first do-step:

After-think-steps:
"Did I miss any appropriate job openings?"

"Did I exclude all inappropriate openings from my list?"

"Is all the information I've gathered legible and accurate?"

"Do I know which entries are incomplete and what additional information I'll need?"

The primary and secondary do-steps in a helpee's program ensure that the helpee can reach the ultimate goal; these steps spell out the specific things that the helpee must do and the order in which they should be done. The check- or think-steps ensure that the helpee will reach the goal by providing a way for the helpee to anticipate, understand, and review each separate do-step.

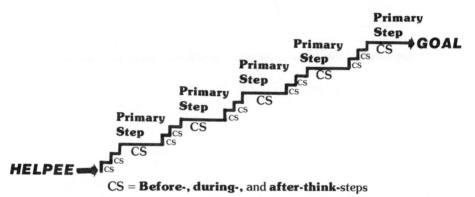

CS = **Before-, during-,** and **after-think-**steps

Helper Skills:

Initiating with the helpee to ensure that the think-steps developed will allow the helpee to monitor progress before, during, and after each action-step.

Every experienced helper is familiar with what might be termed the "law of diminishing probability." Having reached an understanding of a problem and having set a goal, the typical helpee will probably try to figure out some way to reach this goal. It is not very probable that the helpee will try to map out a systematic program of sequential steps leading to the goal. It is even less probable that the helpee will approach such a task in terms of primary steps, which then become new goals to be achieved through a sequence of secondary steps. And it is downright improbable that the helpee will realize the necessity of supporting such a program by developing check- or think-steps. All of this means, of course, that the helper invariably shoulders an increasing responsibility when it comes to initiating with the helpee —

and attending and responding to any signs of helpee confusion.

During this final stage of program development, the helper must continue to promote and support the helpee's development of appropriate steps — in this case those think-steps that will ensure the successful completion of do-steps. But the helper must also be ready to go beyond this if and when the helpee shows signs of floundering. More specifically, the helper must be ready to respond to any problems the helpee encounters in dealing with the *facts, concepts,* and/or *principles* involved in her or his program.

The simplest level of understanding involves factual material. Yet many helpees encounter difficulty at this level. The helpee must know the *facts* bound up in each do-and think-step. Essie, for example, had never heard of a "Service Directory." Her helper responded to her puzzled expression when he suggested this rich source of prospective employers by explaining exactly what a state's "Service Directory" was and where in the library Essie should look for one. By responding in this way, the helper remedied a deficit in Essie's level of factual understanding.

At the next level of complexity, helpees must understand all of the various *concepts* that their separate think- and do-steps entail. In general, concepts tell how something can or should be done while facts simply indicate what something is. Thus concepts have the same relationship to facts as adjectives or adverbs do to nouns or verbs. Returning to Essie's program, her helper found that Essie really did not understand what a "complete" entry on her job list would involve. The helper initiated some exploration of the concept of "completeness," which resulted in Essie outlining the specific items of information that each entry on her list should have.

Principles, of course, are far more complex than either concepts or facts. Simply stated, principles explain why something should be done rather than how it should be done (concepts) or what it is (facts). It is essential that the helpee understand the principles flowing from and influencing her or his own program. Unless the helpee knows why a given activity is important, it is doubtful that he or she will invest it with much thought or effort. Here again, we can see the importance of understanding principles by returning to Essie's program. She initially thought that 10 or 15 employers would be enough for her job list. Once she was helped to understand the principle involved, however — that her chances of landing a really good job would increase in direct proportion to the number of prospective employers on her list — she set her sights much higher.

In summary, then, the task of the effective helper during this final phase of program development is twofold: to assist the helpee in developing a series of before-, during-, and after-think-steps for each secondary and primary do-step; and, at the same time, to make sure that the helpee has a firm grasp of the various facts, concepts, and principles bound up in these steps.

The helper who has successfully promoted a helpee's involvement, exploration, understanding, and preliminary action will invariably be anxious to promote the helpee's development of an effective program of action. Yet it may turn out in some cases that a helper finds himself or herself dealing with a helpee goal that lies outside that helper's field of competency or experience. For example, a helper involved in peer counseling might find that a given helpee's drug-related problem involved reaching a goal of getting off drugs completely within a particular period of time. Unless the helper has a background of experience with similar drug-related situations and has been able to develop successful programs to reach similar goals in the past, he or she will have to proceed very carefully indeed. There are really two options open to the helper in such situations. If the helper knows of another individual who possesses both program-development skills and the required background of experience, he or she can refer the helpee to this individual. If no such person is available, the helper and/or the helpee will have to obtain the necessary information before the helper can develop a program. If the helpee has been functioning at a high level, the helper may ask this helpee to gather necessary information about procedures, consequences, and the like and then come back for a new round of counseling in order to work out a program. If the helpee has been functioning at a relatively low level — and this may be more likely in terms of our hypothetical drug-related case — the helper himself or herself can gather the necessary information before attempting to put together an effective program.

The point, of course, is that program-development skills are as substantive and essential as any other set of skills in the area of human services. The skilled helper knows the limits of his or her specialty knowledge in any area and is not afraid to seek outside advice or help when appropriate. By the same token, however, the skilled helper knows that the helpee's best interests can only be served by conjoining specialty knowledge with concrete and functional program-development techniques. In the terms of our sample situation, the helpee with a drug problem will not be helped by a knowledgeable doctor with no program-development skills any more than he or she will be helped by a counselor with program-development skills but no medical knowledge. The final program must be both systematically developed and substantively appropriate if the helpee is going to succeed in reaching her or his goal.

Bette and Jimmy

Jimmy Bessom squirmed in his seat. "Great — so what I oughta do is work parttime for Morris and go to school like maybe afternoons and nights. Only —"

Bette smiled. "You feel nervous about what'll happen if you try switching everything around like that."

"Yeah." Jimmy nodded his agreement. "I mean — heck, I don't even know if Morris will give me that kinda job — or if I can get the courses I need at night — or — anything!"

"It's pretty confusing when there are so many 'ifs' involved," Bette responded, her expression sympathetic. "But we're not done figuring things out yet, you know. What kind of help would it be if I just helped you figure out where you wanted to get to and didn't help you decide how to get there?"

"Huh?" Jimmy looked at her uncertainly. "But — I mean — what more can you do for me?"

"Let's just find out," Bette said. And she proceeded to tell Jimmy about the ways in which they could go about developing a program of action- and think-steps to get him where he wanted to go.

"The point is," she said, "there's no way you can get where you want if you just start out blindly and try to do everything at once. Instead, what we've got to do is lay out a series of steps for you to take that will lead you to your goal."

Jimmy nodded his understanding. Man, this woman just didn't quit! Even after the way she had listened to him and helped him, Jimmy had still been half-afraid that she would just send him off to make out as best he could on his own. But she was still with him. Incredible!

"Let's start by laying out the really big steps you've got to take," Bette suggested. "And let's really begin by laying out the last major step you have to take."

"How come we start with the last step?"

"Simple. That way you can be sure that the program you have will really get you where you want to go. We'll do the last step first, then the first step, then fill in all the gaps."

Working together, Jimmy and Bette decided that his program would really have two major parts or goals: getting the specific classes he needed and getting the parttime job with Morris.

"I think I ought to work out my schedule first and make getting the parttime job my final goal," Jimmy said, his eyes on the paper that Bette had been using to make some tentative notes.

Bette nodded. "You'll really feel more confident if you know the scheduling problem is all worked out," she said. At the same time she thought to herself that this statement probably said more than Jimmy himself realized about his fundamental priorities. "OK, then. We'll say your final goal is to get the parttime job. Now, what do you think is the last thing you'll actually have to do before getting that job?"

Jimmy thought about this. "I don't know," he said slowly. "I guess maybe just talk Morris into offering me the job. I mean, once he does that I'm home free, right?"

"Right," Bette agreed. "That's good. So we can say that your last big step will be to have a good interview with this guy Morris."

In the end, Bette and Jimmy outlined a series of five major or primary steps leading to Jimmy's ultimate goal. First, he needed to get an academic advisor who was familiar with the evening as well as the day program. Then he needed to determine which of the available courses would fulfill his own requirements. His third step would be to register for these courses. Next, he would develop his job application by deciding just what he had to offer and when he would be able to work. Finally, he would have an interview with Morris. Here is how Jimmy's primary steps look on paper:

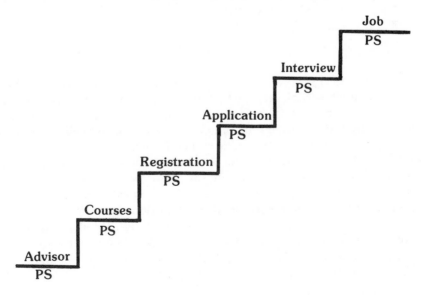

"That's great," Jimmy said. But he still looked uncertain. "The only thing is, how can I do all those things? I mean, like you said, these are all big steps."

So Bette explained to Jimmy how each major or primary step could be turned into a separate goal. "Then all you need to do is develop some smaller, secondary steps to reach each of these goals."

"Hey, yeah!" Jimmy finally saw the light. "I got you! It's like that dumb old joke. You know — how do you eat an elephant?"

Bette grinned. "I don't know. How *do* you eat an elephant?"

"You take one large bite every day for ten years!"

Bette groaned and Jimmy shrugged and grinned. Fairly soon they were knee-deep in secondary steps designed to help Jimmy complete each of his major or primary steps. In order to choose an appropriate advisor, Jimmy would get references from friends in night classes, obtain an appointment with the person who received the strongest recommendation and ask that person if she or he would be willing to serve as his advisor; if this proved impossible, Jimmy would be able to recycle the steps until he secured an advisor. Here is how these secondary steps looked once Jimmy and Bette had plotted them out:

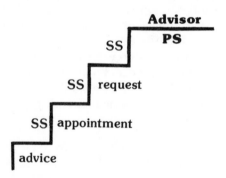

The last thing Bette helped Jimmy do was develop a series of before-, during-, and after-think-steps, which he could use to monitor his progress.

"For example," Bette said. "Before you ask any friends in night school about advisors they would recommend, you can ask yourself 'Is this student someone whose opinion I can really respect?' Then, during your conversation with each of these friends, you can be thinking 'Am I getting the information I need to help me decide which advisor might be most helpful?' And after you've finished talking with your friends, you can ask yourself 'Which of the people that have been recommended sound right for me?'"

Before finishing up this stage of things, Bette helped Jimmy to assign specific time limits to each of his action-steps. They decided to allow one week for Jimmy to switch his registration to the afternoon and night classes and another week to secure an interview with Morris.

"Hot damn," Jimmy exclaimed as they finished with his program. "It looked so hard at first! But — heck, there's nothing here I can't handle pretty well."

Once again, Bette had managed to use appropriate helping skills to work things out for Jimmy. She knew that, even at this stage of Jimmy's movement toward his goal, common sense would not be sufficient to assure his success.

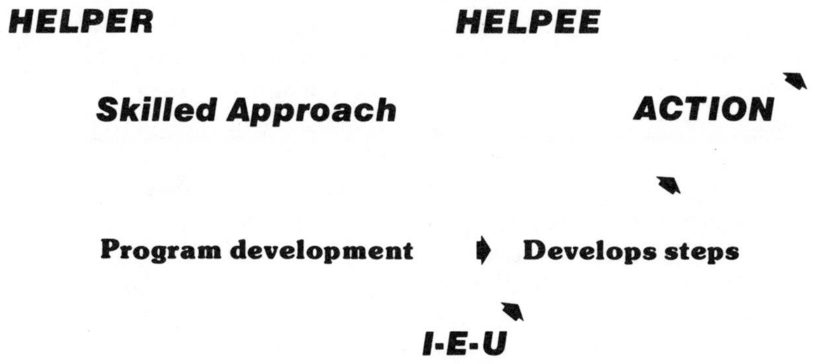

HELPER   **HELPEE**

Skilled Approach   **ACTION**

Program development ▶ **Develops steps**

I-E-U

Figure 6-2: Helper's program-development skills promote helpee's development of functional steps.

In the end, few if any helpees will be able to attain their goals unless they have developed an effective program of action — a program based on systematic and sequential steps; a program that includes think-steps to support each action-step. A program designed to move helpees from where they are to where they want to be.

The Research Background

The development of behavioral steps to enable helpees to achieve observable goals requires a set of helper skills different from those skills required of the helper in the first two phases of the helping process. At one time in the historical development of the field of helping, these helper action-skills were seen not only as different from the more traditional insight-oriented approaches but also as mutually exclusive. Because of antithetical theoretical foundations, helpers rarely if ever tried to achieve changes in both the helpee's insights and actions.

The Conflict Between Insight and Action Goals

As mentioned in an earlier chapter, there are many schools or theories of psychotherapy. A meaningful way of categorizing these schools has been provided by London (1964), who divided the therapeutic schools into either *insight* or *action* approaches to psychotherapy. "Insight" therapists (such as Freudians, Rogerians, or existentialists) believe that the achievement of certain insights by the client would permit him or her to regain a measure of control over his or her problems; for such therapists, the client's insight is the critical goal of psychotherapy, The major differences between various insight approaches revolves around the question "insight into what?"

In contrast, "action" therapist (such as Wolpe, Skinner, Eysenck) believe that the removal of the patient's symptomatic behavior is the most important therapeutic goal, and that the client insight into the cause and development of the symptom is largely irrelevant — and certainly not crucial. London (1964) provides an excellent annotated bibliography that traces the historical development and mutual antagonism that existed between proponents of these two fundamental therapeutic approaches.

In 1966 Carkhuff presented a model for training therapists that, rather than further separating the "insight" and "action" approaches, provided a framework for recognizing the potential contributions of both the schools of therapeutic thought. The "insight" approaches were recognized by Carkhuff as being potentially helpful in establishing a therapeutic relationship and in helping the client to become aware of his or her specific deficits. The action approaches provided the potential means of defining these goals in observable terms and specifying the behaviors necessary to achieve goals in observable terms and specifying the behaviors necessary to achieve these goals. The artificial dichotomy between the "insight" and "action" approaches could be meaningfully bridged; and the research and development of the three-phase helping model occurred, resulting in an eclectic model of helping with continued attempts to integrate the skills of what heretofore had been considered the antagonistic views of the "insight' and "action" approaches (Carkhuff, 1969; Carkhuff & Berenson, 1967, 1977).

Teaching as Treatment

In 1971, Carkhuff suggested that training clients directly in the skills that they need to function in society could be a potent treatment method. In other words, once the helper has established an effective therapeutic relationship, identified with the helpee what specific goals need to be attained, and developed the necessary program steps, the helper can then involve the helpee in skills-training programs designed to achieve these goals. These initial attempts at skills-training of clients form the foundation of the *teaching as treatment* process illustrated in the last chapter. The main difference between the teaching and training approaches is that as a helper moves from training individual clients to teaching groups of clients, the helper-teacher must be much more knowledgeable about the learning-management processes and those teaching skills needed by the helper to facilitate the skill-learning process of groups of clients (Carkhuff & Berenson, 1976). Many different attempts at psychological education have followed the teaching-as-treatment model (Authier, Gustafson, Guerney, & Kasdorf, 1975; Ivey, 1976; Sprinthall & Mosher, 1971).

In addition, there are many types of programs that have emerged from the action-oriented behavioristic approaches (e.g., see Lazarus, 1971). Skills-training programs have been developed for many different clients with many different skills deficits. For example, the literature has reported on such programs as diverse as public speaking for anxious clients (Fremouw & Zitter, 1978); study deficits for students (Lent & Russell, 1978); migraine headache education (Mitchell & White, 1976). To decrease migraines, Mitchell and White taught patients environmental analysis skills, self-recording skills, monitoring skills, and relaxation skills. Randhawa (1978) found that interpersonal skills formed a part of job maintenance across occupations. A variety of programs have taught job-related skills. For example, mentally retarded clients were shown to be capable of learning job-interviewing skills (Grinnell & Lieberman, 1977); offenders with psychiatric histories not only changed their perceptions about their chances for employment through skill training, but also obtained more jobs than the control group (Twentyman, Jenson, & Kloss, 1978); career-decision-making skills can be taught to helpees (Egner & Jackson, 1978). Other researchers have developed social skills programs. Socially anxious men have been taught conversational skills and dating skills (Curran, 1977). Chronic patients taught social skills exhibited a decreased level of arguing and fighting on their hospital wards, a change that was maintained over a three-month follow-up period (Matson & Stephens, 1978). Trower, Bryant, and Argyle (1977) investigated the difference between systematic desensitization and a social skills training package that included training in conversational skills, discrimination of nonverbal cues, and so forth. Twenty unskilled patients and twenty socially phobic patients were trained. The phobic patients responded equally well to both forms of intervention. The social skills training, however, reduced the anxiety level of both groups while also changing behaviors. This approach was further explicated by Trower, Yardley, Bryant, & Shaw (1978). Meichenbaum (1977) developed a program to teach hospitalized schizophrenics self-instruction skills to develop appropriate social behaviors. Patients were able to learn attention skills, coping skills to handle frustration, and observation skills to monitor the effects of their own behavior.

Interestingly enough, however, some of the most ingenious skills-training programs have been designed based on the skills of the insight-oriented approaches. For example, programs have been developed to systematically teach clients the same relationship skills that the effective helper uses in the first two phases of the helping process. That is, skills-training programs have been developed to teach clients how to respond to others and themselves in a skillful manner so that these clients may function more effectively in interpersonal situations.

Some of the earliest skills-training programs trained psychiatric inpatients in responding skills (Pierce & Drasgow, 1969; Vitalo, 1971). Both of these studies found that psychiatric patients could be trained to function at higher levels of interpersonal skills and that these trained patients achieved a higher level of interpersonal functioning than a variety of control and other treatment conditions. Similar results have been found in training parents (Carkhuff & Bierman, 1970; Reed, Roberts, & Forehand, 1977) and mixed racial groups (Carkhuff & Banks, 1970).

The value of teaching as marital treatment has been recently well explored in the literature (Luber, 1978). One study trained married couples who were experiencing marital difficulties in both the responsive and initiative interpersonal skills and then compared their therapeutic outcome with couples counseled by a more traditional insight-oriented approach (Valle & Marinelli, 1975). Therapy-outcome data indicated that the trained group had outperformed the traditionally counseled group on all outcome measures. The efficacy of communication-skill training in marital dysfunction has been further supported by Epstein and Jackson (1978).

Another recent study employed responding-skills training as a means of treating college student clients who had sought help for "personal-social" problems at a university counseling clinic (Cabush & Edwards, 1976). Compared to a control group of clients who were counseled by a more traditional insight-oriented approach, the skills-training helpees significantly outperformed the control group of helpees on six counseling outcome measures. Different approaches have attempted to teach still other interpersonal skills to psychiatric patients (Goldstein, Sprafkin, & Gershaw, 1976; Goldsmith & McFall, 1975).

No doubt the most comprehensive study of the effects of a training-as-treatment approach has been the changeover of an entire institution for delinquent boys from a custodial to a skills-training orientation (Carkhuff, 1974). Correctional personnel with no credentials in mental health were trained in the interpersonal, problem-solving, and program-development skills outlined in this text. Using their program-development skills, the correctional personnel helped develop more than 80 skills-training programs in a variety of physical, emotional, and intellectual areas of functioning.

The results achieved by these correctional personnel were quite dramatic, indicating that they were able to bring about a kind of inmate change of which credentialed mental health professionals would be justifiably proud. A summary of the various outcome criteria used indicates that the delinquents' physical functioning increased 50 percent, their emotional functioning 100 percent, and their intellectual functioning 15 percent. The physical functioning measure assessed seven categories of physical fitness as developed by the American Association for Health, Physical Education

203

and Recreation; the measure of emotional functioning involved a rating of the juveniles' human relations skills; intellectual functioning involved a rating of the juveniles' human relations skills; intellectual functioning was measured by the California Achievement Test. In addition to the gains in physical, emotional, and intellectual functioning, during a one-year period, "elopement" status decreased 56 percent, recidivism rates decreased 34 percent, and crime in the community surrounding the institution decreased 34 percent.

Following this, there were an extensive number of programs utilizing teaching as a preferred mode of treatment with problem youth. For example, delinquent youth with low levels of living, learning and working skills were trained in those skills. The results yielded recidivism rates of approximately ten percent after one year and twenty percent after two years, against base rates for the control groups of fifty percent and seventy percent respectively (Collingwood, Douds, Williams, & Wilson, 1978).

In addition, youthful minority-group dropout learners were taught how-to-learn reading and mathematics skills. The results indicated that the students were able to gain one year or more in intellectual achievement in twenty six two-hour sessions (Berenson, Berenson, Berenson, Carkhuff, Griffin & Ransom, 1978). Clearly, teaching was a preferred mode of treatment in both preventative and rehabilitative modalities.

References

Authier, J., Gustafson, K., Guerney, B., & Kasdorf, J.A. The psychological practitioner as a teacher. *Counseling Psychologist,* 1975, *5,* 31-50.

Berenson, D.H., Berenson, S.R., Berenson, B.G., Carkhuff, R.R., Griffin, A.H., & Ransom, B.M. The physical, emotional and intellectual effects of teaching learning skills to minority group drop-out learners. *Research Reports, Carkhuff Institute of Human Technology,* 1978, Vol. I, Number 3.

Cabush, D.W., & Edwards, J.J. Training clients to help themselves: Outcome effects of training college students in facilitative self-responding. *Journal of Counseling Psychology,* 1976, *23,* 34-39.

Carkhuff, R.R. Training in the counseling and therapeutic practices: Requiem or reveille? *Journal of Counseling Psychology*, 1966, *13*, 360-367.

Carkhuff, R.R. *Helping and human relations.* New York: Holt, Rinehart & Winston, 1969.

Carkhuff, R.R. Training as a preferred mode of treatment. *Journal of Counseling Psychology*, 1971, *18*, 123-131.

Carkhuff, R.R. *Cry twice!* Amherst, Mass.: Human Resource Development Press, 1974.

Carkhuff, R.R., & Banks, G. Training as a preferred mode of facilitating relations between races and generations. *Journal of Counseling Psychology*, 1970, *17*, 413-418.

Carkhuff, R.R., & Berenson, B.G. *Beyond counseling and therapy.* New York: Holt, Rinehart & Winston, 1967, 1977.

Carkhuff, R.R., & Berenson, B.G. *Teaching as treatment.* Amherst, Mass.: Human Resource Development Press, 1976.

Carkhuff, R.R., & Bierman, R. Training as a preferred mode of facilitating relations between races and generations. *Journal of Counseling Psychology*, 1970, *17*, 157-161.

Collingwood, T., Douds, A., Williams H., & Wilson, R.D. *Developing youth resources.* Amherst, Mass.: Carkhuff Institute of Human Technology, 1978.

Curran, J. Skills training as an approach to treatment of heterosexual-social anxiety: A review. *Psychological Bulletin,* 1977, *84*, 140-157.

Dancer, D., Braukmann, C., Schumaker, J., Kirigin, K., Willner, A., & Wolf, M. The training and validation of behavioral observation and description skills. *Behavior Modification,* 1978, *12*(1), 113-134.

Egner, J., & Jackson, D. Effectiveness of a counseling intervention program for teaching career decision-making skills. *Journal of Counseling Psychology,* 1978, *25*, 45-52.

Epstein, N., & Jackson, E. An outcome study of short-term communication training with married couples. *Journal of Consulting and Clinical Psychology,* 1978, *46*, 207-212.

Fremouw, W., & Zitter, R. A comparison of skills training and cognitive restructuring-relaxation for the treatment of speech anxiety. *Behavior Therapy,* 1978, *9*, 248-260.

Goldstein, A., Sprafkin, R., Gershaw, N. *Skill training for community living,* Elmsford, New York: Pergammon Press, 1976.

Grinnell, R., & Lieberman, A. Teaching the mentally retarded job-interviewing skills. *Journal of Counseling Psychology,* 1977, *24,* 332-337.

Ivey, A. The counselor as teacher. *Personnel and Guidance Journal,* 1976, *54,* 431-434.

Lazarus, A. *Behavior therapy and beyond.* New York: McGraw-Hill, 1971.

Lent, R., & Russell, R. Treatment of test anxiety by cue-controlled desensitization and study-skills training. *Journal of Counseling Psychology,* 1978, *25,* 217-224.

London, P. *The modes and morals of psychotherapy.* New York: Holt, Rinehart & Winston, 1964.

Luber, R. Teaching models in marital therapy: A review and research issues. *Behavior Modification,* 1978, *2,* 77-91.

Matson, J., & Stephens, R. Increasing the appropriate behavior of explosive chronic psychiatric patients with a social skills training package. *Behavior Modification,* 1978, *2,* 61-72.

Meichenbaum, D. *Cognitive behavior modification: An integrative approach.* New York: Plenum Press, 1977.

Mitchell, K., & White, R. Self-management of tension headaches: A case study. *Journal of Behavior Therapy and Experimental Psychiatry,* 1976, *7,* 246-254.

Pierce, R., & Drasgow, J. Teaching facilitative interpersonal functioning to psychiatric inpatients. *Journal of Counseling Psychology,* 1969, *16,* 295-298.

Randhawa, B. Clustering of skills and occupations: A generic skills approach to occupational training. *Journal of Vocational Behavior,* 1978, *12,* 80-92.

Reed, S., Roberts, M., & Forehand, R. Evaluation of effectiveness of standardized parent training programs in altering the interaction of mothers and non-compliant children. *Behavior Modification,* 1977, *1,* 323-350.

Sprinthall, N., & Mosher, R.L. Psychological education: A means to promote personal development during adolescence. *The Counseling Psychologist,* 1971, *2*(4), 3-84.

Trower, P., Bryant, B., & Argyle, M. *Social skills and mental health.* London: Methuen Press, 1977.

Trower, P., Yardley, K., Bryant, B., & Shaw, P. The treatment of social failure: A comparison of anxiety reduction and skills acquisition. *Behavior Modification,* 1978, *2,* 41-60.

Twentyman, C., Jenson, M., & Kloss, J. Social skills training for the complex offender: Employment-seeking skills. *Journal of Clinical Psychology,* 1978, *34,* 320-325.

Valle, S.K., & Marinelli, R.P. Training in human relations skills as a preferred mode of treatment for married couples. *Journal of Marriage and Family Counseling,* 1975, 359-365.

Vitalo, R. Teaching improved interpersonal functioning as a preferred mode of treatment. *Journal of Clinical Psychology,* 1971, *27,* 166-170.

Goldsmith, J., and McFall, R. Development and evaluation of an interpersonal skills training program for psychiatric inpatients. *Journal of Abnormal Psychology,* 1975, *84,* 57-58.

What is this chapter all about?

This chapter focuses on the helpee's need to design a series of *primary, secondary,* and *check-* or *think-steps* leading to the goal and on the *program-development skills* the helper must use to facilitate these helpee activities.

Where does this fit in the overall helping model?

Chapter two dealt with helpee *involvement,* chapter three with helpee *exploration,* and chapter four with helpee *understanding.* Each of these concerns represents a primary phase of helpee activity within the prehelping/helping process. In chapter five we focused on defining the goal and choosing a course of action as the first two steps within the primary phase of helpee *action.* The development of a program of action- and check-steps considered in this chapter represents the third stage of helpee concern within this same primary phase of helpee *action.*

PREHELPING ‖ **HELPING**

ACTION
Taking the steps

UNDERSTANDING

EXPLORATION

INVOLVEMENT

Why is it important for the helpee to develop a program?

Just as helpees need more than personalized yet general goals to work toward, so they need more than an optimum yet general course of action in order to reach those goals. The personalized goal is like the statement, "I'm going to get myself out West this summer;" once defined, the statement becomes something like, "I'm going to get to San Francisco by the end of June." In similar fashion, the course of action a helpee has already selected is like the decision to travel to San Francisco by car; now the individual must decide what car, how much money is needed, where he or she will stop each night, and a host of other essential details. *An effective program indicates exactly what the helpee must do and think at each point on the way to the goal.* Thus it ensures that the helpee will be able to reach the destination successfully.

Who must do what in developing a program?

Program development requires helpees to enter a new round of exploration, understanding, and action. Helpees must *explore* the territory between their present location and the goal. Helpees must *understand* what behaviors are required and how these may be affected by their unique strengths and limitations. And the helpees must *act* in order to design the systematic series of steps that will lead to the goal. Thus the helper will have to continue to use *attending, responding,* and *personalizing* skills with the helpees. More specifically, the helper must make sure that the helpees' primary and secondary action-steps are appropriate in nature and scope, that they lead directly to the major goal without leaving any gaps into which the helpees could fall and that each of these action-steps has been defined in concrete and measurable terms. Going on, the helper must make sure that the helpees develop a series of check- or think-steps to accompany each action- or do-step in the program — for only in this way will the helpees be able to control and focus their efforts at each level in the program. Helpee check-steps ensure that the helpee fully understands all of the *facts, concepts,* and *principles* inherent in each action- or do-step.

When should program development begin?

The helper should initiate program-development activities with the helpee once the goal has been defined and the optimum course of action selected. Under no circumstances should the helper encourage or even allow the helpee to try reaching the goal until a careful and comprehensive program has been developed to meet the unique needs of that helpee.

The comprehensiveness of the program that is developed will vary as a function of the helpee's level of functioning and the complexity of the skill area. The general principle is: The more simple and brief the program is the better — *as long as it gets the client to the goal.* However, the skilled helper must be capable of writing a very lengthy and complex program, consisting of many primary, secondary, and check-steps, if that is what the helpee needs in order to reach the goal.

How can you practice the skills of program development?

Start by setting and defining a real goal for yourself. Maybe you are a smoker who wants to quit. Or maybe you would like to make a major purchase during the next year — a new car or even a home. Or maybe you have some definite career plans that can be stated in terms of a concrete goal. Once you have defined your goal, use the helper skills outline in the last chapter to select your best course of action to reach this goal. Now you will be ready for program development. First, chart a series of primary steps. Then treat each of these primary steps as a goal in its own right and develop a series of secondary steps to reach it. Make sure that there are no gaps in your action-program and that each step is defined in terms of the amount of time and the specific behaviors involved. Ask yourself if you are sure you can complete each secondary and primary step successfully. Now develop a series of check- or think-steps to allow you to monitor your progress before, during, and after your performance of each primary and secondary action-step. Repeat the entire procedure for a number of different goals, both small and large. You will find that you gradually become quite comfortable with the specific procedures involved in program development. It is, after all, nothing more than a matter of simplifying the difficult and ensuring the uncertain, by separating large tasks into smaller ones and then making sure that each small task can and will be completed successfully.

helping people take steps 7
to reach their goals: INITIATING SKILLS III

Overview

1. Once a helpee has defined the goal, chosen a course of action, and developed a program, he or she must complete the action-phase of the helping process by actually *taking the steps to reach the goal.*

2. The effective helper promotes the helpee's ability to take the steps in the program successfully by employing *program-implementation skills.*

3. The helpee must *master* each step in the final program — an especially critical concern when new behaviors or skills are involved.

4. In order to master each step, the helper works with the helpee to outline in advance a series of procedures focusing on *repetition, review, rehearsal,* and *possible rewriting* of specific activities.

5. In order to *master* some steps, the helper may have to *teach* the helpee by using the *Tell-Show-Do* teaching process.

6. The helpee must develop specific ways of *reinforcing* performance at each step-level in the program.

7. At this stage, the helper outlines with the helpee a series of both *positive and negative reinforcements* flowing from the helpee's own frame of reference.

8. Finally, the helpee must be able to *recycle* the important new skills and procedures developed in order to make personal growth self-sustaining in every living, learning, and working area.

9. The helper works to ensure that the helpee can recycle not only the skills involving *program development* and *program implementation* but also the fundamental phases of *exploration, understanding,* and *action.*

10. The helpee's concern here with program mastery, reinforcement, and recycling *ensures that no loose ends remain and that the helpee can reach the goal successfully.*

11. The helper's aim must embrace not only the helpee's attainment of the immediate goal but also the helpee's *development of skills that will allow continued and self-sustaining growth.*

In earlier chapters we considered the initial importance of helpee *involvement* as promoted and sustained by the helper's use of basic attending skills. Whatever their reasons for seeking aid, helpees cannot begin to deal with their problems until they have been drawn into full and active involvement in the helping session to the point where they are able to present personally relevant material. We have considered the critical role of helpee *exploration,* promoted by the helper's use of specific *responding skills.* Helpees, like all the rest of us, tend to view most troublesome situations at first in externalized terms: "Here's what's happening, here's what they're doing to my life, here are all the outside forces that are making things a mess for me." We considered the way in which, as the skilled helper begins to *personalize* with helpees at deeper and more meaningful levels, these same helpees begin to gain a fuller and more meaningful *understanding* of their individual roles in and responsibility in their situations. As exploration showed the helpees where they are, so understanding allows them to see where they are in the light of where they want or need to be. Finally, we considered the importance of those initial stages of helpee *action* that the helper promotes through use of *goal-development, problem-solving,* and *program-development skills.* Having accepted and articulated specific and personalized goals, helpees begin to act by defining these goals in meaningful, measurable, and realistic terms. And having developed these goals by defining them and selecting optimum courses of action, the helpees continue to act on their own behalfs by developing specific, systematic, and detailed programs comprising a series of action-steps and a supporting series of check-steps. Their own efforts in the area of program development assure that the helpees can reach the goals they have set for themselves.

As before, the question that confronts the helper at this point is a simple yet critical one: "Is my job over? Have I done enough?" And as before — and as one final story will show — the answer must again be no.

Ruth Tanaka was pleased by the way the Hardys handled themselves. A solidly middle-class couple with (presumably) a solid, middle-class commitment to the American dream of the Good Life, they had undoubtedly assumed in the past that the only people who needed counseling or related types of professional help were "sickies." John Hardy's words and actions still reflected his belief that the strong person was able to take care of himself. And Marge Hardy obviously felt that the mere fact of their appearance in Ruth's office was a tacit admission that she and John were weak people. Yet here they were, their love and concern for their children clearly far stronger than their socially conditioned aversion to seeking outside help. They were proud people, Ruth realized — and yet their pride did not deny them flexibility. They were self-righteous people — and yet they refused to allow their feelings of righteousness to cut them off from their children.

It was not difficult for Ruth to involve the Hardys in the helping situation. For one thing, they were both motivated in constructive directions. And for another thing, everything about Ruth's office and Ruth's own manner conspired to put the Hardys at their ease and tell them, in effect, "You've come to the right place. I want to help you. I can help you." Nor was it difficult for Ruth to promote the Hardys' own exploration of their situation. On the contrary, they seemed immensely relieved to have found someone at last who was willing to hear them out.

"It's like they don't even recognize we're their parents," Marge said. "Just last night I tried to talk to Mikey about how he was doing in school. He's a junior this year, so his grades will really count when he starts applying to colleges. And I knew he hadn't been studying much. Hardly at all. But when I sat down to talk, all he could say was 'Oh, Ma, knock it off, will you? Let me live my life!' "

Ruth noted the way Marge's hands clung to one another, her fingers twining and untwining. "So you felt hurt because he couldn't see that it was his life you cared about," she responded. Marge nodded dumbly.

"It's the same way with all three of them," John said. "Mike, Sharon, Billy — they all seem to be pulling away from us." He shrugged and looked around the room. "Sure, I know what everyone says — that it's just a stage kids have to go through. But I think that's bull. Me and Marge, neither one of us ever throught of treating our parents the way our own kids treat us. Like we weren't even there, for God's sake!"

"It makes you angry that they don't even seem to know you're around," Ruth responded.

215

"You're damned straight it makes me angry," John blurted. Then he colored slightly and shook his head. "I don't mean to get upset. After all, it's not your problem, is it?"

"No, of course it's not," Marge put in. "But we still thought — that is, we hope — that maybe you'll be able to help us out with it," she finished lamely, looking at Ruth with an entreating expression.

Ruth nodded. "You feel badly about coming to someone else with your problems," she said. "But the problems themselves still seem pretty overwhelming."

She continued to respond to the Hardys as they explored the various aspects of their troubled relationship with their children. And gradually, making sure that the Hardys were with her at each step, she began to initiate more fully with them, helping them to reach an understanding of the ways in which they themselves were responsible for their own feelings of inadequacy and frustration.

"It sounds to me as though you feel weak as parents because you can't figure out how to get your real concern — your love — across to the children," Ruth said at one point. And both of the Hardys were right there with her.

"Yeah, it's like — like we're not doing something we should be doing," Marge agreed. And John added, "I mean, the way I see it now, there's no good to be served by blaming everything on the kids. They aren't perfect by a long shot. But there's also no way we can hope to control everything they do. So maybe what we have to do is figure out a better way of handling ourselves in our relationship with them."

Ruth smiled. It was always a real pleasure to work with people whose sincerity of purpose wiped out any vested interest they might have in preserving their own precious self-images. Going on, she helped the Hardys to translate their personalized understanding into a goal: to develop the specific interpersonal skills they needed to communicate on a meaningful and constructive level with their children. Once this goal had been set, Ruth helped the Hardys to develop it more effectively. She outlined for them the specific behavioral ingredients that made up "interpersonal skills": attending, observing, listening, responding, and so on. They talked at length about what each of these separate behaviors or activities involved, and Ruth outlined some sample responses they could use in dealing with their children's expressions of personal feeling, meaning, and problems. Finally, she worked with the Hardys to develop a careful program of activity that would take them from where they were to where they wanted to be.

"It's funny," John said as he and Marge rose to leave. "We all talk a lot about skills. I mean, I've had young guys come on the job and do well and others come on and do a lousy job — and the difference is always the kinds of skills they've picked up along the way. But I never thought before about people needing real kinds of skills just to get along with other people. Now that I do think about it, I see it couldn't be any other way!"

Both the Hardys thanked Ruth profusely for her time and help. It was obvious that they felt far, far better about themselves and their situation than they had in many weeks. For the first time they knew where they were going in their relationship with their children — and they knew how to get there.

Success story? Perhaps so, perhaps not. Given the quality of help they received from Ruth, the Hardys may well have been able to improve their relationship with their children. But they may also have failed to reach their common goal. Despite everything that Ruth did for them — promoting exploration and understanding, helping them to see things in personalized terms over which they could exert control, facilitating their development of a goal and a program of action designed to take them to this goal — there was still a major element of chance in the Hardys' subsequent endeavors. For Ruth — beguiled, perhaps, by her admiration for the Hardys and their honest expressions of need — did not carry things as far as she should have. Instead, she allowed herself at the last moment to slip into what we have come to recognize as the "common sense" approach to helping. Convinced that the Hardys had everything they needed for success, she did not follow up her program-development efforts with an equal degree of attention to the question of program implementation. More specifically, she made sure they had a program but did not make sure that they had mastered this program to the point where they could put it to practical and successful use. Ruth did not go over various ways in which the Hardys could *master* every new step or level in their program. She did not deal with the need for them to *reinforce* their successful completion of each new step in the program. Finally, she did not spend any time at all going over the ways in which the Hardys could *recycle* their new skills for subsequent use in a wide range of situations.

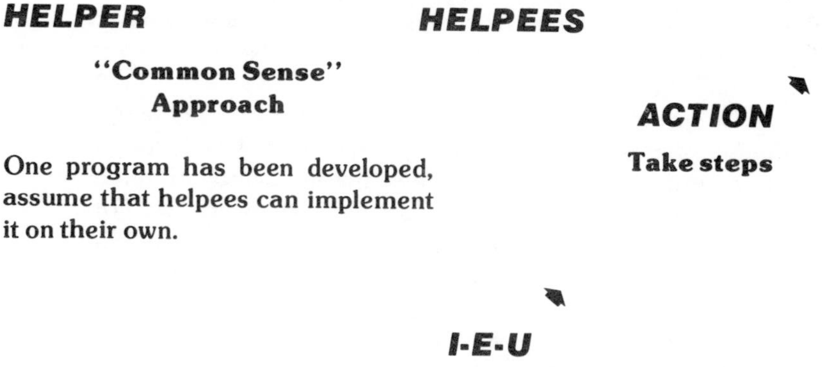

HELPER   **HELPEES**

> "**Common Sense**"
> **Approach**
>
> One program has been developed, assume that helpees can implement it on their own.

ACTION

Take steps

I-E-U

Figure 7-1: Impact of Ruth's "common sense" approach on helpee's ability to act.

Once again, the commitment of the truly effective helper must be to helpee success — nothing more and nothing less. And the best way to ensure helpee success is to eliminate any and all chances of failure in the helpee's movement toward the goal. Among other things, this means that helper efforts in program development must be followed by an equal degree of attention to modes of program implementation. In this chapter, then, we will focus on the ways in which the helper can promote success by treating methods of *mastering, reinforcing,* and *recycling* the steps in any program — the key ingredients in program implementation.

Mastering
The
Steps

Helpee Goal:

To ensure successful completion of eech step in the program.

The ultimate test of any program of action is not how easy or difficult it may have been to develop nor how few or how many steps it may include but how well it works for the helpee once implemented. With program implementation, as with program development, the most important criterion is success. Thus it is important for helpees to begin the process of program implementation by making sure that they master each separate step. This will involve a fourfold process of *repetition, review, rehearsal,* and possible *rewriting*. In situations where the helpee is completely unfamiliar with the program steps, mastery will involve the helper *teaching* the steps.

The program developed to reach a goal may contain a number of specific steps that the helpee can already do. In other words, the helpee may have already demonstrated a mastery of the particular behaviors these steps involve. For example, one young helpee might set a goal in terms of her school life of earning an honors grade in a science course. One of her primary steps could well involve writing a research paper. And one of the secondary steps leading to completion of this paper might involve visiting the library. It could well turn out that this helpee has made frequent trips to the library in the past. Thus she has, in effect, mastered the "going to the library" behavior required by this particular secondary step.

But what of those action-steps that a helpee has not

previously mastered? The key to such mastery is *repetition*. Only by learning and then repeating a particular behavior or set of behaviors can a helpee really master the skills involved.

Our sample helpee knows how to get to the library because she has been there before. A simple action like going to the library can be mastered with relatively few repetitions. But let us assume that this helpee has never had occasion to use the card catalog in the library before and that she is now required to do so by another secondary step in her program. She can get instruction from one of the librarians on the use of the catalog. But the helpee will not have mastered the skill of using the card catalog until she has repeated the activity at least six times — and perhaps many more times than this.

Simple repetition of an activity or behavior accomplishes a great deal. In physiological terms, it conditions the muscles and nervous system to perform a new task effectively — regardless of whether the task involves using chopsticks instead of a fork or physically attending to study materials that demand a high level of concentration. Repetition also enforces the creation of constructive psychological habits; after a number of conversations in which we have gone out of our way to make frequent eye contact, making such contact begins to seem both netural and beneficial. Although there can be no had-and-fast rule concerning the number of repetitions required to master a skill, there is an obvious and important rule of thumb: the more complex a task, the higher the number of repetitions required for mastery.

In summary, then, the helpee can only hope to master new and unfamiliar behaviors required by the program through frequent and correct repetition of these same behaviors.

Now let us look at the second procedure required for real program mastery: *review*. As we have seen, each of the primary and secondary steps in a helpee's program involve specific activities or behaviors. If the program has been developed effectively, the helpee's behaviors at the level of any given step will be dependent upon successful performance at the previous step-level. For example, a helpee whose physical fitness program requires her to jog one-half-mile at the third primary step-level will be prepared to do so if she has already shown herself able to jog one-quarter-mile at the second primary step-level. Making each new step dependent upon each previous step ensures that the helpee will have the practical skills necessary to master all of the steps in the program. Having developed and begun the program, however, the helpee cannot afford to take success at any step-level for granted. Rather, the helpee must pause when each new set of behaviors is mastered in order to *review* all previous behaviors. In this way, the helpee can spot any weaknesses in performance and take steps to correct them.

This process of review involves more than the *after-think*-steps that should accompany completion of any single *do*-step. In reviewing, the helpee should look back over the whole range of behaviors mastered up to this point and ask, "Have I really built a solid foundation for taking my next step?" The female helpee working on a physical fitness program, for example, might respond to this question by saying, "Well, I did all right on the eighth-mile run that was my first primary step. But I just barely made it through the quarter-mile run. I was so bushed at the end I could hardly stand." While she has certainly completed the primary step involving a quarter-mile run, her review shows her that she has not really mastered it to the point where she can go on to the next step. The skills foundation she has sought to build is still not strong enough to support her efforts at the next step-level. Having come to this conclusion, the helpee decides to go back and repeat her efforts at the last step-level until she has really mastered the skill of running a quarter-mile.

Once helpees have reviewed their progress through all previous steps, they are ready to go on. Rather than leaping into the next activity immediately, however, helpees should begin by *rehearsing* the specific behaviors required by the step in question. Rehearsal of this sort really means practicing the skills involved in the new step in a preliminary manner. It means getting ready to perform the behaviors in the step. For our sample runner, rehearsing the next step may simply involve getting warmed-up and ready to go. For another helpee whose goal of developing interpersonal skills requires the primary-step behavior of responding to feelings, rehearsal may involve actually repeating the format for such responses a number of times before actually attempting to respond to another person during an interaction.

In summary, then, the helpee's implementation of any given step should be preceded by a review of progress through all previous steps and a rehearsal of the specific behaviors required by the new step. Only in this way can mastery of the separate steps that make up the overall program be ensured.

Finally, the helpee must be able to *rewrite* any step in the final program if the need arises. Sometimes a program may appear perfect in every respect until the helpee actually begins to take the steps; it may then be discovered that a given primary or secondary step really does not "work" — or that a given check-step does not provide the sort of accurate feedback on progress that is required. For example, a secondary step may turn out to involve unexpectedly difficult or complex behaviors. The helpee must be able to rewrite any given segment of the program so that movement from step to step may continue in a smooth, gradually incremental fashion. Such rewriting may involve breaking one step into several steps, adding new steps, or modifying the specific behaviors previously referred to by a particular step. The ability to rewrite elements within a program ensures that the helpee can maintain mastery over the entire program once he or she has actually begun moving toward the goal.

Helper Skills:

Initiating with the helpee to ensure full mastery of and control over the program of action.

The helper may or may not be present during any given phase of the helpee's implementation of the program. Thus it is crucial that the helper spend time in advance working out procedures for repetition, review, rehearsal, and possible rewriting with the helpee.

The helper should begin by making sure that the helpee understands the basic principles involved in repetition, review, and rehearsal for program mastery. Most importantly, the helper must emphasize that only frequent and correct repetition of new behaviors or tasks will enable the helpee to add these new skills to her or his repertoire. Again, repetition is the critical key to mastery of each new step.

The principle underlying the review process has already been touched upon: By reviewing past performance at every step, the helpee can correct weaknesses and strengthen and reinforce the foundation upon which all subsequent steps will be based. The helper must promote the helpee's understanding that performance at any new level can never be stronger than the cumulative strength and level of skills reflected at previous step-levels. By the same token, the helper must ensure that the helpee understands the principle underlying rehearsal: That by getting ready for or practicing the actual behaviors required by a new step, the helpee can ensure mastery of that step.

The helper can suggest particular methods of repetition, review, and rehearsal based on the unique characteristics of a given helpee's program. In terms of repetition, for example, the helper must recognize which program behaviors are familiar to the helpee and are ones the helpee has already fully mastered. Any behaviors or activities that do not fall into this category are, by definition, new ones the helpee has yet to master. The helper must make sure that the helpee has an effective method of repeating each of these new behaviors: by taking half-a-dozen or more "dry runs" through a library's card catalog, for example; by practicing the same greeting skills on at least 10 people each day; or perhaps by going over and over again the complex substeps required to get up, bathe, dress, eat a good breakfast, and leave the house for work in less than 45 minutes.

In outlining possible review procedures, the helper may develop a series of questions for the helpee. We have already noted one question of this sort for the helpee: "Have I really built a solid foundation for taking my next step?" Depending upon the particular program involved, the helper may suggest any number of other questions that the helpee can ask and answer:

"Have I been performing within the time limits set for each step?"

"Have I been completing the number of behaviors or activities required by each step?"

"Has the quality of activity at each step been high enough?" (For example, a man completing a physical fitness step involving completion of 10 push-ups may have actually done 10 but allowed his lower body to remain on the floor during the last 3; thus he could determine that the quality of his push-ups at this level had not been sufficiently high.)

The helper can work with the helpee to outline appropriate rehearsal procedures for each new step, beginning this process, perhaps, by asking the helpee, "How might you practice this new set of skills before you actually try them out?" By exploring the helpee's answer to questions of this sort, the helper can arrive at a specific and concrete set of rehearsal strategies for every new step in the helpee's program.

Finally, of course, the helper should clarify for the helpee the procedures required if the helpee has to *rewrite* any step or steps in the final program. In essense, the helpee must know that rewriting invariably means breaking complex behaviors down into simpler steps, adding new behaviors or steps where gaps appear in a program, or modifying the description of behaviors required at any particular step-level. If both helper and helpee have worked effectively in developing the original program, the helpee may never have to rewrite; yet the ability to do so if the need arises can sometimes make the difference between helpee success and failure.

There are many occasions when the helper's focus on repetition, review, rehearsal, and rewriting are all that is needed to ensure that the helpees can master the program steps. However, on many other occasions the helper needs to *teach* the helpees how to perform certain program steps. At times helpees have no understanding of what a particular program step involves. They are totally unfamiliar with the particular skill step. Thus they would not be able to master such a step and acquire the skill without specific instruction. For example, a psychiatrically disabled client may be involved in a program to improve her or his job-seeking skills. One of the primary steps in his or her program is to "verbally describe his or her job assets to the interviewer." This particular client has rarely, if ever, been able to say positive things about him or herself. Even with detailed secondary steps as to how to accomplish this skill-step, the client still cannot understand exactly what the behavior should be. These primary and secondary steps, though seemingly simple to many other people, are totally removed from this client's previous experience.

An example from a non-client situation would be an adult who is trying to learn how to ice skate. Although the steps involved in an ice skating program could be objectively described, the mastery of ice skating skills could be more effectively achieved if an instructor taught some of the steps. In this situation the learner has no familiarity or previous experience with how this skill is mastered.

Although effective teachers do incorporate in their teaching program the principles of repetition, review, rehearsal, and rewriting, they also use a systematic teaching process to ensure that the helpee learns most efficiently. The particular teaching process that has been most effective in teaching skills to helpees can be most simply described as a Tell/Show/Do teaching process. Each primary or secondary program step for which the helpee needs instruction should include each of these components. The Tell-step involves explaining the program step to the helpee; the Show-step involves demonstrating the program step to the helpee; and the Do-step involves setting up practice situations for the helpee to perform the step. With this teaching process, a helpee who is totally unfamiliar with a particular step will be provided with an auditory, visual, and kinesthetic learning experience.

In essence, the Tell-step is composed of the specific instructions for performing the skill. Being told what steps to do is a common method by which many of us learn. Thus, the Tell-step is a fundamental step in a teaching program. The problem in many teaching programs, however, is not that the Tell-step is forgotten, but that the Tell-step is often not followed by the Show- and Do-steps. Merely telling a person exactly what to do does not ensure that it will be done differently or better. This is especially true of helpee behavior that is well established. For example, simply telling a helpee to "increase the number of times each week he verbally praises his spouse" does not ensure that the helpee will be able to perform this behavior very effectively. He must be shown what this step involves and be given opportunities for practicing it.

The importance of the Show-step in mastering skills has achieved increasing recognition. The opportunity to see the skill step being performed is a fundamental part of any systematic teaching program. The helper will routinely want to include a demonstration of the step before the helpee actually attempts the skill. By means of both the Tell- and Show-steps, the helper will have maximized the possibility of success in the helpee's initial practice attempts. In developing the Show-step, it is important to remember that before helpers observe a demonstration, they should be given an explanation of exactly what they will be observing. The preceding Tell-step of the teaching process informs them what to look for. For example, "The first step involved in describing your job assets to an interviewer is to say to the interviewer all the facts about yourself that indicate that you can do the job. As you watch the videotape demonstration of this step, listen for the two sentences that describe these job assets."

The Do-step ensures that the helpee has the opportunity to actually perform the skill-step. The teaching of skills must culminate in the helpee's performance or doing of the skill. The number and variety of practice situations that are included in the teaching program is a function of the helpee's needs. The particular practice situations can be sequenced in terms of their approximation to the natural setting in which the helpee must actually apply the skill. For example, the components of a job interview could be practiced first with the helper role-playing the interviewer, then a stranger to the helpee role-playing the interviewer, and finally simulated interviews in the office of a job interviewer. In general, the helper will want to ensure that some practice does take place in the most realistic and natural environments.

By promoting the development of program-mastery procedures, the helper can do a great deal to prepare the helpee for program implementation. Some helpees finish their program-development activities full of fire and enthusiasm; they cannot wait to get started. By outlining repetition, review, rehearsal, and rewriting strategies, the effective helper can ensure that these helpees do not go off half-cocked. By directly teaching helpees those steps with which they are totally unfamiliar, the helper can prevent implementation failure. Some helpees experience misgivings even after they have developed a comprehensive program designed to lead them to their goals; in effect, they say, "Sure, it looks great — but can I do it?" By taking the time to work out effective mastery procedures, the helper can do a great deal to promote self-confidence in such helpees.

Reinforcing
The
Steps

Helpee Goal:

To develop methods of reinforcing successful completion to each step in the program.

Regardless of the attitudes with which helpees may enter into a helping situation, the great majority of them are positively motivated by the time they have finished developing an effective program of action. They see — perhaps for the first time — that they can get where they want to go. They really want to make it. The world being what it is, however, much of this initial motivation can often be eroded by the pressures of performing well in the world at large. Thus it is important for each helpee to guard against such loss of motivation by developing ways of reinforcing performance at every step.

The simplest sort of reinforcement involves developing a specific set of rewards and punishments. The helpee decides how successful completion of a given step can be rewarded — and how failure to complete that step may be punished. The male helpee involved in a study-skills program, for example, might decide to reward himself for completing each step in his program by watching a favorite TV program at night — and to punish himself for failure to complete a step satisfactorily by missing the program. Another helpee might decide to reward herself for successful efforts during the week by making a date for the weekend. She could then determine that inadequate performance at any step-level during the week would be punished by staying home alone rather than spending the time with someone whose company she enjoys.

As with repetition, review, and rehearsal procedures, reinforcement schedules should be worked out by the helpee in advance of actual program implementation. Such schedules are, in effect, subprograms carefully designed to support and promote effective effort at every level of the major program of action. Developing ways of reinforcing successful performance allows helpees to build continuing motivation into their programs. In the absence of reinforcement of any kind, helpees may begin strongly but lose that essential "drive" partway through their programs. With appropriate rewards and punishments built into the major program, however, the helpees will invariably be able to function at peak energy and motivation throughout their movement toward the goal.

Helper Skills:

Initiating with the helpee to ensure that all positive and negative modes of reinforcement are appropriate and effective.

In working with the helpee to develop appropriate modes of reinforcement, the helper must remember one thing: It is absolutely essential that all rewards and punishment flow from the helpee's own frame of reference. Regardless of how effective the helper may feel a given mode of reinforcement is, that reward or punishment will be worse than useless unless the helpee assigns it the appropriate positive or negative value.

The problem of inappropriate or helper-centered reinforcement may seem a simple one, but this is often not the case. For example, one helper was working with a woman who had developed a program designed to help her make better and more effective use of her time. The helper knew that this woman enjoyed spending time relaxing by herself. He also knew she liked to spend time out of doors. For these reasons, he suggested that she reward her own successful completion of steps each day by scheduling a half-hour walk after supper. The woman admitted that this would certainly be pleasurable yet seemed strangely hesitant. After further talk, she revealed that rewarding herself in this way would actually prompt feelings of considerable guilt because of her invalid husband!

The most effective way in which the helper can assist in developing modes of reinforcement that reflect the helpee's own frame of reference is to go back through the initial phases of the helping process itself. The helper should promote further helpee exploration in order to pinpoint those things the helpee values positively and negatively. The helper should promote new helpee understanding of the ways in which certain of these positive and negative things may be used to reinforce performance throughout the program. And finally, the helper should promote new helpee action to select and define the specific rewards and punishments that will be most effective at each step in the program.

It will be simplest if the helper begins by promoting the helpee's selection of appropriate rewards for successful performance. Depending on the particular program and the specific steps involved, a single type of reward may be used throughout or separate rewards may be linked with separate steps. Again, the most important thing for the helper to remember is that all rewards must come from the helpee's own unique frame of reference. The effect of each reward should be to reinforce successful completion of a given step and enhance the positive aspects of helpee behavior during the next step.

Once the system of rewards has been set, the helper can work with the helpee to develop an equally appropriate set of punishments. In most if not all cases, these punishments can be simply the "flip side" of the rewards already scheduled. If a helpee is to be rewarded for success by having dessert, for example, the punishment can be to accept the denial of dessert. By the same token, a helpee who has decided to reward success by spending $5 on recreational activities at the end of the week can decide to punish any failure by putting that same $5 in a special savings account that can only be tapped once the final goal has been successfully reached.

In promoting helpee development of modes of reinforcement, the helper should also stress the importance of helpee vigilance. The problem with rewards and punishments that are self-imposed, of course, is that everyone wants the former and no one wants the latter. Having set up a simple schedule of rewards and punishments, some helpees may be tempted to rationalize any future failures: "I know I could have done it if it hadn't been for —" The helper should emphasize the need for the helpee to keep a vigilant eye on performance at each step-level and to judge the performance of each behavior as objectively as possible. Yes, there are often extenuating circumstances that promote helpee failure. But the fact remains that failure is failure. Regardless of the reasons, a helpee who fails is a helpee who has not and may not reach the goal. The temptation to rationalize such failure may be great at times. But unless the helpee resists such temptation and persists in punishing all failures and rewarding only success, he or she may have to live with failure a long time. The effective helper knows this — and emphasizes the importance of vigilance in order to make sure that the helpee stays on track and moves toward the goal.

Recycling
The
Steps

Helpee Goal:

To transfer skills and strategies to new areas of personal concern.

If the helpee has moved successfully through all of the separate prehelping and helping phases, the goal will be reached. This goal may have been a relatively minor one (e.g., to earn a better grade in a particular class in school) or it may have been a major one (e.g., to acquire the interpersonal skills necessary for better communication with family and friends). Regardless of the scope of the original goal, however, there is one constant: the skills reflected in the helping process itself. Each helpee has learned to perform a number of specific activities. In particular, the helpee can now set goals, develop programs designed to reach these goals, and then implement these same programs. All of the skills involved in these activities can and should be *recycled* by the helpee.

To see the process of recycling at work, let us go back for a moment to Essie, the helpee in the last chapter who developed a program designed to get her a new and higher-paying job that carried with it some real chance for promotion. In developing her program, Essie charted a series of primary steps (PS) that included the following activities:

PS: Developing a job list.

PS: Developing application materials.

PS: Developing personal contact materials.

PS: Getting in touch with employers.

PS: Developing interview skills.

Each of these primary steps, as we saw, entailed a separate series of secondary steps. For example, Essie's second primary step (developing application materials) included the following secondary steps:

PS: Developing application materials.

SS: Developing assets based on educational background.

SS: Developing assets based on previous work experience.

Once Essie has landed a new job, she can recycle the various skills she has acquired in order to set a new goal related to promotion within the company, develop a program to reach this new goal, and implement the program. Her new promotion-oriented program would almost certainly reflect the same primary step referred to as "developing application materials." But now Essie could amend the secondary steps to reflect her new position:

PS: Developing application materials.

SS: Developing assets based on educational background.

SS: Developing assets based on previous work experience.

SS: *Developing assets based on present work experience.*

Of these secondary steps, the last one cited would almost certainly prove the most valuable in helping Essie reach her goal of promotion within the company.

We can see, then, that programs and skills can be recycled within the same area in order to achieve new goals in that area. Many programs recycled in this manner, like Essie's programs in her career area, will closely resemble one another. But the helpee can also recycle critical skills and develop additional programs to reach goals in totally new areas. For example, Essie found that her very success in her career or working area was causing problems in other areas. Specifically, she found that her husband — who had seemed relatively untroubled by her stalled career — was now increasingly irritated by the way in which more and more of her energy and interest was focused upon her new job. At the same time, Essie found that her new job was making demands on her that she had not really been trained to meet. She felt as though she wanted to learn more within the framework of either a training program or a series of classes.

Essie had reached her goal in the area of working. In doing so, she had acquired more than the specific skills required by her particular program. She had also learned about the whole process of goal setting and program development itself. Thus, confronted by real concerns in the areas of living and learning, she could set new goals in these areas and then develop comprehensive programs to reach them. For example, she decided that her goal in terms of her marriage was to improve her relationship with her husband to the point where they had fewer than one serious quarrel every two weeks; one critical step in the program she developed to reach this goal involved the acquisition of some basic interpersonal skills. Similarly, she decided that she had to improve her repertoire of working skills to the point where she needed to ask her superior no more than one procedures-oriented question each week. In order to reach this goal, she developed a program that included enrolling in two company-sponsored training seminars.

Like Essie, then, a helpee can and should recycle all those program-development and program-implementation skills that have been acquired during the helping process. These skills can be recycled to achieve new goals in the same area, like Essie's new goal of promotion in the original career area — or to achieve goals in new areas, like Essie's goals in the new living and learning areas. Helpees are like everyone else: they certainly have many different aims in all the areas of living, learning, and working. By reaching initial goals, helpees show that they are capable of growing. By recycling skills and steps in order to reach new goals, helpees can show that they are capable of continued growth.

Helper Skills:

Initiating with the helpee to ensure that she or he can recycle skills within the same area and within other living, learning, and working areas.

The helpee who has finished the several previous phases of program development and program implementation will be focusing primary concern on reaching the original goal. This is as it should be. However, the effective helper knows that the helpee should gain more from the helping process itself than the limited ability to reach a single, isolated goal. Thus, the helper should do everything possible to promote the helpee's ability to recycle steps and skills. If necessary and appropriate, additional helping sessions can be scheduled to deal with the concept and procedures of program recycling.

The essential skills the helper must promote in the helpee are those of goal development (i.e., defining the goal and choosing a course of action), program development, and program implementation. The helpee must be able to set new and meaningful goals in concrete and measurable terms. He or she must be able to go on to develop a comprehensive program of primary and secondary *do*-steps and supporting check- or *think*-steps. Finally, the helpee must be able to implement the program by outlining specific methods of program mastery, reinforcement, and recycling.

The helper committed to promoting recycling skills must be concerned with the specifics of all of the above activities. But the helper's concern must also extend beyond these activities. For the helper knows full well that these and all other human skills and activities rest upon the foundation of individual *exploration*, individual *understanding*, and individual *action*. Consequently, the helper must ensure that the helpee is capable of self-exploration at any time; then the helpee will always be able to answer the question, "Where am I?" The helper must ensure that the helpee knows how to gain an understanding of his or her situation in accurate and personalized terms; then the helpee will always be able to answer the question, "Where am I in relation to where I want or need to be?" Finally, the helper must ensure that the helpee knows how to develop and implement an effective program of action; then the helpee will always be able to answer the question, "How can I get from where I am to where I want to be?"

Recycling is the last step the helpee takes. But it is far from the least important. In fact, promoting the helpee's ability to recycle steps and skills may be the most crucial thing the helper does. For by promoting the ability to recycle strategies, the helper transforms the helpee from a dependent person into an independent and autonomous individual — that is, from a loser on his or her own terms into a winner on anyone's terms.

Bette and Jimmy

"That's it, then, huh?" Jimmy said, eagerness written all over his face. Bette laughed.

"You're really ready to go," she responded. "It must feel good to have a definite idea of where you're going and what you're going to do."

"You said it! First off, I've got to find out which of the kids I know are taking night classes so's I can ask them about advisors."

"You got it! But — before you rush off, let's just take a couple more minutes to sort of polish things up."

Jimmy hesistated. Once he might have resented anyone's attempt to slow him down or get him to wait. But somehow Bette seemed different. She had really helped him get his head straight. It only made sense for him to hear her out — even though everything was pretty much set as far as he was concerned.

"Sure," Jimmy said, sitting back in his chair again. "I guess we ought to check everything out before I really get started."

What Bette had in mind, of course, were the several steps involved in program implementation. She knew that Jimmy had a great deal of energy and enthusiasm right now. But she did not want to take any chances lest that motivation dissipate.

"There are a few things you should be able to do for yourself as you get started with your program," she told Jimmy. "In the first place, you ought to have some way of *reviewing* what you've done so far at any given point in your program." And she spent several minutes outlining some review procedures that Jimmy could use.

"What it sounds like is that I should always be able to tell whether I'm ready to go on to the next step," Jimmy said. Bette nodded. "That's it. You've got to be able to look back at all the progress you've made and ask yourself 'Are there any gaps or holes in what I've done? Am I really sure that I'm set to move ahead?' If you can answer this kind of question positively, you'll be ready to move on. On the other hand, if you spot any weak places in your progress — like maybe overlooking some courses that you'd need for graduation — this kind of review procedure allows you to fix things up before going any further."

Next Bette outlined some specific ways in which Jimmy could *rehearse* the behaviors involved in each new action step before he actually tried to take that step. "A good example would be your interview with Mr. Morris," she told him. "Once you've completed all the secondary steps we designed for you — outlining your work skills, getting some recommendations, and so on — you can actually practice what you'll do in the interview by asking someone else to play the part of Morris while you rehearse what you'll say. The more realistic you can make your rehearsal, the better practice it will be and the better your chances will be of handling the real interview effectively."

Jimmy nodded, then grinned. "I get you. Listen, my old man is gonna be so happy that I'm staying in school, I bet I can get him to play Morris's part and help me practice!"

The last thing Bette discussed with Jimmy was the idea of *recycling* the skills and procedures he had acquired. "See, you're going to feel differently about a lot of things once you've got this school and work situation straightened out. And one thing's for sure — you're eventually going to want to set some new goals for yourself. Maybe one will involve going on to a four-year college. Or maybe it will be getting a really good job. And there'll be a lot of little goals besides the big ones. It doesn't matter. What you've learned to do here will work to get you from wherever you are to wherever you want to be."

Bette took Jimmy back over the steps he had already taken. He had *explored* his situation to find out what was really happening in his life. He had translated the fruits of this exploration into terms that allowed him to *understand* where he was in light of where he wanted to be. And he had learned to *act* by taking the steps involved in program development and program implementation.

HELPER   **HELPEE**

Skilled Approach

                                                              ACTION ↖

  Program implementation   **Takes steps**

                            I-E-U ↖

Figure 7-2: Program-implementation skills used by the helper to promote helpee action.

"It's incredible," Jimmy said, turning back to Bette in the doorway. "My head feels like it's cramed with stuff I never thought about before. But — but — it's like I know it will just start falling into place when I start doing the steps in my program."

Bette smiled. "You're right, Jimmy. The key to the whole thing is actually doing the things you've learned — not just thinking about them. And certainly not sitting around letting yourself get hassled by them. The more you do in an organized and wide-awake way, the more you learn to do."

Jimmy nodded and turned to leave. At the last minute he turned again in the doorway, pausing awkwardly. "I'm not much good at this kind of thing," he said "But — thanks for your help! I really mean that."

Bette smiled again. "Go do it," she said. "And make sure you keep me posted on how it's working out."

"I sure will." Jimmy grinned. "The best thing is that now I really know it *is* working out!" And he was gone.

The Research Background

Clearly, the behavior modification approaches have emphasized the action-phase of helping. Whether they represented schools of classical conditioning (Eysenck, 1960; Salter, 1961; Wolpe, 1958) or instrumental conditioning (Bandura, 1961; Frank, 1961; Krasner & Ullman, 1965; Salzinger, 1959), these behavior theorists employed directive forms of control and manipulation of primary drives. The therapist was often seen as a programmed therapy machine or computer that administered specified reinforcement schedules to the response system of a machinelike patient. Unfortunately, the patient had to fit the model.

Other learning theorists attempted to incorporate a more humanistic view of therapy within the framework of learning or social reinforcement theory (Dollard & Miller, 1950; Miller, 1959; Mowrer, 1953; Murray, 1963; Shaffer & Lazarus, 1952). Their attempts, however, were theoretically limited since they only translated counseling and therapy into learning theory terminology without usually offering any new treatment techniques (Lazarus, 1977).

In general, however, there has been a proliferation of behavioristic techniques. Some of the techniques derived from classical conditioning have been the following procedures: counter-conditioning; direct conditioning; reciprocal

inhibition; extinction. Evolving from instrumental conditioning have been the following procedures: shaping; environmental manipulations; punishment; omission learning
(Carkhuff & Berenson, 1967, 1977).

Although these treatment procedures offered a wide
variety of rehabilitative techniques, they only represented a
limited number of dimensions of generic program-
development skills (Carkhuff, 1969, 1972). In other words,
all action-steps moving systematically toward operational
goals are programs. Among these behavior-therapy programs are the variety of rehabilitative techniques derived
from classical and instrumental conditioning approaches.
However, the variety of programs remaining to be developed
is multitudinous. They are as varied as there are individuals
with personalized problems and goals. In addition, the
generic concept of program development allows for the development of proactive or preventative helping programs
rather than the reaction or rehabilitative programs typically
emphasized by the behavioristic approaches.

Learning Theory — Neither Necessary nor Sufficient

Getting people to learn new behaviors by means of a
reinforcement process has been a longstanding concern of
"action" therapists. These helpers, typically referred to as
behavior modifiers or behavior therapists, have examined
the reinforcement process in great detail. In the process, they
have developed a set of principles, a complex theory, and a
new jargon. The helper who wishes to employ straightforward reinforcement strategies in the action-phase may
wonder if she need master this new language and theory
before she is capable of employing a reinforcing technique.

Although the mastery of new concepts and theories may
be a valuable learning experience in and of itself, the helper
who wishes to implement action-steps need not be a knowledgeable learning theorist. There is, in fact, no single learning theory that can account for all the various behavioral
techniques that have emerged. Naive adherents to a
learning-theory approach may themselves not be aware of
all the controversy generated by the inadequacy of learning
theory to explain and predict why and how certain behavioral techniques work. Indeed, it has been the commitment of the behaviorist to ongoing research and technological development that has undermined the relevance and

applicability of learning theory. At present there is a raging debate among behaviorists as to whether or not the introduction of a new variant of reinforcement techniques is "truly" behavioral. The use of cognitive variables as behaviors that can be reinforced has led to the thought that perhaps reinforcers do not, as has been traditionally believed, need to immediately follow a behavior in order to be effective (Mahoney, 1977; Meichenbaum, 1977). As researchers, some behaviorists see the pitfalls of their adherence to old explanations (Bandura, 1977; Lazarus, 1977; Thoreson & Coates, 1978), while others have a desire to maintain their previous reductionist beliefs (Greenspoon & Lamal, 1978; Jones, Nelson, Kazdin, 1977; Kantor, 1978; Skinner, 1977; Wolpe, 1978).

London (1972) has written a provocative article that addresses the need for "action" therapists to devote their energies to developing new learning techniques rather than trying to stretch learning theory to account for the effectiveness of each new technique that emerges. London maintains that all the theorems and principles espoused by the behaviorists of the 1960s can be " . . . reduced to one or one-and-a-half principles — namely, that learning depends on the connections in time, space, and attention between what you do and what happens to you subsequently." Armed with this principle, the helper can devise various reinforcement strategies designed to encourage helpers to implement their skills programs. Hints for helpers who wish to learn more about various reinforcement strategies are also available (Watson & Thorp, 1972).

What Is Reinforcing?

As mentioned in this text, the actual reinforcement must come from the helpee's frame of reference. This often necessitates further exploration for the helper and helpee. To assist the helper in expanding all the possible activities that might possess reinforcement properties, various reinforcement survey schedules have been developed (Cautela and Kastenbaum, 1967).

However, it must not be overlooked that helpers who possess high levels of responding and initiating skills are themselves very potent reinforcers for their helpees (Mickelson & Stevic, 1971; Vitalo, 1970). Verbal comments of the high-level functioning person can increase the efficiency and outcome of the learning process. Thus, statements of praise made by a skilled helper can serve as powerful reinforcement from the helpee's frame of reference.

Another source of reinforcement for the helpee's attempts at developing new skilled behavior is the ability of the helper to model the behavior the helpee is learning to perform. A helper who has established personal reinforcement potency by means of a skillful therapeutic relationship and who can also perform the actual skill-steps the helper is trying to learn can function as a constructive model for the helpee. As a result, the helpee's willingness and ability to perform the program steps may be enhanced by a process of imitative learning on the helpee's part.

A recent research study was designed to test the hypothesis that an interpersonally skilled model would enhance the process of imitative learning (Dowling & Frantz, 1975). These researchers found that high-level functioning models generated significantly more imitative learning from their group members than either control group models or low-level functioning models, regardless of the particular behavior that was being modeled.

The major implication for the action-phase of helping — suggested by the various research investigations into the effects of helper level of interpersonal functioning on skill learning — is that the high-level functioning helper can improve a helpee's skilled performance by being both a reinforcing agent and a reinforcing model. By making reinforcing statements and by modeling the skill being learned, the helper can have a constructive impact on the skill-learning process.

The potency of these same interpersonal skills on the classroom learning process is also well documented (Aspy, 1972; Aspy & Roebuck, 1977). That is, students of teachers who possess high levels of responding and imitative skills learn more than the students of teachers who possess low levels of interpersonal skills. A recent text has been designed to teach teachers how to learn and apply these interpersonal skills in the classroom (Carkhuff, Berenson, & Pierce, 1977).

The Tell-Show-Do Teaching Process

Only recently have counselors started to learn how to teach skills — either to themselves or to their clients. Historically, counselor education programs taught counseling students only facts, concepts, and theories. Professional skills were learned primarily on the job, often through trial and error. Little if any specific skill-training occurred in the class-room or in the field. However, the realization gradually came that some of the apparently qualititative skills of counseling could be systematically and effectively taught to counselors-in-training, as well as to paraprofessionals (Carkhuff, 1966, 1969; Carkhuff & Berenson, 1967; Truax, Carkhuff, & Douds, 1964).

Based on their increasing ability to teach counseling skills to counseling students, the helping professionals have gradually moved to the teaching-as-treatment approaches referred to in chapter six. This emphasis on teaching as treatment, as well as the increasing popularity of skills-based counselor-training programs, has naturally focused more attention on the skills-teaching process (Carkhuff, 1971; Carkhuff & Berenson, 1976). Thus, it has only been relatively recently that a great many counselors have started not only to think of helping as a learning process but also of themselves as teachers (Carkhuff, 1971; Alschuler & Ivey, 1973; Ulmer & Franks, 1973). The technology involved in teaching *skills* has been described as comprising at least three elements: (1) providing verbal or written didactic in-structions; (2) proving models; and (3) providing or arrang-ing feedback on performance (Authier, Gustafson, Guerney, & Kasdorf, 1975) — or simply stated: *Tell, Show,* and *Do* (Carkhuff, 1972). A number of studies have attempted to tease out the differential effects of each of these specific components of the skill-teaching process (Edelstein & Eisler, 1976; Friedman, 1972; McFall & Twentyman, 1973; Payne, Weiss, & Kapp, 1973; Stone & Stein, 1978; Stone & Vance, 1976). Some investigators have directed their re-search at particular populations, ranging from psychotic patients to the therapists themselves (Jaffe & Carlson, 1976; Uhlemann, Lea, & Stone, 1976; Tosi & Eshbaugh, 1978; Teevan & Gabel, 1978). Others have studied the differential effects of the components of the teaching process by focusing on the training of particular skills — such as counselor empathy, assertiveness skills, and social skills (Hodge, Payne, & Wheeler, 1978; Kung, 1975; McFall & Lillesand, 1971; Peters, Cormier, & Cormier, 1978; Ronnestad, 1977; Wallace, Horan, Baker, & Hudson, 1975). Overall, the majority of the investigators found that teaching skills to various groups of clients is best done when using a combina-tion of didactic, modeling, and experiential components.

Refinements of these basic findings reinforce the princi-ples of *helping* that have been explicated thus far: (1) The level of *skill acquired,* using a *Tell/Show/Do* approach is *related to* the levels of *skill of the trainer/counselor/teacher* (Carkhuff, 1969; Carkhuff & Berenson, 1976). Still to be determined is the level of trainer's or supervisor's skills (Seligman, 1978). (2) The blending of experiential and didactic elements has most impact when the *learning is related to the learner's frame of reference;* this point of view is a growing trend in the world of business as well as counseling (Bell & Margolis, 1978). (3) The blend of these *teaching* modalities *must be individualized for different populations,* just as helping techniques are individualized according to *helpee deficits.* In a study that compared the use of behavioral rehearsal versus systematic training with and without modeling techniques, Eisler, Blanchard, Fitts, & Williams (1978) found that nonpsychotics could learn social skills without the modeling component. Modeling, however, was *essential* to the learning of the group labeled "schizophrenic." Systematic training was found to increase learning across all groups. Rehearsal alone was not effective. (4) Lastly, the best blend of Tell/Show/Do steps depends to a certain extent upon the content of the module being learned. In other words, the *skills employed* by the trainer/counselor *are determined by* the outcome *objectives* of the modules being taught. Understanding of material may be best achieved by simple didactic techniques; performance of a skill may necessitate all three components (Hersen, Eisler, & Miller, 1973).

Recycling — The Ultimate Therapy Outcome Criterion

Recycling should be the long-range goal of any helping effort. That is, long-term follow-up evaluations of therapy outcome should not only indicate that the helpee has maintained the gains achieved at the end of therapy but also that the helpee has continued to improve even after therapy has ceased. In other words, the helpee should be able to continue the learning and growth process in the absence of the helper.

The concept of *further improvement* after therapy termination (as opposed to simply *maintaining improvement*) has heretofore not been an area of significant concern for therapeutic researchers. It appears that only one study has systematically examined this concept (Palau, Leitner, Drasgow, & Drasgow, 1975).

These authors reported on a sequence of follow-up

studies (up to five years in length) of interpersonal-skills training programs. As expected, the follow-up-group averages were significantly higher than the pretraining-group averages; but what was most interesting to these authors was the finding that 8% to 30% of each training group continued to improve after training. These researchers hypothesized that those trainees who continued to improve were largely responsible for their own continued growth, based on their ability to emulate their trainer and to internalize the skill-learning process so as to ultimately make themselves their own model.

The issue of recycling the learning process so as to continue the process even after therapy is terminated remains a fruitful area for research. Enabling the helpee to recycle the learning process and grow in new and better ways must certainly be the ultimate goal of the skilled helper.

References

Alschuler, A., & Ivey, A. Getting into psychological education. *Personnel and Guidance Journal*, 1973, 5, 682-691.

Aspy, D. *Toward a technology for humanizing education*. Champaign, Ill.: Research Press, 1972.

Aspy, D., & Roebuck, F. *Kids don't learn from people they don't like*. Amherst, Mass.: Human Resource Development Press, 1977.

Authier, J., Gustafson, K., Guerney, B., & Kasdorf, J. The psychological practitioner as teacher: A theoretical-historical and practical review. *The Counseling Psychologist*, 1975, 5, 31-49.

Bandura, A. Psychotherapy as a learning process. *Psychological Bulletin*, 1961, 58, 143-157.

Bandura, A. Self-efficacy: Toward a unifying theory of behavioral change. *Psychological Review*, 1977, 84, 191-215.

Bell, C., & Margolis, F. Blending didactic and experiential learning methods. *Training and Development Journal*, August 1978, 16-18.

Carkhuff, R.R. Training in counseling and therapeutic practices: Requiem or reveille? *Journal of Counseling Psychology*, 1966, 13, 360-367.

Carkhuff, R.R. *Helping and human relations*. New York: Holt, Rinehart & Winston, 1969.

Carkhuff, R.R. Training as a preferred mode of treatment. *Journal of Counseling Psychology*, 1971, *18*, 123-131.

Carkhuff, R.R. The development of systematic human resource development models. *The Counseling Psychologist*, 1972, *3*, 4-11.

Carkhuff, R.R., & Berenson, B.G. *Beyond counseling and therapy*. New York: Holt, Rinehart & Winston, 1967, 1977.

Carkhuff, R.R., & Berenson, B.G. *Teaching as treatment*. Amherst, Mass.: Human Resource Development Press, 1976.

Carkhuff, R.R., Berenson, D.H., & Pierce, R.M. *The skills of teaching: Interpersonal skills. Teacher's guide*. Amherst, Mass.: Human Resource Development Press, 1977.

Cautela, J.R., & Kastenbaum, R. A reinforcement survey schedule for use in therapy, training and research. *Psychological Reports*, 1967, *20*, 1115-1130.

Dollard, J., & Miller, N.E. *Personality and Psychotherapy*. New York: McGraw-Hill, 1950.

Dowling, T.H., & Frantz, T.T. The influence of facilitative relationship on initiative learning. *Journal of Counseling Psychology*, 1975, *22*, 259-263.

Edelstein, B.A., & Eisler, R.M. Effects of modeling and modeling with instruction and feedback on behavioral components of social skills. *Behavior Therapy*, 1976, *6*, 382-389.

Eisler, R., Blanchard, E., Fitts, H., & Williams, J. Social skills training with and without modeling for schizophrenics and non-psychotic hospitalized psychiatric patients. *Behavior Modification*, 1978, *2*, 147-172.

Eysenck, H.J. (Ed.), *Behavior therapy and the neuroses*. New York: Pergamon, 1960.

Frank, J.D. *Persuasion and healing*. Baltimore, Md.: Johns Hopkins University Press, 1961.

Friedman, P.H. The effects of modeling, role-playing and participation on behavior change. In B.A. Maher (Ed.) *Progress in experimental personality research* (Vol. 6). New York: Academic Press, 1972, pp. 42-81.

Greenspoon, J., & Lamal, P. Cognitive behavior modification: Who needs it? *Psychological Record*, 1978, *28*, 343-351.

Hersen, M., Eisler, R., & Miller, P. Effects of practice instructions and modeling components of assertive behavior. *Behavior Research and Therapy*, 1973, *11*, 443-451.

Hodge, E., Payne, P., & Wheeler, D. Approaches to empathy training: Programmed individual supervision and professional vs. peer supervision. *Journal of Counseling Psychology*, 1978, *25*, 449-453.

Jaffe, P.G., & Carlson, P. Relative efficacy of modeling and instructions in eliciting social behaviors from chronic psychiatric patients. *Journal of Clinical Psychology*, 1976, *44*, 200-207.

Jones, R., Nelson, R., & Kazdin, A. The role of external variables in self-reinforcement. *Behavior Modification*, 1977, *1*, 147-178.

Kantor, J. Cognition as events and as psychic construction. *Psychological Record*, 1978, *28*, 329-342.

Krasner, L., & Ullman, L. *Research in behavior modification*. New York: Holt, Rinehart & Winston, 1965.

Kung, D. Lecturing, reading and modeling in counselor restatement training. *Journal of Counseling Psychology*, 1975, *22*, 542-546.

Lazarus, A. Has behavior therapy outlived its usefulness? *American Psychologist*, 1977, *32*, 550-554.

London, P. The end of ideology in behavior modification. *American Psychologist*, 1972, *27*, 913-920.

Mahoney, M. Reflections on the cognitive-learning trend in psychotherapy. *American Psychologist*, 1977, *32*, 5-13.

McFall, R., & Lillesand, D. Behavior rehearsal with modeling and coaching in assertive training. *Journal of Abnormal Psychology*, 1971, *77*, 313-323.

McFall, R., & Twentyman, T. Four experiments on relative contributions of rehearsal, modeling and coaching to assertive training. *Journal of Abnormal Psychology*, 1973, *81*, 199-218.

Meichenbaum, D. *Cognitive behavior modification: An integrative approach*. New York: Plenum Press, 1977.

Mickelson, D.J., & Stevic, R.R. Differential effects of facilitative and nonfacilitative behavioral counselors. *Journal of Counseling Psychology*, 1971, *18*, 314-317.

Miller, N.E. Liberalization of basic S-R concepts. In S. Koch (Ed.),

Psychology: A study of a science (Vol. 2). New York: McGraw-Hill, 1959.

Mowrer, O.H. *Psychotherapy: theory and research.* New York: Ronald, 1953.

Murray, E.J. Sociotropic — learning approach to psychotherapy. In P. Worshell and D. Burns (Eds.), *Personality change.* New York: Wiley, 1963.

Palau, J., Leitner, L., Drasgow, F., & Drasgow, J. Further improvement following therapy. *Group Psychotherapy and Psychodrama,* 1975, *27,* 1-4.

Payne, P., Weiss, B., & Kapp, R. Didactic, experiential and modeling factors in the learning of empathy. *Journal of Counseling Psychology,* 1973, *19,* 425-429.

Peters, L., Cormier, L., & Cormier, W. Effects of modeling, rehearsal feedback and remediation on acquisition of a counseling strategy. *Journal of Counseling Psychology,* 1978, *25,* 231-237.

Ronnestad, M. The effects of modeling, feedback and experiential methods on counselor empathy. *Counselor Education and Supervision,* 1977, *16,* 194-201.

Salter, A. *Conditional reflex therapy.* New York: Capricorn, 1961.

Salzinger, K. Experimental manipulation of verbal behavior: A review. *Journal of General Psychology,* 1959, *61,* 65-95.

Seligman, L. The relationship of facilitative functioning to effective peer supervision. *Counselor Education and Supervision,* 1978, *17,* 254-261.

Skinner, B.F. Why I am not a cognitive psychologist. *Behaviorism,* 1977, *5,* 1-10.

Stone, G., & Stein, M. Effects of modeling and instruction as a function of time, task and order. *Journal of Counseling Psychology,* 1978, *25,* 150-156.

Stone, G., & Vance, A. Instructions, modeling and rehearsal: Implications for training. *Journal of Counseling Psychology,* 1976, *23,* 272-279.

Teevan, K., & Gabel, H. Evaluation of modeling, role-playing and lecture discussion training techniques for college student mental health paraprofessionals. *Journal of Counseling Psychology,* 1978, *25,* 85-95.

Thoreson, C., & Coates, T. What does it mean to be a behavior therapist? *The Counseling Psychologist,* 1978, *7,* 3-21.

Tosi, D., & Eshbaugh, D. A cognitive-experiential approach to interpersonal and intrapersonal development of counselors and therapists. *Journal of Clinical Psychology*, 1978, *34*, 494-500.

Truax, C.B., Carkhuff, R.R., & Douds, J. Toward an integration of the didactic and experiential approaches to training in counseling and psychotherapy. *Journal of Counseling Psychology*, 1964, *11*, 240-247.

Uhlemann, M.R., Lea, G., & Stone, G. Effect of instructions and modeling on trainees low in interpersonal communication skills. *Journal of Counseling Psychology*, 1976, *23*, 509-513.

Ulmer, R., & Franks, C. A proposed integration of independent mental health facilities into behavioral social training programs. *Psychological Reports*, 1973, *32*, 95-104.

Vitalo, R. The effects of facilitative interpersonal functioning in a conditioning paradigm. *Journal of Counseling Psychology*, 1970, *17*, 141-144.

Wallace, W.G., Horan, J., Baker, S., & Hudson, G.R. Incremental effects of modeling and performance feedback in teaching decision-making counseling. *Journal of Counseling Psychology*, 1975, *22*, 570-572.

Watson, D.L., & Thorp, R.G. *Self-directed behavior: Self modification for personal adjustment*. Belmont, Calif.: Brooks/Cole, 1972.

Wolpe, J. *Psychotherapy by reciprocal inhibition*. Stanford, Calif.: Stanford University Press, 1958.

Wolpe, J. Cognition and causation in human behavior and its therapy. *American Psychologist*, May 1978, 437-446.

What is this chapter all about?

This chapter deals with the procedures that helpees must follow in *taking the steps* to reach their goals and with the specific *program-implementation skills* that the helper must use to promote helpee success.

Where does this fit in the overall helping model?

Again, the four major phases of helpee activities focus on helpee *involvement*, helpee *exploration*, helpee *understanding*, and helpee *action*. The procedures outlined in this chapter complete the sequence of activities entailed by the last of these four major phases; by actually *taking the steps* in the program, the helpee completes the *action*-phase of the overall helping process.

PREHELPING   **HELPING**

ACTION
Taking the steps

UNDERSTANDING

EXPLORATION

INVOLVEMENT

Why are the procedures in this chapter important to the helpee?

Like all of us, helpees can become so fired with enthusiasm that they go off half-cocked. In such cases, the most carefully developed program may not be sufficient to guard against failure. Thus, it is essential that helpees know clearly in advance how they can *master, reinforce,* and *recycle* the skills recently acquired. The helper who sends a helpee off without using those *program implementation* skills designed to facilitate program mastery, reinforcement, and recycling may undo all that has so far been accomplished with the helpee.

Who must do what to ensure that the helpee takes the steps in the program successfully?

The helper must continue to attend and respond to the helpee. At the same time, the helper must initiate with the helpee to ensure that "all systems are go." In particular, the helper must outline specific methods of *repetition, review, rehearsal,* and *rewriting* to promote helpee mastery of each step in the program. The helper must be sure to *teach* those steps with which the helpee is totally unfamiliar. Next, the helper must be certain that the helpee has an adequate system of *positive and negative reinforcements* to support successful completion of each program step: Such reinforcements must always flow from the helpee's own unique frame of reference. Finally, the helper must work to ensure that the helpee can *recycle* not only the specific program-development and program-implementation procedures used, but also the basic procedures involved in helpee exploration, understanding, and action.

When should the helper make use of program-implementation skills?

Once the goal has been defined, a course of action chosen, and a full program of action and check-steps developed, the helpee will usually be anxious to start taking the steps to reach the goal. Since the helpee will usually be taking these steps independently (i.e., outside of the specific helping setting), the helper must initiate with the helpee by employing program-implementation strategies before the helpee actually begins the program. A good program ensures that the helpee *can* reach the goal; helper use of program-implementation skills ensures that the helpee *will* reach the goal.

How can you practice your program implementation skills?

Begin with one of the practice programs you developed at the end of the last chapter to reach a specific personal goal. To promote your *mastery* of each step in this practice program, make sure that you answer each of the following questions accurately and completely: "In what contexts can I *repeat* the new skill or behavior involved in each step?"

"What must I look for in my *review* of past performance at each new step-level?" "What procedures can I follow in *rehearsing* each new step before I actually take it?" "What would be involved in *rewriting* any of the primary or secondary steps in my program if that became necessary?" Try taking some of the steps and develop a Tell/Show/Do teaching process. For your own practice, *teach some of these steps to a friend.* Next, develop some specific modes of positive and negative *reinforcement* for all of the steps in your program. Make sure that each of the specific rewards and punishments you outline is both realistic and effective. Finally, go over what you must do to *recycle* both the basic E-U-A procedures and the specific program-development and program-implementation skills in terms of both a new goal in the same area as that of your practice program and a new goal in another area entirely.

helping culminates **8** in learning: THE MODEL REVISITED

Overview

1. All efforts by one person to help another have an inevitable impact — *for better or for worse.*

2. In all successful efforts to promote constructive change in helpee or client behavior, *the common denominator is helper skills.*

3. The helper uses basic *attending skills* — preparing, positioning, observing, and listening — to promote helpee *involvement.*

HELPER **HELPEE**
A ━━━━━▶ **I**

4. The helper uses *responding skills* — responding to content, to meaning, to feelings, to feelings plus reasons — to promote helpee *exploration.*

HELPER **HELPEE**
A-R ━━━━━▶ **I-E**

5. The helper uses *personalizing skills* — personalizing the meaning, personalizing the problem, personalizing the feelings, personalizing the goal — to promote helpee *understanding.*

HELPER **HELPEE**
A-R-P ━━━━━▶ **I-E-U**

6. The helper uses *initiating skills* — goal development, problem solving, program development, and program implementation — to promote helpee *action.*

HELPER **HELPEE**
A-R-P-I ━━━━━▶ **I-E-U-A**

7. The helpee's ultimate aim should go beyond the resolution of any single problem or situation to the acquisition of those skills needed for a lifetime of exploration, understanding, and action — *a lifetime of learning.*

8. The helper's ultimate objective must be *to deliver to the helpee all those specific skills that will be needed for lifelong learning.*

We have, in a very real sense, come full circle. We started with the idea that helping itself begins with learning: The individual helpee must learn how the present situation or problem can be resolved through the development of new and more constructive patterns of behavior; and the aspiring helper must learn how to facilitate helpee growth and change through the acquisition and use of specific helping skills. Helping begins with learning. But helping also culminates in learning — a lifelong process of self-controlled achievement that embraces helper and helpee alike. The single interaction or series of interactions between helper and helpee — conducted in an outpatient clinic or school guidance counselor's office, in a dorm advisor's simple room, or the privacy of a family's own home — can and should have an impact far beyond its visible context.

The helpee who sought to resolve only a single problem should discover that she or he is capable of resolving almost all problems, reaching almost all goals.

The helper who sought to provide aid only in a limited situation should discover that she or he is capable of delivering an ever-increasing repertoire of skills to those people who need them most.

Again, we began with the idea — in reality, a demonstrable fact — that all helping is for better or worse. The single certainty in any counseling or helping situation is that neither the helper nor the helpee will emerge unchanged. The helper is always changed to the extent that specific skills have been honed or blunted, reinforced or modified, or shown as inadequate through involvement in the helping interaction. The helpee is always changed to the extent that he or she has either grown or deteriorated in individual capability. And again, this same learning is implicit in the climactic stage of any helping interaction. The helper's use of specific skills in one situation affects the subsequent use of those skills in all situations. The helpee's resolution of an individual problem serves to clarify the ways in which ever-greater control can be exerted in various other areas of life.

The effective helper knows all of this, of course. And he or she also knows that what ensures a positive rather than a negative transformation of each helpee is *skills* — not just ideas or theories or common sense or good intentions — but skills! Skills are what the helper must use to effect positive and constructive change and growth in each helpee. And skills are what the helpee must acquire and use to exert a greater degree of constructive control over her or his own life

— control that itself is expressed not through thought or feeling alone but also through practical action.

In this text we have focused on the concrete and functional skills that the effective helper must use in order to make a positive difference with helpees. These skills are not artificial or arbitrary procedures that the helper imposes upon the helping session. Rather, they are systematic and technological responses flowing from a model that is itself biological and organic in nature. A surgeon plies her skills not because they happen to have been taught at the particular medical school she attended, but because years of collective experience have shown these skills to be appropriate in dealing with the organic phenomena of human illness and disease. By the same token, the helping skills we have considered do not reflect the vested interest of any one group or collection of professional helpers. Rather, they have been shown by experience and outcome alike to be effective modes of response to the human condition that can and do promote measurable growth in individual helpees.

Attending
Promotes
Involvement

As we have seen, all effective helping must begin by promoting helpee *involvement*. Nothing positive can be done for helpees until they are drawn into and fully involved in the helping process itself. The first stage of helpee involvement, obviously, requires that helpees *appear*. As involvement increases, helpees *express themselves* nonverbally through physical behaviors and *express themselves verbally* through initial statements and comments. Finally, helpees signal full involvement by shifting from superficial conversation to some *expression of personally relevant material*.

The skills the helper uses to achieve full helpee involvement are basic ones. By *preparing*, the helper promotes helpee appearance. The helper then *positions* in order to gather information and to communicate genuine interest and concern. The helper *observes* in order to pick up those visual cues that indicate where the helpees are and how they are experiencing their world. The helper *listens* in order to hear both what the helpees say and (through tone as well as content) what they really mean. We can group these four helper skills together and refer to them collectively as *attending* skills.

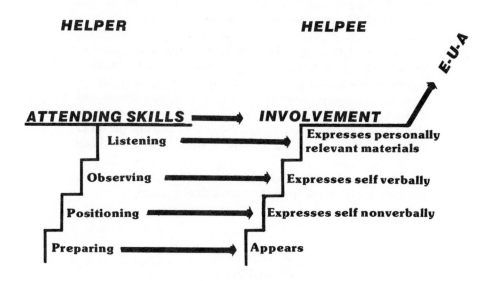

*Figure 8-1: Helper **attending skills** promote helpee **involvement.***

From the outset, then, we can see the organic nature of the helping model. Helpee involvement is not an arbitrary or contrived goal endorsed by one particular school of thought. Rather, it is the necessary but not sufficient condition of initiating a helping interaction with any person.

Responding
Promotes
Exploration

Once helpees are involved in a helping session, they must undertake a process of *exploration*. Here again, exploration is a natural and inevitable prelude to all meaningful human growth. The budding artist or poet explores a wide range of creative styles before focusing on that approach that will be most productive. The student or recent graduate explores a number of career options before focusing attention on any one area. In the same way, the helpees begin by exploring many different aspects of a particular situation to ensure that nothing relevant to the present problem is overlooked. Such exploration starts as the helpees, already involved in the discussion of personally relevant material, are encouraged to explore the *immediate situation*. What is really going on in the helpee's world? Who else is involved? How does the external situation affect the helpee? Where, when, and how are important things happening? Once helpees have explored the immediate situation, they can go on to explore the *immediate meaning* the situation has for them, the *immediate feelings* the situation provokes, and the *immediate reasons* for each of these feelings. In effect, helpees at these several stages of exploration are saying, "Here's what's going on, here's what it means to me, here's how that makes me feel, and here's why I feel that way."

The effective helper promotes helpee exploration by continuing to use attending skills. These basic skills ensure that the helper is communicating real interest (which serves to maintain a high level of helpee involvement) at the same time that she or he is learning more about the helpee's own unique frame of reference — the way the helpee sees and experiences the world. In addition, the helper now *responds* to the helpee — *to the content* of the helpee's expressions concerning specific situations: "So you're saying that _____"; to the helpee's meaning: "So you mean _____"; to the helpee's experiential *feelings:* "You feel _____"; and to the externalized *reasons* for these feelings: "You feel _____ because he/she/it _____." Throughout, the helper seeks to pinpoint those external areas of greatest concern to the helpee. At no time during the helpee's period of exploration does the helper attempt to shape or control the substance of the helpee's expressions. At most, the helper will prompt new and/or deeper exploration by asking some simple questions. The helpee's job at this stage is simply to explore; the helper's job is to promote and monitor this exploration and begin to form some initial and private discriminations concerning important and unimportant material based on visual and verbal data provided by the helpee. We can refer collectively to the skills the helper uses to facilitate helpee exploration as *responding skills.*

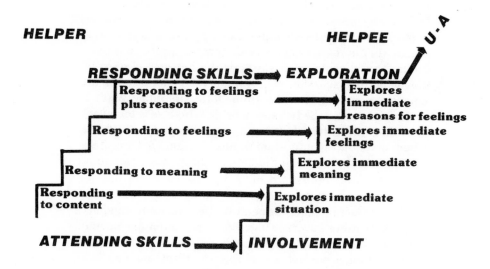

Figure 8-2: Helper **responding skills** *promote helpee* **exploration**

Personalizing
Promotes
Understanding

One of the most critical stages in the entire helping process involves the helpee's shift from exploration to *understanding.* By exploring their present situation and feelings, helpees have come to terms with where they are. This present position is invariably seen by helpees in external terms; any problems discussed during exploration are usually treated by the helpees as being "their" fault: "They hassle me all the time." "They're not fair." "It really makes me mad." "She won't listen to me." "He's totally incapable of understanding me." "The job market just doesn't have room for me." "The whole thing's stupid." Were a helpee allowed to drift forever as a victim of these externalized agencies or forces, he would quite literally remain helpless. Now, therefore, the helpee must begin to put himself back into the equation in a controlling role. The meaning of the situation developed earlier must be transformed into *personalized meaning:* no longer, "It means that they're not fair," but "It means that I get dumped on." As understanding increases, this personalized meaning is expanded to include some statement that *personalizes the problem* or deficit: "I get dumped on because I can't figure out how to get them to treat me with respect." At last the helpee is beginning to view the situation in terms that, by focusing on individual responsibility and limitations, pave the way for individual growth and control. Inevitably, of course, the helpee's new understanding of his personal role in the problem awakes a new set of *personalized feelings:* "I feel stupid because I can't figure out how to get them to respect me instead of giving me a hard time." Finally, the helpee focuses on a *personalized goal:* "I feel dumb because I can't figure out how to handle the situation and I really want their respect."

Without help, few if any helpees can effect the shift from an externalized perspective, which makes a scapegoat of someone or something else, to a personalized perspective, which promises control by acknowledging responsibility. And yet it is just such a shift that lies at the heart of all helpee movement through exploration to understanding. At this point, therefore, the helper must begin to initiate with the helpee: first by *personalizing the meaning* implicit in (but has not yet been expressed through) the helpee's exploratory expressions; then, once the helpee signals acceptance of this personalized meaning, by *personalizing the problem;* by going on to *personalize the new feelings;* and finally, by

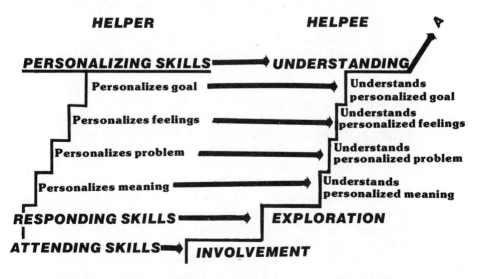

Figure 8-3: Helper **personalizing skills** *promote helpee* **understanding.**

personalizing the helpee's goal, which is invariably nothing more than the flip-side of the personalized problem. Thus, the helper goes beyond the monitoring and discriminating functions attendant upon helpee exploration by actively seeking to focus and personalize the helpee's understanding in specific areas. For the helper knows that only full and personalized understanding on the helpee's part will make constructive action possible.

Initiating Promotes Action

The last major phase of the helping process, of course, involves helpee *action.* Having arrived at an understanding of the personalized goal, the helpee must now *define this goal* in meaningful, measurable, and realistic terms and *select the most appropriate course of action* that will make goal achievement possible without infringing upon critical helpee values. Once the goal has been developed in this way, the helpee must go on to develop *action-steps* that lead in a systematic yet gradual manner to the goal and an attendant series of *check-steps* that ensure that the helpee will be able to monitor progress throughout each period of activity. Finally, the helpee must actually *take the steps* designed to lead to the goal.

As with the transformation from helpee exploration to helpee understanding, so the helper must effect the shift to initial helpee action by *initiating* with the helpee. At first, the helper will use *goal-development skills* to facilitate helpee definition of the goal and *problem-solving skills* to promote the helpee's choice of an optimum course of action. Next, the helper must use specific *program-development skills* that involve the creation of both action- and check-steps for the helpee. And finally, the helper will use *program-implementation skills* to show the helpee how each step in the program of action can be reviewed and rehearsed and how the entire cycle of goal development and program development (as well as the far larger cycle of exploration, understanding, and action) can be recycled for new use in any number of different areas. All of these helper techniques or strategies can be referred to collectively as *initiating skills.*

*Figure 8-4: Helper **initiating skills** promote helpee **action.***

Toward
Lifelong
Learning

As we have emphasized throughout this text, the goal of all helping is a change for the better in helpee behavior: a change that is reflected in concrete and measurable movement toward a goal. Such constructive change is at the heart of that process often characterized as "growth" or "learning." For the helpees who have truly changed as the result of receiving help from other persons do far more than achieve single, isolated goals; they acquire the ability to exert ever-greater control over each and every living, learning, and working area. By the same token, truly effective helpers do more than aid helpees in resolving particularly difficult situations. They deliver to helpees the greatest number of interpersonal, program-development, and program-implementation skills that the helpees can handle. For the ultimate aim of the best helpers is not to perpetuate their careers by allowing helpees to remain dependent upon them. Rather, their aim is, quite literally, to work themselves out of a job. And their method involves making a maximum delivery of skills to every helpee so that each one can take over the management of all aspects of individual life. Incompetent helpers deliver nothing to their helpees beyond fruitless advice and private, often irrelevant or even destructive theories. Minimally effective helpers promote their helpees' abilities to solve particular problems. Fully effective helpers eventually turn the people with whom they work into helpers in their own right.

In the last decade or so, the term *revolution* has become a catchphrase. Yet the overwhelming majority of people who have attempted to stage a revolt, whether on an individual or a collective basis, have failed miserably. Seizing the power that others previously held over their lives, they have squandered this power wantonly; seeking to assert new power over others, they have only shown how easy it is for even the most righteous revolutionaries to fall into their predecessors' old habits. It is perhaps significant that such people have set their sights on revolution rather than evolution; after all, it is far easier to go around in circles than it is to climb upward toward new heights and new challenges.

Despite the popularity of the term, most revolutions have failed to promote real human growth. And yet such revolution — or evolution — is both possible and essential. It begins with the realization by each individual that a life lived without constructive goals and the skills needed to achieve these goals is a life abandoned to mere chance. If we would change the world for the better rather than the worse, we must begin by acquiring the skills we need to promote such change — in our own lives and in the lives of others.

The skills of helping — these are the tools of meaningful and positive revolution. Stated somewhat differently, they are the technological means whereby we can promote real biological evolution. For they are the tools we need to realize the goals of helping.

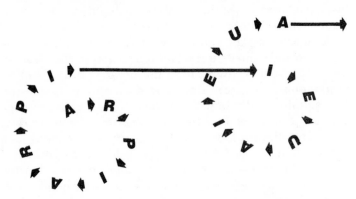

Figure 8-4: Helper **initiating skills** *promote helpee* **action**

Attending skills to promote individual *involvement.*

Responding skills to promote individual *exploration.*

Personalizing skills to promote individual *understanding.*

Initiating skills to promote individual *action.*

And each new action becomes the starting point for further exploration, deeper understanding, more effective action.

Helping begins with learning. Given the necessary skills, such learning never stops.

Index

Positioning, 39-42, 52-53, 59
Posture, 45, 110
Pre-helping. *See* Involvement
Preparing, 36-39, 59
Principle of Inevitable Effect, 8
Problem, personalized, 95, 106-109
Problem-solving skills. *See* Goal-development and problem-solving skills; Decision-making matrix
Program-development skills, 175-176, 183, 186-204 *passim*, 209-211
Program-implementation skills, 213, 218, 221-225, 235, 245-247
Psychoanalysis, 126-127
Psychotherapy, 165, 200-201
Psychotic/non-psychotic learning, 239

Questioning technique, 69-71, 92-93, 144-145, 153

Recycling, 17-18, 213-214, 228-232, 239-240
Rehearsal, 213, 220-221
Reinforcement, 213, 225-228, 235-237
Repetition, 213, 219
Responding skills, 61-62, 68-69, 92-93, 96, 100, 110-111, 144, 249, 252-254
Response, interchangeable, 103-104, 117-118
Review, 213, 219-220
Revolution vs. evolution, 258
Rewards and punishments. *See* Reinforcement

Rewrite, 213, 221
Role "owning," 95, 100-102, 106-107, 112

Set, 67-68
Setting, 37-39
Situation, responding to, 69-72, 92
Skills, 1, 4, 250-251. *See also* Attending skills; Goal-development and problem-solving skills; Personalizing skills; Program-development skills; Program-implementation skills; Responding skills
Skills training, 201-204, 237-240
Specialty knowledge, 196
Systematic training vs. behavioral rehearsal, 239

Teaching as treatment, 201-204
Tell-Show-Do teaching process, 237-239
Terminology, 143-145
Theory and practice, counseling, 123-126
Think steps, 175, 183, 191-196, 209, 210
Time-frame, 187
Training vs. teaching, as treatment, 201-204
Trait-and-factor approach, 167

Understanding, 1, 14-15, 22-23, 95, 96, 101-102, 121-122, 123-127, 131-132, 254-256
Values, 135, 148-154, 174
Verbal expressions, 47-49; vs. nonverbal expressions, 72-73